Minneapolis St. Paul

Second Edition

by Rick Nelson

John Muir Publications
Santa Fe, New Mexico

Thanks to my parents, Judy and Don, for encouraging and facilitating my affection for the Twin Cities. And a special thanks to David Anger, Claude Peck, and Scott Winter for their invaluable assistance.

John Muir Publications, P.O. Box 613, Santa Fe, New Mexico 87504

Second edition. First printing April 1999.
Printed in the United States of America.

ISBN: 1-56261-471-1
ISSN: 1088-9310

Editors: Peg Goldstein, Heidi Utz
Graphics Editor: Heather Pool
Production: Janine Lehmann
Design: Janine Lehmann
Cover Design: Suzanne Rush
Maps: Julie Felton
Typesetter: Fabian West
Printer: Publishers Press
Front cover photo: © Unicorn Stock Photos/Alice M. Prescott (Third Avenue Bridge)
Back cover photo: © Unicorn Stock Photos/Phyllis Kedl (Golden Horses on the Capitol)

Distributed to the book trade by
Publishers Group West
Berkeley, California

CONTENTS

MAP CONTENTS

See Minneapolis and St. Paul the CiTY·SMaRT™ Way

The Guide for Twin Cities Natives, New Residents, and Visitors

In *City•Smart Guidebook: Minneapolis/St. Paul,* local author Rick Nelson tells it like it is. Residents will learn things they never knew about their cities, new residents will get an insider's view of their new hometowns, and visitors will be guided to the very best Minneapolis and St. Paul have to offer—whether they're on a weekend getaway or staying a week or more.

Opinionated Recommendations Save You Time and Money

From shopping to nightlife to museums, the author is opinionated about what he likes and dislikes. You'll learn the great and the not-so-great things about the Twin Cities' sights, restaurants, and accommodations. So you can decide what's worth your time and what's not; which hotel is worth the splurge and which is the best choice for budget travelers.

Easy-to-Use Format Makes Planning Your Trip a Cinch

City•Smart Guidebook: Minneapolis/St. Paul is user-friendly—you'll quickly find exactly what you're looking for. Chapters are organized by travelers' interests or needs, from Where to Stay and Where to Eat to Sights and Attractions, Kids' Stuff, Sports and Recreation, and even Day Trips from the Twin Cities.

Includes Maps and Quick Location-Finding Features

Every listing in this book is accompanied by a geographic zone designation (see pages vi–vii for zone details) that helps you immediately find each location. Staying in the Warehouse District and wondering about nearby sights and restaurants? Look for the Downtown Minneapolis label in the listings and you'll know that statue or café is not far away. Or maybe you're looking for the Science Museum of Minnesota. Along with its address, you'll see a Downtown St. Paul label, so you'll know just where to find it.

All That and Fun to Read, Too!

Every *City•Smart* chapter includes fun-to-read city trivia (did you know that Rollerblades were invented in the Twin Cities?) and tips to help make your stay more enjoyable. You'll also find illuminating sidebars. For a guide to the best bakeries in town, for example, see page 79. For a guide to Mary Tyler Moore's TV Minneapolis, see pages 6 and 7.

GREATER TWIN CITIES

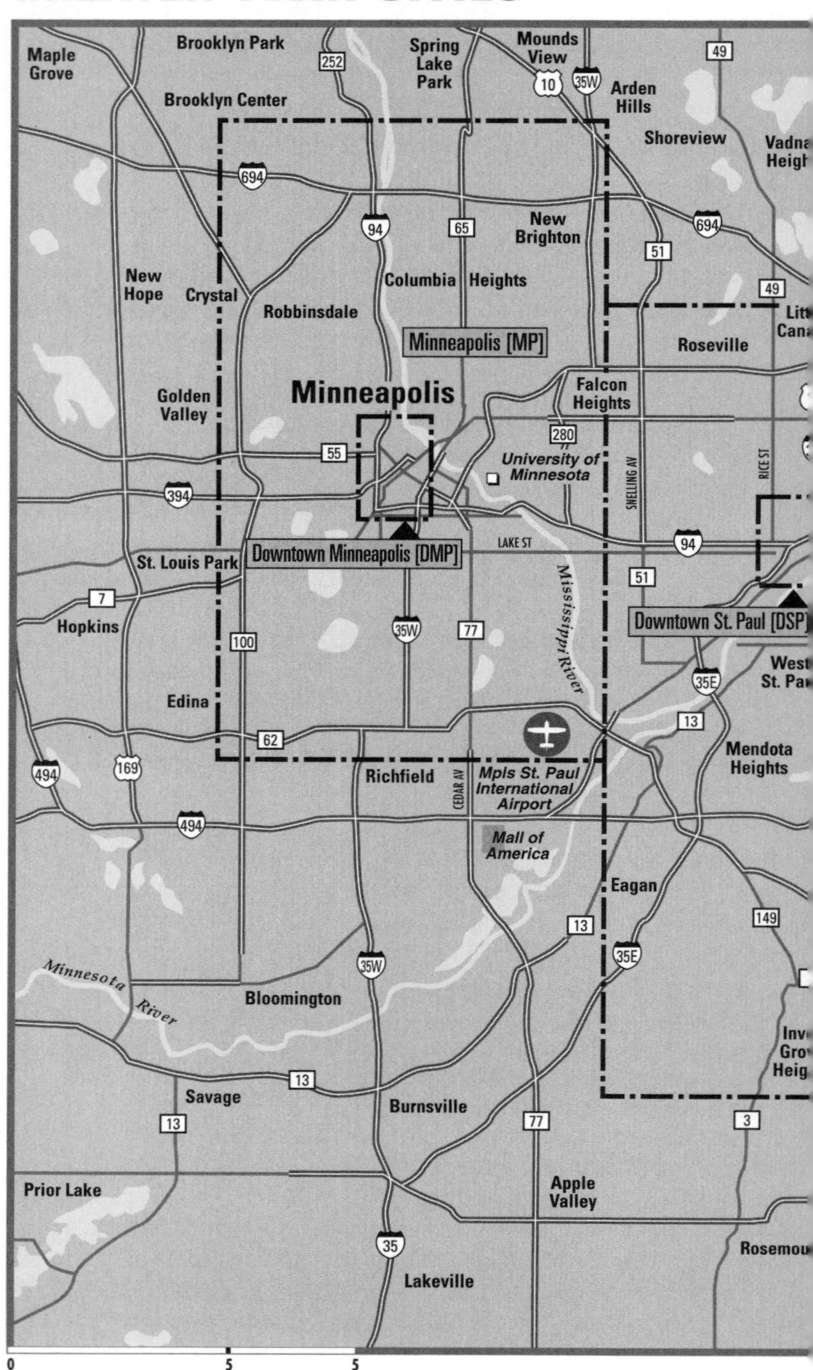

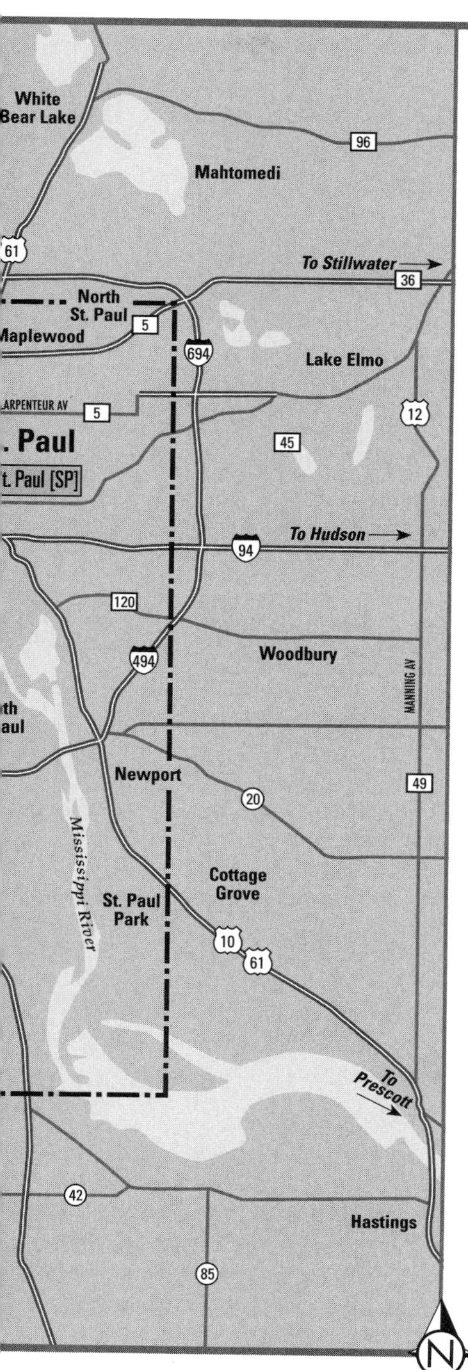

MINNEAPOLIS/ ST. PAUL ZONES

Downtown Minneapolis (DMP)
Bounded by Nicollet Island on the north, Chicago Avenue on the east, 15th Street on the south, and I-394 on the west

Downtown St. Paul (DSP)
Bounded by University Avenue on the north, Lafayette Road on the east, Harriet Island on the south, and Marion Street on the west

Minneapolis (MP)
Bounded by Lowry Avenue on the north, Highway 280 on the east, 54th Street on the south, and France Avenue on the west

St. Paul (SP)
Bounded by Larpenteur Road on the north, I-494 on the east, Mendota Road on the south, and Highway 280 on the west

Greater Twin Cities (GTC)
Includes Mall of America and outlying communities such as Richfield, Edina, Bloomington, Eden Prairie, Hopkins, Plymouth, Maple Grove, and Maplewood

Greater Minneapolis CVA

1
WELCOME TO THE TWIN CITIES

Although their nickname implies a pair of clones, the cities of Minneapolis and St. Paul are really more fraternal than identical twins. Both have distinctive histories, topographies, and identities, as well as a rivalry stemming back almost 150 years.

St. Paul's roots are in transportation. The city grew up just outside the army outpost at Fort Snelling, which guarded the strategic junction of the Minnesota and Mississippi Rivers. The landing at St. Paul marked the northernmost navigable destination on the Mississippi, a choice location that later attracted the railroads and became the state capital.

From its very early years, Minneapolis's fortunes were based almost entirely upon the power of the 25-foot St. Anthony Falls, about eight miles north of Fort Snelling, the only falls on the "Father of Waters." Within two decades of the city's settlement, more than two dozen lumber and flour mills harnessed the falls' considerable power. By the end of the nineteenth century, boomtown Minneapolis was the flour-milling capital of the world.

Early settlers of both cities were determined to make their hometowns centers of commerce, education, and culture. Their work ethic and dedication to philanthropy have set a civic example that continues to this day, making the Twin Cities one of the nation's most livable and lively urban areas.

Tim Rummelhoff

Learn about Twin Cities' history at the James J. Hill House in St. Paul.

A Brief History of the Twin Cities

Geologists estimate that the last glaciers inched their way across the area that is now Minnesota more than 12,000 years ago, leaving in their wake a landscape dotted with lakes and ponds. Minnesota's nickname is "the Land of 10,000 Lakes," although there are actually about 16,000 lakes in all. And Minneapolis (from a combination of Sioux and Greek words meaning "city of waters") isn't called the "City of Lakes" for nothing; 22 lakes exist within city limits.

The area's original residents were members of the rival Dakota (Sioux) and Ojibwa (Chippewa) tribes. Their first contact with Europeans came in 1680, with the arrival of Father Louis Hennepin, a Franciscan missionary. Hennepin was perhaps the first European to see the Mississippi's falls, which he named for his patron saint, Anthony of Padua. As white settlement increased, the natives were driven from the area and were almost entirely gone by the 1860s.

New Englanders moved into the region in the 1850s and 1860s to seek their fortunes in the rustic Minnesota territory. Pioneers like James J. Hill, Charles Pillsbury, and Thomas Washburn made their marks on the region, founding major companies, creating civic institutions, and establishing government posts.

The New England settlers were followed by waves of German, Swedish, Norwegian, and Irish immigrants, and by the turn of the century, nearly a half-million people lived in the Minneapolis–St. Paul area. Tremendous growth occurred from 1900 to the end of World War I, as both cities began to mature and build infrastructures, cultural institutions, schools, and parks.

The advent of the streetcar in the late nineteenth century pushed the

Twin Cities Architecture—Recommended Reading

For a closer look at local architecture past and present, try these titles:

A Guide to the Architecture of Minnesota, *by David Gebhard and Tom Martinson (University of Minnesota Press). A thorough catalog of significant works, half of which are located in the Twin Cities*

Lost Twin Cities, *by Larry Millett (Minnesota Historical Society Press). A fascinating walk down memory lane, this chronicle of long-gone buildings reconstructs a lost urban world with an engaging text and hundreds of pictures.*

cities far beyond their original boundaries. New neighborhoods sprang up as workers arrived for jobs in busy flour mills, grain elevators, and factories—including the mighty Minneapolis Moline plant, the world's largest farm-implement manufacturer.

The prosperity and building boom continued in both cities through the 1920s but came to a screeching halt with the Great Depression. Little growth occurred during the 1930s, and most of the construction that took place was done under the auspices of government relief programs. As the crippling years of the Depression wore on, the Twin Cities became a center for the nation's organized labor movement and the Communist and Socialist Parties.

World War II brought great change to the Twin Cities. With wartime and postwar prosperity, the cities gained national prominence as leaders in progressive government, business, and the arts. In 1946 the Dayton Company founded the Five Percent Club, pledging to donate 5 percent of its annual pretax profits to charity and asking other businesses to follow suit. Since then, more than 200 companies have signed on to the club (now known as the Keystone Program) and donated billions to support the area's rich array of cultural, social, and educational institutions.

An explosion in suburban development began in the early 1950s and has gone on, unabated, for nearly half a century. The two once relatively compact cities are now surrounded by a sprawling, seven-county metropolitan area. Two-thirds of the region's 2.5 million residents live in suburban areas.

Such unchecked growth led to problems, which in turn led to the creation of a unique government body to direct the booming metropolis.

TWIN CITIES TIME LINE

1680 Father Louis Hennepin names the falls on the Mississippi for his patron saint, Anthony of Padua.

1763 France relinquishes its claim to territory that includes much of the future state of Minnesota.

1767 Explorer and cartographer Jonathan Carver surveys the region for the English Crown.

1803 The United States purchases the Louisiana Territory, and the remaining area around the Twin Cities is placed under American domain.

1805 Colonel Zebulon Pike signs a treaty with the Dakota Indians that establishes a military post at the confluence of the Mississippi and Minnesota Rivers.

1820 Fort St. Anthony is founded by Captain Josiah Snelling. Five years later it is renamed in his honor.

1823 The first steamboat arrives at Fort Snelling from St. Louis.

1837 Saloon keeper Pierre "Pigs Eye" Parrant builds a cabin a few miles downstream from Fort Snelling. It becomes the first building in what is now St. Paul.

1841 Father Lucien Galtier builds a chapel in Pigs Eye and dedicates it to Saint Paul. The hamlet takes on the same name.

1849 St. Paul becomes the capital of Minnesota Territory.

1850 The town of St. Anthony is founded on the east bank of the Mississippi River at the falls. John Stevens builds the first house on the west bank of the river.

1854 The first bridge spanning the Mississippi, connecting Minneapolis with Nicollet Island, is built.

1855 Minneapolis is founded on the west bank of the river opposite St. Anthony.

1858 The University of Minnesota is founded.

1862 The area's first railroad opens.

1872 Minneapolis annexes the city of St. Anthony.

1881 The world's largest flour mill, the Pillsbury "A" mill, opens in Minneapolis.

1882 The nation's first hydroelectric plant opens at St. Anthony Falls.

1883 Charles Loring establishes the Minneapolis Park Board, and James J. Hill's Northern Pacific Railroad connects the Twin Cities with the West Coast.

The heated rivalry between the cities goes into overdrive as Minneapolis surpasses St. Paul's census. Both cities are later revealed to have padded their numbers heavily.	**1890**
The Minneapolis Symphony (later the Minnesota Orchestra) plays its first concert.	**1903**
Cass Gilbert's imperial State Capitol is dedicated.	**1905**
The Cathedral of St. Paul is dedicated, and the Minneapolis Institute of Arts opens.	**1915**
The 32-story Foshay Tower is dedicated in downtown Minneapolis. It remains the tallest building west of Chicago for decades.	**1929**
St. Paul native Frank B. Kellogg wins the Nobel Peace Prize.	**1930**
Sister Elizabeth Kenny opens a polio clinic in Minneapolis.	**1940**
Minneapolis Mayor Hubert Humphrey's impassioned speech at the Democratic National Convention sparks the beginning of the civil rights movement.	**1948**
Southdale, the country's first enclosed shopping mall, opens in Edina.	**1956**
The beloved Metropolitan Building is demolished ("the most inexcusable act of civic vandalism in the city of Minneapolis," according to one critic) in the name of urban renewal.	**1961**
The Guthrie Theater opens in Minneapolis to great acclaim.	**1963**
The first interstate freeway opens in Minneapolis, clearing the way for large-scale suburban development and simultaneous inner-city decay.	**1965**
Nicollet Mall is dedicated in downtown Minneapolis, and its design is copied the world over.	**1967**
Historic preservationists score a huge victory when St. Paul's Old Federal Courts Building (now Landmark Center) is saved from the wrecking ball.	**1972**
Philip Johnson's 52-story IDS Center opens in downtown Minneapolis, surpassing the Foshay Tower's 44-year dominance on the city's skyline.	**1973**
The Minnesota Twins win the World Series, a feat they repeat in 1991.	**1987**
The Twin Cities host the first winter-city Super Bowl game.	**1991**
Mall of America, the nation's largest shopping and entertainment complex, opens in Bloomington.	**1992**
Former pro wrestler Jesse Ventura elected governor of Minnesota.	**1998**

Founded by the state legislature in 1967, the Metropolitan Council attempts to solve disputes among municipalities and to provide regional urban management. The council presides over transit, parks, water and sewer service, and airports. But suburban sprawl—unchecked by natural barriers such as mountains or large bodies of water—continues to challenge the Twin Cities area.

The People of the Twin Cities

Although Minneapolis and St. Paul have traditionally been overwhelmingly white, an influx of new residents in the past few decades has greatly improved racial diversity. Still, the area is almost relentlessly homogeneous. According to the U.S. Census Bureau, nearly 91 percent of the population is Caucasian, 4 percent is African American, almost 4 percent is Asian, and

Love Is All Around

To most Americans, Minneapolis will always be the home of Mary Richards, the quintessentially spunky, all-American career gal of the 1970s. The opening credits of The Mary Tyler Moore Show *put Moore all over Minneapolis, and it's fun to retrace her steps today.*

Phyllis Lindstrom's rambling Victorian house—where Mary lived on the second floor and Rhoda Morgenstern lived on the third floor—is two blocks west of Lake of the Isles Parkway, at 2104 Kenwood Parkway. The house is now owned by the director of the Minneapolis Institute of Arts. When Mary moved to a high-rise apartment later in the series, she took up residence in Chase House, the luxury building of Cedar Square West (now Riverside Plaza), near the West Bank of the University of Minnesota campus. WJM-TV, the ratings-basement station where Mary worked as a news producer, was located in the Midwest Plaza Building in downtown Minneapolis (801 Nicollet Mall).

Three shots of the then-brand-new IDS Center were incorporated into various versions of the show's opening credits. One shot has Mary, holding a potted chrysanthemum, riding the escalator in Crystal Court; the second shows her lunching on the balcony of the Gallery Restaurant (now Basil's), and the third depicts her window-

1 percent is Native American. German Americans are the largest single ethnic group, followed by Scandinavians, Irish, and Hispanics.

Minneapolis has the nation's largest urban concentration of Native Americans, in a community centered primarily around the Minneapolis Regional Native American Center (the nation's first Native American community center) on East Franklin Avenue in South Minneapolis. Hmong, Vietnamese, and Laotian refugees began arriving in the Twin Cities in the late 1970s, and today enjoy thriving communities, particularly around Nicollet Avenue South in Minneapolis and University Avenue East in St. Paul. The Hispanic population has traditionally been anchored on the east side of St. Paul.

The African American community is making great strides in the Twin Cities. Minneapolis was the first major American city to elect an African American female mayor; the Honorable Sharon Sayles Belton has held the top title in the City of Lakes since her election in 1992. Alan Page, for-

shopping at Mary Jane Shoes (now Badiner Jewelers), at the base of the IDS Tower at Eighth Street and Nicollet Mall.

Mary's grocery-shopping scene was shot at the Red Owl (a now-defunct chain), at Hennepin Avenue South and 25th Street in South Minneapolis. There, she's exasperated because she's buying Juicy Burger II, a low-priced hamburgerlike product the store introduced when beef prices skyrocketed in the mid-1970s.

The opener's most memorable moment—and the show's signature—has Mary so overcome with the thrill of being young, single, and in downtown Minneapolis that she twirls on her heel and hurls her tam into the air. The scene was shot on the corner of Seventh Street and Nicollet Mall. The big Donaldsons store in the background was destroyed by fire in 1982; it is now the site of Saks Fifth Avenue.

In the show's closing credits (just before the meow of the MTM kitten), Mary and a male friend are seen strolling hand in hand down Nicollet Mall between Third and Fourth Streets in front of the Sheraton-Ritz Hotel. The mall has since suffered an unpleasant facelift, and the hotel was replaced by a parking lot in the early 1990s.

mer Vikings football legend, has sat on the Minnesota Supreme Court since 1994.

The Twin Cities is home to a large, visible gay and lesbian population. There isn't a gay neighborhood per se in either city, although downtown Minneapolis's Loring Park area tends to attract gay residents.

While the Twin Cities are strong Catholic enclaves, they also remain heavily Protestant, reflecting their German and Scandinavian roots. The American Lutheran Church, now part of the Evangelical Lutheran Church of America, was headquartered in Minneapolis for years, and the nation's three largest Lutheran congregations still call the Twin Cities home.

Calendar of Events

JANUARY

New Year's Eve, Historic Main Street, Minneapolis
St. Paul Winter Carnival

MARCH

Hollywood Oscar Party, State Theatre
Minneapolis State high school tournaments, St. Paul RiverCentre
St. Patrick's Day Parade, downtown St. Paul

APRIL

Festival of Nations, St. Paul RiverCentre

MAY

May Day Parade and Festival, Minneapolis
Cinco de Mayo, St. Paul
Syttende Mai, Minneapolis

JUNE

Gay, Lesbian, Bisexual, Transgender Pride Festival, Loring Park, Minneapolis
Grand Old Days, Grand Avenue, St. Paul
Juneteenth Celebration, Theodore Wirth Park, Minneapolis
Stone Arch Festival of the Arts, St. Anthony Falls, Minneapolis
Svenskarnes Dag, Minneapolis
Symphony Ball, Minneapolis

JULY

Basilica Block Party, Basilica of St. Mary, Minneapolis
Le Grand Aioli Bastille Day Celebration, Minneapolis
Minneapolis Aquatennial
Rondo Days, St. Paul
Taste of Minnesota, State Capitol Mall, St. Paul
Viennese Sommerfest, Orchestra Hall, Minneapolis

AUGUST

Cedarfest, Cedar-Riverside, Minneapolis
Minnesota Renaissance Festival, Shakopee
Minnesota State Fair, St. Paul
Powderhorn Festival of the Arts, Minneapolis
Uptown Art Fair, Minneapolis

SEPTEMBER

American Indian Movement Pow Wow, Minneapolis

OCTOBER

Twin Cities Marathon
University of Minnesota Homecoming, Minneapolis

NOVEMBER

Holidazzle, Nicollet Mall, Minneapolis

DECEMBER

Capital City Lights, downtown St. Paul
Holidazzle, Nicollet Mall, Minneapolis

Twin Cities Weather

One of the lures of the Twin Cities is experiencing Minnesota's dramatic theater of seasons. Of course, winter is what most Americans think of when they consider Minnesota, and with good reason. Although International Falls (called "the Nation's Icebox" and often the most frigid place in the Lower 48) is thankfully more than 300 miles to the north, it does get cold during winter.

St. Paul Winter Carnival ice carving

St. Paul CVB

How cold? Temperatures can plummet—and remain—below zero degrees Fahrenheit for days on end (the local record is a bone-chilling 40 below, set in January 1996). The average January temperature is a comparatively balmy 10 degrees Fahrenheit.

On the flip side, summers can be hot and humid. Temperatures can easily climb into the nineties, accompanied by stifling humidity. But that's an extreme, too. Most August days hit an average high of 80 degrees, and summers tend to be

TRIVIA

Movies Filmed in the Twin Cities

Airport
Beautiful Girls
Drop Dead Fred
Equinox
Fargo
Feeling Minnesota
Foolin' Around
Grumpier Old Men
Grumpy Old Men
Jingle All the Way
Mallrats
The Mighty Ducks
The Mighty Ducks 2
The Mighty Ducks 3
The Personals
Twenty Bucks
Untamed Heart

dry, much to the angst of area farmers.

Spring and fall in the Twin Cities are lovely but painfully brief. Winter can drag—literally—well into April. Suddenly, spring will arrive (much to the relief of residents) and segue into summer in a matter of weeks. Ditto the autumn months. Summer often lingers into late September, and the snow can fly as early as November 1, leaving but a few weeks for the autumn colors to work their magic.

How much does it snow in the Twin Cities? An infamous blizzard dropped more than 30 inches of snow on Halloween in 1991, and a more deadly (and entirely unexpected) storm on Armistice Day in 1940 left nearly 50 inches of snow and killed scores of Minnesotans. But most winters average 50 inches of the white stuff scattered across the entire season.

Truth to tell, Minnesota winters really don't deserve the bad rap they have around the rest of the country, or even in their own backyard. While it's true that the city made famous by Mary Tyler Moore is most hospitable in spring and summer, the Twin Cities can be a great destination in the dead of winter as well. Minnesota winters can be very beautiful, with gleaming snow, soaring pine trees, and clean crisp air. Local and regional parks offer all kinds of wintertime activities, including skating, sledding, and alpine and Nordic skiing. Kids (and adults) temporarily enlarge families with front-yard snow siblings.

Dressing in the Twin Cities

The first rule is to dress for the weather, and in winter that means layers. A heavy, well-insulated coat is a wardrobe staple, and a hat, gloves, scarf, and sturdy waterproof boots are also critical when the temperatures fall. In spring and autumn, a lightweight waterproof jacket is advised, as well as a light sweater or two. Most locals break out the shorts as soon as the temps top 60 degrees, sometime in early May, and keep them out until the autumn leaves start to fall.

Both Minneapolis and St. Paul are informal cities, and few upscale restaurants require coats and ties for men. Black tie is reserved for very special—and increasingly rare—occasions. Business dress is also becoming more relaxed. On Friday, legions of downtown and suburban office workers revert to casual dress, and many companies allow relaxed apparel on other days, too. At Orchestra Hall, the Guthrie Theater, and the Ordway Music Theatre, you'll see outfits running the gamut—from dark suits and conservative ties to blue jeans and T-shirts.

Business and Economy

A number of major American corporations call the Twin Cities home. These include Cargill, a commodities concern widely considered to be the world's largest privately held company (its annual revenues exceed $50 billion). West Publishing, the legal publishing and information systems behemoth, is headquartered in suburban Eagan, as is Northwest Airlines, the nation's fourth largest airline. In the manufacturing sector, the list includes 3M

Mother of Invention

Minneapolis and St. Paul are fountains of invention, churning out products that are sold the world over. The list of hometown creations includes:

Post-It Notes and cellophane tape, both from 3M
Pacemakers by Medtronic
The entire Big G family of cereals from General Mills
GM's Betty Crocker line of packaged foods
Cream of Wheat hot cereal
Poppin' Fresh rolls and every other Pillsbury product, including Totino's frozen pizzas and Green Giant vegetables
Tonka toys
Thermostats (invented by Honeywell)
Supercomputers (perfected by Cray Research)
Rollerblades
The Tilt-A-Whirl carnival ride
Salted Nut Roll and Nut Goodie candy bars
Mini-Donuts

Famous Natives

Eddie Albert*—actor,* Roman Holiday, Green Acres

Loni Anderson*—actor,* WKRP in Cincinnati

Siah Armajani*—sculptor*

James Arness*—actor,* Gunsmoke

Merrill Ashley*—principal dancer, New York City Ballet*

Joel and Ethan Coen*—film directors and producers* Raising Arizona, Blood Simple, Fargo, Barton Fink

Julia Duffy*—actor,* Newhart, Designing Women

Mike Farrell*—actor,* M*A*S*H*

F. Scott Fitzgerald*—author,* The Great Gatsby, Tender Is the Night

Al Franken*—actor,* Saturday Night Live, *and author,* Rush Limbaugh Is a Big Fat Idiot

John Paul Getty*—billionaire industrialist*

Peter Graves*—actor,* Mission: Impossible

Tippi Hedren*—actor,* The Birds

George Roy Hill*—Oscar-winning director,* The Sting

Greg Howard*—cartoonist,* Sally Forth

Hubert H. Humphrey*—Minneapolis mayor, U.S. senator, U.S. vice president, presidential candidate*

Meridel Le Sueur*—author,* Harvest Song, Little Brother of the Wilderness, North Star Country, Song for My Time, Winter Prairie Women

Kelly Lynch*—actor,* Drugstore Cowboy

Harvey Mackay*—author,* Sharkproof, Swim with the Sharks Without Being Eaten Alive, Beware the Naked Man Who Offers You His Shirt

Walter Mondale*—U.S. senator, U.S. vice president, presidential candidate, ambassador to Japan*

Bob Mould*—lead singer, Sugar*

Leroy Neiman*—painter*

Mike Nelson*—actor,* Mystery Science Theater 3000

The Artist Formerly Known as Prince*—musician and actor* Purple Rain

Gordon Parks*—author,* The Learning Tree, *and film director,* Shaft

Dave Pirner*—lead singer, Soul Asylum*

Harry Reasoner*—journalist,* 60 Minutes

Charles Schulz*—creator of* Peanuts

Eric Severeid*—journalist*

Kevin Sorbo*—actor,* Hercules

Lea Thompson*—actor,* Caroline in the City

Cheryl Tiegs*—model*

Robert Vaughn*—actor,* The Man from U.N.C.L.E.

Paul Westerberg*—lead singer, The Replacements*

R. D. Zimmerman*—novelist,* Closet, Hostage

(Minnesota Mining and Manufacturing), Honeywell, and Weyerhauser. Medical manufacturers are a key segment of the local economy, led by Medtronic, inventors of the pacemaker.

Service giants include American Express Financial Advisors, which operates one of its most successful divisions in Minneapolis; Carlson Companies, a $2 billion company whose holdings include the Radisson hotel chain, Carlson Wagonlit Travel, and TGIFriday's; U.S. Bank and Norwest Corporation, the region's two largest banks; the St. Paul Companies, one of the nation's largest underwriters of professional and property insurance; and the University of Minnesota, the state's fourth largest employer and the nation's largest land-grant university.

Retail is big business in the Twin Cities. Dayton Hudson Corporation, the nation's fourth largest retailer, was born—and is still headquartered—on Nicollet Mall in downtown Minneapolis. The $21 billion company owns three of the country's largest department store chains (Marshall Field's, Hudson's, and Dayton's), the midpriced Mervyn's chain, and Target, the upscale discounter. SUPERVALU, the nation's largest food wholesaler (annual sales top $16 billion), is based in suburban Eden Prairie, as is Best Buy, one of the country's largest electronics chains. Fingerhut, the $2 billion discount catalog business, calls suburban Minnetonka home. The Musicland Group, the brash music retailer (Sam Goody, Musicland, and Media Play), is located in St. Louis Park.

Food processing put Minneapolis on the map, and more than a century after the city's rise to preeminence in the flour-milling industry, the area remains a giant food-processing town. The roster of name-brand companies includes General Mills, Pillsbury (now a division of Grand Metropolitan PLC), Land O' Lakes, Cream of Wheat, and International Multifoods.

Billion-Dollar Twin Citians

Nine Twin Citians made Forbes *magazine's 1998 list of billionaires. The names include:*

Members of the Cargill and MacMillan families, who control Cargill, the Minnetonka-based grain giant and the world's largest privately held company

Radisson Hotel magnate Curt Carlson

Dwight Opperman, former chairman of West Publishing

Stanley Hubbard, the man behind U.S. Satellite Broadcasting

Virginia McKnight Binger, whose family helped create 3M

Celebs in Residence

Dominick Argento*, composer, lives in Minneapolis.*

Judith Guest*, author of* Ordinary People, *lives in Edina.*

Garrison Keillor*, the man behind public radio's* A Prairie Home Companion, *lives in St. Paul.*

Oscar-winning actress ***Jessica Lange,*** *(and playwright/actor* ***Sam Shepherd****) live in Stillwater.*

inger and composer ***Bobby McFerrin*** *lives on Lake of the Isles in South Minneapolis.*

Greg LeMond*, three-time Tour de France–winning bicyclist, lives in Medina.*

The Artist Formerly Known As Prince *lives in Chanhassen.*

Lynne Rossetto Kasper*, cookbook author and radio host, lives in St. Paul.*

Because of its diversified economy, major corporations, and well-educated workforce, business and government leaders often consider the Twin Cities area to be recession-proof. Indeed, the area's economy remains consistently strong, and its cost of living is low compared to other major American cities. While Minnesota's personal income tax is the second highest in the nation (how else to pay for the state's highly touted quality of life?), the 6.5 percent sales tax is waived for food and clothing, which tends to even things out. Here's what you'll pay in the Twin Cities for some typical goods and services:

Five-mile taxi ride:	$7
Double hotel room:	$75
Dinner for one:	$15
Movie admission:	$7
Daily newspaper:	$.50 (Minneapolis)
	$.25 (St. Paul)
Tube of toothpaste:	$2.50
Hot dog (downtown vendor):	$1.50

Homes

Housing is considerably more affordable in the Twin Cities than in many major American metropolitan areas. Starter homes within Minneapolis/St.

Paul city limits can start at $85,000. New suburban construction often begins at $95,000. A three-bedroom home averages $105,000.

Rents are similarly moderate. A one-bedroom apartment in a decent inner-city neighborhood can run around $600, slightly more in a new suburban complex.

Schools

The Twin Cities have more than 50 separate public school districts, often following municipal borders. Public education is one of state government's top priorities, a fact that is reflected in high tax rates. A large percentage of revenues from the state's steep commercial and residential property taxes (the nation's second highest) are diverted to education.

The investment pays off. The state's students routinely rank among the top in the nation in test scores. A relatively new open-enrollment law means that high school students can attend any school of their choice, regardless of residence.

Marc Caryl

2
GETTING AROUND THE TWIN CITIES

Orienting yourself in Minneapolis and St. Paul is easy. Both cities are essentially large rectangles laid out along a bend in the Mississippi River. Minneapolis hugs the river on a basically north-south axis, and St. Paul lies on top of the river on an east-west axis.

Minneapolis's primary streets run north-south. Hiawatha Avenue is the principal thoroughfare between Minneapolis/St. Paul International Airport and downtown Minneapolis. Other major north-south streets in South Minneapolis are Cedar, Portland, Park, First, Blaisdell, Nicollet, Lyndale, and Hennepin Avenues. On the city's north side, the principal north-south streets are Lyndale and Penn Avenues and Victory Memorial Drive. The city's busiest east-west streets include Broadway on the north side; Washington and University Avenues on the northern end of downtown, through the University of Minnesota campus; and Franklin, Lake, and 50th Streets in South Minneapolis.

In St. Paul, the primary east-west routes include Seventh Street; Shepard and Warner Roads; and Summit, Marshall, University, Minnehaha, Arlington, and Como Avenues. Primary north-south routes include Cleveland, Snelling, and Hamline Avenues; Lexington Parkway; Dale and Rice Streets; Johnson Parkway; and McKnight Road.

Streets in Minneapolis fall into a fairly predictable and easy-to-follow pattern. East-west streets are numbered, starting at Washington Avenue. In South Minneapolis, Franklin Avenue is also 20th Street, and Lake Street is also 30th. Avenues, running north-south, are numbered east of Nicollet Avenue. West of Lyndale, avenues are named, in alphabetical order, for 52 blocks.

The most accurate Twin City street maps are made by the Hudson Map Company (2510 Nicollet Ave. S., Minneapolis; 612/872-8818). The company's *Twin Cities Street Atlas* sells for $16.95.

Finding an address in St. Paul can be more confusing. Downtown streets are numbered, but the order stops there. Throughout most of the city, street names follow no apparent pattern. It's wise to have a good street map on hand when navigating St. Paul.

Freeways crisscross the Twin Cities metropolitan area. The major north-south artery is Interstate 35. Coming north into the Twin Cities, I-35 splits in two in suburban Burnsville, with I-35W heading north into Minneapolis and I-35E turning north and east into St. Paul. The two freeways reconnect about 20 miles north of the Twin Cities in Forest Lake. From there, I-35 continues to its northern terminus, the port city of Duluth.

The major east-west freeway is Interstate 94, which splits St. Paul in half, crosses the Mississippi River just south of the University of Minnesota campus, and hooks around the southern and western edges of downtown Minneapolis before heading north and west out of the city, on its way to western Minnesota, North Dakota, and points beyond.

The western suburbs are connected to downtown Minneapolis via Interstate 394, a $400 million expressway with separate lanes for carpools and buses. The entire Twin Cities is ringed by Interstate 494 (on the south and west) and Interstate 694 (on the north and east). The western edges of the metropolitan area are served by two north-south freeways: Highway 100 is just west of Minneapolis city limits, and Highway 169 is about five miles further west. Crosstown 62 hugs the southern edges of Minneapolis, connecting Minneapolis/St. Paul International Airport with I-35W, then heading west past the Southdale area and onto I-494.

Public Transportation

Metro Transit

Not very long ago, the Twin Cities area was crisscrossed by one of the world's largest electric streetcar systems. The streetcars made their debut in downtown Minneapolis in 1889, and by the 1920s the Twin City Rapid Transit Company had more than 1,000 cars on 500 miles of track. The system was so extensive that it was possible to travel via streetcar to nearly every corner of the metropolitan area—from Stillwater on the St. Croix River in the east to Lake Minnetonka's shores in the west, from Anoka 40 miles south to Hastings—although most of the area back then was rural.

The streetcars disappeared in 1954, replaced by the buses that still constitute mass transit in the Twin Cities. Today, Metro Transit (612/373-3333, 612/341-0140 TDD/TTY, 612/341-4587 automated route information; www.metrotransit.org) transports more than 65 million passengers a year over 115 routes on its fleet of more than 1,000 vehicles.

Buses are generally safe and are patrolled by a 150-member police force. Metro Transit manages to run during even the most brutal of blizzards and is often the safest and least nerve-racking way to get around in winter. Inner-city service is the most frequent and dependable, and it is possible—but not always easy—to live in Minneapolis or St. Paul and not own a car (the same cannot be said about the suburbs). Downtown Minneapolis, downtown St. Paul, Uptown Minneapolis, and the Mall of America are Metro Transit's four main hubs, at which a number of routes converge and transferring is easy.

Service to most suburban areas is spotty at best outside morning and evening rush hours. Still, commuting from the suburbs by bus is often preferable to battling freeway traffic, particularly since new lanes allow buses and other multipassenger vehicles to bypass the often bumper-to-bumper traffic in ordinary lanes. Metro Transit also operates more than 120 "park-and-ride" lots across the Twin Cities, allowing commuters to park free and hop buses to their destinations.

Metro Transit operates three Transit Stores, which sell passes and offer information on routes, fares, and discounts. In downtown Minneapolis, the Transit Store is located at 719 Marquette Avenue (look for the front of a bus coming out of the building). In downtown St. Paul, the Transit Store is located on the skyway level of the American Bank Building, at 101 East Fifth Street. The Mall of America store is in the Transit Hub, just outside the mall's East Broadway entrance (between Bloomingdale's and Sears).

Metro Mobility

Metro Mobility (651/221-1932) offers door-to-door transportation for people with disabilities. The service provides more than 1.2 million rides per year in its fleet of 150 specially equipped vans. Rides can be scheduled up to two weeks in advance.

Minnesota RideShare

Designed to encourage fewer cars on the road, Minnesota RideShare

TWIN CITY TAXI COMPANIES
Airport Taxi, 612/721-0000
Blue & White Taxi, 612/333-3333
Suburban Taxi, 612/884-8888
Yellow Cab Minneapolis, 612/824-4444
Yellow Cab St. Paul, 651/222-4433
Yellow Cab Suburban, 612/824-4000

(612/349-RIDE, 612/349-SIGN TDD/TTY) is a free carpool and van-pool service operated by Metro Transit. RideShare drivers use the bus freeway lanes and receive inexpensive or free parking in many downtown Minneapolis/St. Paul facilities.

Taxis

Unless you're waiting in a few rare stretches of downtown Minneapolis or at the airport, don't expect to hail a cab from the curb in the Twin Cities. Call instead and have a dispatcher send one to your door.

Fares vary among companies but average about $1.50 per mile. There's often a surcharge for extra passengers and trips to the airport. Expect to pay $25 for a taxi from the airport to downtown Minneapolis, $15 for an airport–downtown St. Paul run, and $10 from the airport to Mall of America. Most cabs accept major credit cards.

Airport Express

If you're staying at a hotel and don't need to rent a car, consider Airport Express (612/726-6400). This quick, affordable one-way or round-trip van service runs from the airport to a number of hotels and condominiums in downtown St. Paul, downtown Minneapolis, and a few suburban locations. Cost is about one-third of taking a taxi.

Driving in the Twin Cities

The Twin Cities have never been particularly compact, and suburban sprawl during the last 25 years has pushed metropolitan area borders far into the countryside. Outside of the two downtowns and adjoining urban neighborhoods, little of the area is easily walkable, and Metro Transit covers few suburban destinations. So if you plan to venture outside of either downtown, you will probably need a car.

Once you're in that car, however, navigating the area is easy. Drivers are generally courteous but not particularly charitable. Don't expect a lot of kindness when merging or changing lanes.

Driving the area's overtaxed freeways can be a trying experience during morning and evening rush hours. I-35W between downtown Minneapolis and the Minnesota River, I-94 between the two downtowns, and I-394 west of downtown Minneapolis can be particularly maddening. Almost all freeway on-ramps are metered during peak hours, meaning that a computerized system of stop lights limits access to manage traffic flow.

An old joke notes that there are two seasons in Minnesota: winter

TIP

For an update on highway conditions, call 651/297-4103 (651/296-9930 TDD/TTY).

If your car is towed in Minneapolis, call 612/673-5777. The impound lot is located at 51 Colfax Avenue North, adjacent to I-394 just west of downtown. In St. Paul, call 651/292-3642. St. Paul's lot is behind Holman Field, at 830 Bard's Channel Road, near the intersection of Highway 52 and Concord Street. Both facilities accept cash, checks, and major credit cards.

and highway construction. And indeed, road crews take full advantage of the brief snowless months to make repairs. Currently, two of the area's main interstate freeways are undergoing several years of reconstruction. Expect delays on both I-35W from downtown Minneapolis to the Minnesota River, and I-94 from Cretin Avenue in St. Paul to the Lowry Hill Tunnel in Minneapolis.

Winter Driving

Wintertime driving can be a real test of will in the Twin Cities. Maintenance crews are surprisingly skilled at clearing roads and keeping them passable with copious amounts of sand and salt. Still, driving on icy roads isn't anyone's idea of fun. The heinous phenomenon known as "black ice" (frozen car exhaust) has caused many a fender-bender and worse. So be sure to drive slowly, give the vehicle in front of you plenty of room, use your brake gingerly, and steer in the direction of a spin should one occur.

The Minnesota Highway Patrol suggests keeping an emergency winter survival kit in your car. It should include a flashlight, a candle, matches, and chocolates or hard candy. It's also wise to include a bag of salt, a blanket or two, and a window scraper and brush among your emergency supplies.

If you've never driven in a cold-weather city before, you may be alarmed to happen upon a street sign that reads "Snow Emergency Route." Fear not. This sign means that after a particularly heavy snowfall, the city will declare a "snow emergency," and that thoroughfare will be plowed first. Less-traveled residential streets will be cleared within 24 to 48 hours.

During a snow emergency, parking is banned on streets according to their priority, and both cities (in what some residents joke is the primary means of filling city coffers) vigorously tag and tow vehicles in violation of plowing regulations. Call 612/348-SNOW in Minneapolis and 651/266-7569 in St. Paul for information about snow emergency procedures.

Winter conditions also affect parking. If snowfalls are heavy enough, Minneapolis allows parking only on the even-numbered side of most residential streets. Mounds of snow also eliminate metered and unmetered spots everywhere.

Winter is not easy on automobiles, which is one reason classic vehicles and expensive new models are rarely seen during winter. The sand and

Parking meters within Minneapolis city limits accept only quarters. Be sure to note the meters' hours of operation, because Minneapolis meter-readers watch their beats like prison guards. If you let your meter expire, you'll be hit with a $10 ticket. Most meters are enforced Monday through Friday 8 a.m. to 6 p.m., although Metrodome and Minneapolis Convention Center area meters are enforced daily until 10 p.m.

salt that is liberally spread across area roads play havoc on a car's exterior, and the extreme cold can and will freeze just about anything inside a car engine, including the fuel.

The weather isn't easy on roads, either. Half of the fabled 10,000 Minnesota lakes are really waterlogged potholes—or so you will begin to believe when taking a drive after a long, harsh winter.

Parking Tips

Twin Citians love to complain about parking—and the lack thereof in both downtowns. Actually, each has enormous parking facilities. In Minneapolis, three gargantuan city-owned ramps straddle a blocks-long section of I-394, providing space for several thousand cars. By day, commuters from the western suburbs fill the ramps (accessed directly from I-394). By night, they are busy with patrons visiting Target Center (connected by skyway), as well as downtown bars, theaters, and restaurants.

Most downtown Minneapolis parking ramps and lots participate in the "Do the Town" program, a joint effort between the city and the Downtown Council. Under the program, drivers park free with a $20 purchase at any of 200-plus stores, restaurants, clubs, and theaters. Just enter a ramp or lot (look for the green "Do the Town" sign) after 4 p.m. on weekdays or any time on weekends, and don't forget to get validation from a participating merchant or restaurateur.

Downtown St. Paul has a similarly huge stockpile of parking—particularly in city-owned ramps and the Kellogg Boulevard area, home to RiverCentre and the new Science Museum of Minnesota. St. Paul also has its own validation program. A $20 purchase from a participating merchant entitles you to three hours' parking.

Biking in the Twin Cities

Both cities are starting to see the wisdom of dedicated commuter bike paths, and each has begun realigning city streets to accommodate bikers. In Minneapolis, several principal streets (including Hennepin, Portland, and Park Avenues, and Second, Fourth, Fifth, Ninth, and Tenth Streets) have dedicated bike lanes. Minneapolis also has an extensive system (nearly 40

TIP

Commuter Connection (235 Pillsbury Center, Minneapolis; 612/348-2062) sells maps of bike trails in the seven-county metro area, as well of state trails maintained by the Department of Natural Resources.

miles) of interconnected paved bike paths running through its parks and along its Grand Rounds parkways.

In 1995 the city opened a 3.5-mile bike corridor along a little-used railroad right-of-way that connects downtown with Cedar Lake and the rest of the extensive bike path system. The downtown entrance is at the intersection of Glenwood Avenue and 12th Street. Call 612/673-2411 for details. A similar path will soon follow several miles of railroad right-of-way in south Minneapolis near 28th Street, stretching from France Avenue to the west to the Mississippi River on the east.

St. Paul recently created a bike path running the full length of Summit Avenue that connects to paths running along Mississippi River Boulevard. Many suburbs also have trails designed for both serious cyclists and recreational pedalers.

Hennepin County maintains a large system of groomed trails. One of the most popular is a 16.5-mile trail that follows an old streetcar route, connecting Hopkins with Victoria. Along the way, the trail skirts Lake Minnetonka, comes within a mile of the University of Minnesota Landscape Arboretum, and goes through the lovely Carver Park Reserve. Another former streetcar trail, this 10.5-mile stretch runs through rolling countryside from Hopkins to Chaska, ending at the Minnesota Valley Wildlife Refuge. Picnicking and parking are available on both trails. For more information, call 651/559-9000.

The state of Minnesota also maintains a number of trails, the majority outside the seven-county metropolitan area. For more information, call 651/296-6157 or 800/ 766-6000.

Woodside biking

Minnesota Office of Tourism

Walking in the Twin Cities

The same trails that serve bikers also allow pedestrians to circle city lakes, stroll along the river, and safely walk

Calhoun Cycle (1622 W. Lake St., Minneapolis; 612/827-8231) rents a large selection of single and tandem bicycles by the hour, half-day, day, and weekend at reasonable rates.

along parkways from one park or lake to the next. Downtown and neighborhood streets are fairly pedestrian friendly, with many shops and cafés accessible by foot.

In 1997 the Washington, D.C.–based Surface Transportation Project and the Environmental Working Group named the Twin Cities the nation's sixth safest metropolitan area for pedestrians. In the suburbs, however, foot travel is less viable.

Airports

The Twin Cities area is served by a number of airports, all managed by the Metropolitan Airports Commission, a division of the Metropolitan Council. Minneapolis/St. Paul International Airport (MSP) was recently ranked among the world's five safest airports. The busy facility, located at Wold Chamberlain Field, was named after Ernest Wold and Cyrus Chamberlain, two Minnesota aviators killed in action during World War I.

An airport has existed on the MSP site since 1923, when an old auto racetrack was retrofitted as an airfield. Northwest Airlines, formerly Northwest Airways, started with a mail route at the field in 1926. Three years later, the company began regular passenger service. Northwest is

Major Airlines Serving the Twin Cities

Air Canada, 800/241-6522
America West Airlines, 800/247-5692
Continental Airlines, 800/525-0280
Delta Air Lines, 800/241-1212
Frontier Airlines, 800/432-1359
Northwest Airlines, 800/225-2525
Sun Country Airlines, 612/726-1218
Trans World Airlines, 800/221-2000
United Airlines, 800/241-6522
US Airways, 800/428-4322
Vanguard Airlines, 800/826-4827

still the big name here, and 80 percent of the airport's gates are controlled by the Eagan-based airline, the nation's fourth largest.

More than 30 million people pass through MSP every year, arriving or departing on more than 1,100 daily flights via 18 national and regional carriers. The airport has direct flights to 160 destinations, including 20 cities outside the United States.

The airport's urban location, just 16 miles south of downtown Minneapolis and 12 miles east of downtown St. Paul, causes consternation among nearby residents, who have to live with the constant roar of aircraft. But the accessible location is a boon to visitors and residents alike.

MSP consists of two separate terminals. The main terminal, named for Minnesota native Charles Lindbergh, is located on Highway 5 just off I-494, west of Highway 55 and Fort Snelling. The terminal is somewhat dowdy but easy to manage. It is currently undergoing a major renovation that will considerably enhance its dining, shopping, and parking facilities.

Parking is available in a series of large ramps just opposite passenger drop-off and pickup points; it is accessible via skyway from the ticketing floor. The airport also offers valet parking, and the entire facility is wheelchair-accessible. Car rental and additional parking ramp access are available through a tunnel; enter at the baggage pickup area.

The second terminal—named for the late Hubert H. Humphrey, former Minneapolis mayor, U.S. vice president, and Minnesota senator—is

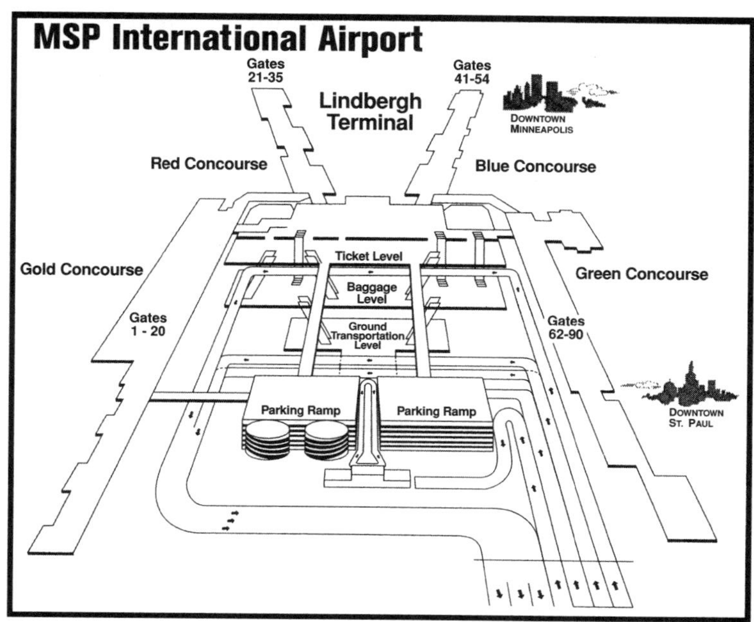

Dining on the Fly

Like many American airports, Minneapolis-St. Paul International has become more shopping mall than airline terminal. A number of quick-service restaurants are scattered throughout MSP, on its four concourses and in its attractive and comfortable new main-terminal food court, North Star Crossing.

For great sausage and fries, check out ***Jodi Maroni's****, a branch of the Venice, California, chain (Blue Concourse, Gate 47). Pizza lovers will relish the beauties coming out of the wood-burning oven at* ***California Pizza Kitchen ASAP*** *(Red Concourse, Gate 26). Share a big bowl of hearty Irish stew (and a side of great soda bread) at* ***Lake Line Pub*** *(Red Concourse, Gate 28). Quick pastas, sandwiches, prepared salads, and tasty desserts are available at* ***D'Amico & Sons*** *(Northstar Crossing). The best bagels come from* ***Big Apple Bagels*** *(Gold Concourse, Gate 7).*

located just north of I-494 on 34th Avenue South in Bloomington. This cheerless facility is reserved for charter flights and a number of international arrivals and departures. Its best feature is its manageability: crowds are thin, traffic is almost nonexistent, and parking is very easy. But unfortunately, beyond a small snack bar and gift shop, few amenities exist to ease the waiting time. The airport's main long-term parking lot is just north of the terminal; enter on 34th Avenue. A new terminal is scheduled to open in 2002.

A free shuttle bus connecting the two terminals runs frequently. Metro Transit offers service—but, alas, no express routes—to Lindbergh and Humphrey from downtown Minneapolis. Route 54 is an "almost-express" route to and from downtown St. Paul.

Many business travelers and private aviators prefer the small St. Paul Downtown Airport (644 Bayfield St., 612/224-4306) to MSP. This airport, also called Holman Field, offers inexpensive services and a convenient location, right across the Mississippi River from downtown St. Paul. Other local small airports include AirLake Airport (8140 220th St. W., Lakeville; 612/469-4040), Anoka County Airport (2289 85th Ave. N., Blaine; 612/784-6614), Crystal Airport (Bass Lake Rd. and Hwy. 52, Crystal; 612/537-2058), Flying Cloud Airport (10110 Flying Cloud Dr., Eden Prairie; 612/941-3545), and Lake Elmo Airport (12402 N. 30th St., Bayport Township; 651/777-6300).

Train Service

Marc Caryl

MSP International Airport

The Empire Builder, Amtrak's major east-west train between Chicago and Seattle, stops at the Amtrak passenger station in St. Paul's Midway area (730 Transfer Rd., 651/644-1127). Because of the long distances between destinations, however, train travel in the Midwest is significantly less convenient or popular than in other parts of the country, making traffic in this drab, utilitarian station fairly light.

Currently, the train to Chicago departs from St. Paul at 8:20 a.m. and arrives in Chicago's Union Station at 4:20 p.m. One-way tickets average $75. The daily train to Seattle departs St. Paul at 11:55 p.m. and arrives in Seattle's King Street Station two days later at 10:30 a.m. One-way tickets average $219. For more information, contact Amtrak at 800/872-7245.

Located two blocks north of the intersection of University and Cleveland Avenues, about 10 minutes from both downtowns, the station is open daily from 6:30 a.m. to midnight. Metro Transit service is via Route 16. Expect a $10 taxi fare from downtown St. Paul and a $15 fare from downtown Minneapolis. Parking at the station is free.

Bus Service

Greyhound (800/231-2222) was founded in Minneapolis, and the company operates two bus stations in the Twin Cities. The Minneapolis station (29 N. Ninth St., 612/371-3323) is located across the street from the Orpheum Theatre and two blocks from the major Metro Transit routes along Hennepin Avenue and Seventh and Eighth Streets. The St. Paul station (166 W. University Ave., 651/222-0509) sits a few blocks west of the Minnesota State Capitol. Both terminals are also served by Jefferson Bus Lines (612/332-3224), which operates an additional passenger pickup station at Minneapolis/St. Paul International Airport's Lindbergh Terminal.

Tim Steinberg—Embassy Suites

3

WHERE TO STAY

Thanks to building booms during the 1980s and 1990s, hotel and motel rooms are available in just about any price range and at any Twin Cities location. Most national chains are represented, along with a number of unique hotels and bed-and-breakfasts. Most of the five thousand hotel rooms in downtown Minneapolis are connected to the skyway system. The pickings in downtown St. Paul are much slimmer, but several fine hotels—and significant bargains—do exist.

The I-494 strip is lined with an unusually large number of motels and hotels, all near the Minneapolis/St. Paul International Airport and the gargantuan Mall of America, built on the Metropolitan Stadium site in 1992. The mall's popularity can sometimes make it difficult to book a room anywhere in the area; many visiting mall shoppers must stay in downtown Minneapolis or St. Paul (both about 15 minutes away) if they don't plan ahead.

Each listing contains a price-rating symbol that indicates the cost of a double room. These rates include lodging tax. In Bloomington and Minneapolis, the tax is 12 percent; in St. Paul it's 13 percent.

Price-rating symbols:

$	**Under $50**
$$	**$51 to $75**
$$$	**$76 to $125**
$$$$	**$126 and up**

DOWNTOWN MINNEAPOLIS

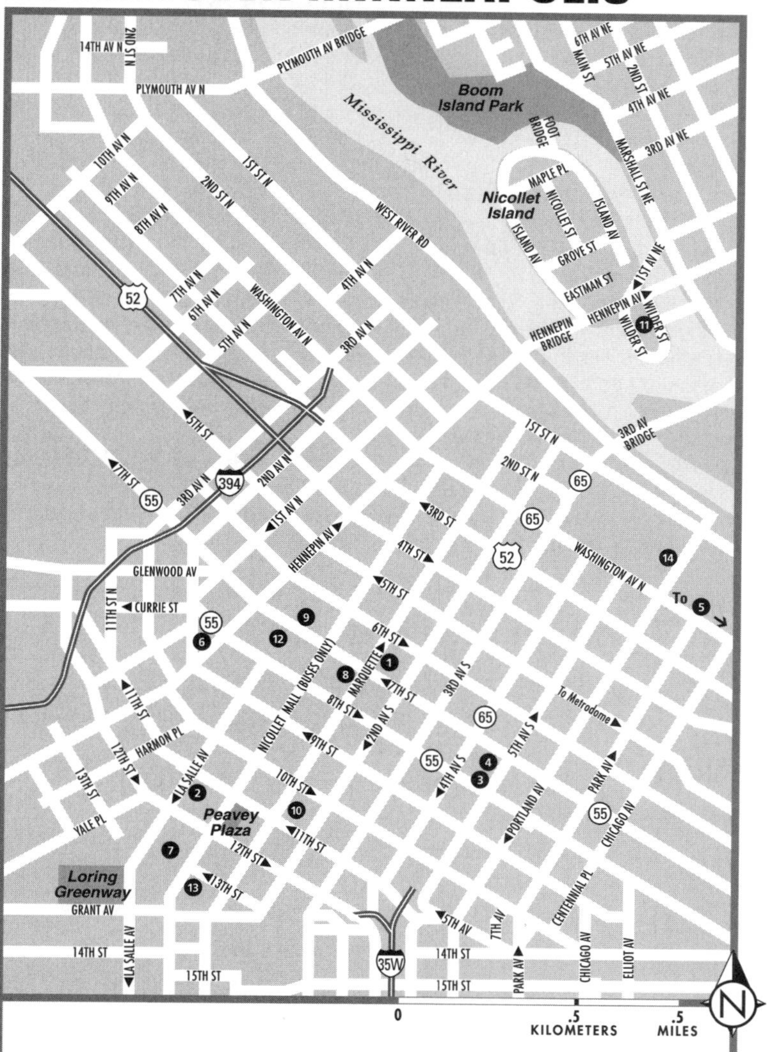

Where to Stay in Downtown Minneapolis

1 Crown Plaza Northstar
2 Doubletree Suites
3 Embassy Suites Minneapolis
4 Executive Suites
5 Holiday Inn Metrodome
6 Hotel Amsterdam
7 Hyatt Regency Minneapolis
8 Marquette Hotel
9 Marriott City Center
10 Minneapolis Hilton and Towers
11 Nicollet Island Inn
12 Radisson Plaza Hotel
13 Regal Minneapolis Hotel
14 Whitney Hyatt Hotel

DOWNTOWN MINNEAPOLIS

CROWN PLAZA NORTHSTAR
618 Second Ave. S.
Minneapolis
612/338-2288
$$

This sensible, comfortable 1960s hotel recently underwent a multimillion-dollar renovation. It is located in the heart of downtown, across the street from the Minneapolis Athletic Club. Several nonsmoking floors are available. The Rosewood Room, the hotel's restaurant, is a reliable though dull dining alternative. The Northstar's summer terrace—eight floors above Seventh Street—is a great spot for an inexpensive lunch or happy hour cocktail. Skyway connected. ♿ (Downtown Minneapolis)

DOUBLETREE SUITES
1101 LaSalle Ave.
Minneapolis
612/332-6800 or 800/662-3232
$$

One of the best deals in the city, the Doubletree is a hospitable alternative to the big chains. Its 230 attractive suites aren't particularly large but include a bedroom, kitchenette, and sitting room (complete with sleeper sofa). The hotel also maintains a small workout room. Just beyond the snug lobby is Cafe Luxx, a hopping jazz joint. No skyway connection, but the hotel is a half-block from Orchestra Hall. ♿ (Downtown Minneapolis)

EMBASSY SUITES MINNEAPOLIS
425 S. Seventh St.
Minneapolis
612/333-3111

Top Ten Hotel Bars:

1. **St. Paul Hotel**, 350 Market St., St. Paul; 651/292-9292
2. **Marquette Hotel**, 710 Marquette Ave., Minneapolis; 612/332-2351
3. **Lumber Barons Hotel**, 127 S. Water St., Stillwater; 651/439-6000
4. **Nicollet Island Inn**, 95 Merriam St., Minneapolis; 612/331-1800
5. **Hotel Sofitel**, 5610 W. 78 St., Bloomington; 612/835-1900
6. **Lowell Inn**, 102 N. Second St., Stillwater; 651/439-1100
7. **Whitney Hyatt Hotel**, 150 Portland Ave., Minneapolis; 612/339-9300
8. **Radisson Plaza Hotel**, 35 S. Seventh St., Minneapolis; 612/339-4900
9. **Crown Plaza Northstar Hotel**, 618 Second Ave. S., Minneapolis; 612/338-2288
10. **Embassy Suites St. Paul**, 175 E. Tenth St., St. Paul; 651/224-5400

When making a hotel reservation, call the local number rather than the toll-free 800 number. You could get a lower rate.

$$$
The Embassy is an all-suites hotel in Centre Village, a mixed-use complex near the Metrodome, City Hall, and the Hennepin County Medical Center. It offers 218 two-room suites, modest on-site workout facilities, a so-so in-house restaurant (Cornell's), free breakfast, and this chain's standard soaring atrium. Skyway connected. ♿ (Downtown Minneapolis)

EXECUTIVE SUITES
431 S. Seventh St.
Minneapolis
612/339-9010
$$
An extended-stay bargain, this Centre Village operation offers a collection of furnished studio and one-bedroom apartments, complete with fully equipped kitchens, cable TV, voice mail, and pleasant views. On-site ramp parking is available. Studios run $80 per night for five nights or more; one bedrooms go for $90 per night. Skyway connected. ♿

HOLIDAY INN METRODOME
1500 Washington Ave. S.
Minneapolis
612/333-4646 or 800/448-3663
$$$
This quasi–art deco 1980s hotel with 265 rooms anchors the Seven Corners neighborhood, home to many theaters, nightclubs, and restaurants. The Metrodome is six blocks to the west. The rooms are pleasantly, if forgettably, furnished, and there is an adjacent parking ramp. Amenities include a small indoor pool and workout area, a mediocre restaurant (The Grille), and free shuttle service to downtown and the Metrodome. ♿ (Downtown Minneapolis)

HOTEL AMSTERDAM
828 Hennepin Ave.
Minneapolis
612/288-0459
$
A small (24 rooms) bare-bones hostelry. Many of the rooms have shared baths, but this gay- and lesbian-oriented establishment is clean and relatively quiet, despite its situation above one of the city's most popular gay bars. Although it lacks downtown's requisite skyway connection, the location, a block from Hennepin Avenue's theaters and restaurants, can't be beat. (Downtown Minneapolis)

HYATT REGENCY MINNEAPOLIS
1300 Nicollet Mall
Minneapolis
612/370-1234
$$$$
One of the city's major convention hotels, the Hyatt boasts a choice location but is just as impersonal as its big-name rivals. The hotel has 532 comfortable rooms and 20 suites, plus four restaurants (including Manny's for steak and the Oceanaire for seafood). Other attractions include

TRIVIA

If a celebrity is staying in Minneapolis, chances are he or she has booked a room—or, more likely, a suite—at the Marquette Hotel. In St. Paul, the hostelry of choice is the St. Paul Hotel.

the Regency Athletic Club and Spa (612/343-3131), a well-appointed facility available to hotel guests for a $9 fee, a number of large ballrooms, and the city's largest exhibition hall outside of the Minneapolis Convention Center. The Hyatt is a two-block stroll from the convention center, Orchestra Hall, shops, and restaurants. Skyway connected. ♿ (Downtown Minneapolis)

MARQUETTE HOTEL
710 Marquette Ave.
Minneapolis
612/332-2351 or 800/445-8667
$$$$

Probably the top spot in town, the Marquette is the luxury hotel of choice for most out-of-town celebrities, who enjoy its big, well-appointed rooms, discreet and thoughtful staff, and prime IDS Center location. The Marquette's 277 rooms are managed by Hilton International. Shopping, business, and entertainment are all within a short walk. The hotel offers a small fitness facility on the fifth floor and a banquet and meeting room on the 50th floor of the IDS Tower. Basil's, the hotel's so-so restaurant, serves breakfast, lunch, and dinner daily, but it's worth a visit for its thrilling view, high above the Crystal Court. The Marq VII bar in the hotel's first-floor lobby is a stylish place to conclude a long day of work or play. Skyway connected. ♿ (Downtown Minneapolis)

MARRIOTT CITY CENTER
30 S. Seventh St.
Minneapolis
612/349-4000
$$$$

This 31-story triangular glass monolith in the City Center shopping and office complex offers nearly 600

Downtown Minneapolis on a Budget

Several moderately priced—and comfortable—hotel options do exist in downtown Minneapolis. These include the Normandy Inn (405 S. Eighth St., 612/370-1400), Holiday Inn Express & Suites (225 S. 11th St., 612/341-3300), Regency Plaza Hotel (41 N. 10th St., 612/339-9311 or 800/528-1234), and the Residence Inn (45. S. Eighth St., 612/677-1000).

rooms and suites. The hotel has an enormous ballroom and a well-equipped conference center, as well as Gustino's restaurant (singing waiters but predictable, overpriced food) and the more informal Allie's American Grill. Downtown shopping, entertainment, and business addresses are all within easy walking distance. Skyway connected. ♿ (Downtown Minneapolis)

MINNEAPOLIS HILTON AND TOWERS
1001 Marquette Ave.
Minneapolis
612/376-1000 or 800/445-8667
$$$$

This is the city's primary convention hotel, built specifically to complement the Minneapolis Convention Center, a block and a half to the south and adjacent to Orchestra Hall. The mammoth Hilton has 814 rooms (including 52 suites), and while its pompous public spaces are grand in a schlocky kind of way, the rooms are comfortable and well appointed. The hotel has two restaurants (including Carver's, an expensive steakhouse), an on-site health club and pool, and an enormous ballroom. Skyway connected. ♿ (Downtown Minneapolis)

NICOLLET ISLAND INN
95 Merriam St.
Minneapolis
612/331-1800
$$$

Built within the limestone walls of a nineteenth-century door factory, this antique-filled romantic getaway is smack-dab in the middle of the largest island in the Mississippi River. From here, it's a 10-minute walk to the heart of downtown. The inn has 24 distinctive guest rooms, as well as a popular restaurant and picture-perfect views of the river and downtown Minneapolis. The restaurants and movie theaters of Southeast Main Street are just a two-minute stroll across a vintage iron bridge. ♿ (Downtown Minneapolis)

RADISSON PLAZA HOTEL
35 S. Seventh St.
Minneapolis
612/339-4900 or 800/333-3333
$$$

This flagship of local zillionaire Curt Carlson's worldwide Radisson chain is geared toward the business traveler, with big, modern, nicely appointed rooms and plenty of amenities, including an excellent on-site health club and a service with-a-smile staff. The 288-room hotel has two restaurants, The Festival and The Cafe, but skip them both; far better establishments are just footsteps away, including Goodfellow's, right across the street (see Chapter 4, Where to Eat). Skyway connected. ♿ (Downtown Minneapolis)

REGAL MINNEAPOLIS HOTEL
1313 Nicollet Mall

TRIVIA

The Radisson Hotel chain was born in Minneapolis in 1909, on Seventh Street between Nicollet and Hennepin Avenues. The original Radisson, a swank, 350-room hotel, was razed in 1982. The current Radisson Plaza Hotel was built on the site in 1987.

DOWNTOWN ST. PAUL

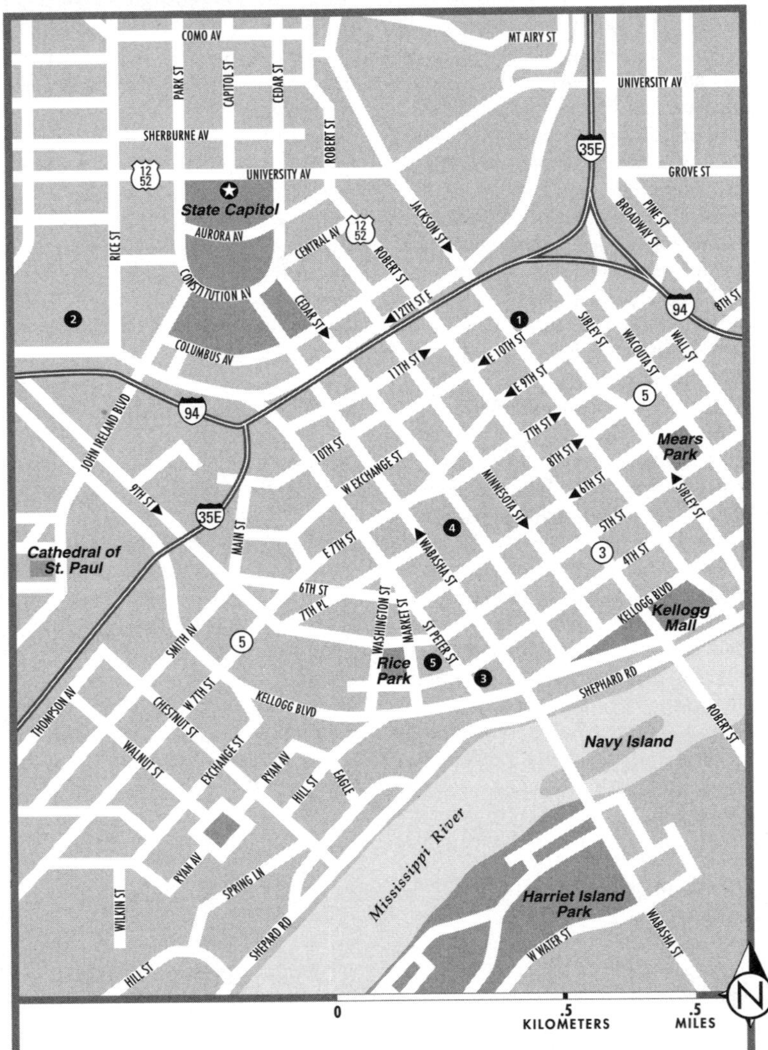

Where to Stay in Downtown St. Paul

1 Embassy Suites Saint Paul
2 Kelly Inn State Capitol
3 Radisson Hotel St. Paul
4 Radisson Inn
5 Saint Paul Hotel

Minneapolis
612/332-6000 or 800/522-8856
$$$
A smart choice for conventioneers on a budget, the Regal is two short blocks from the Minneapolis Convention Center and close to parks, entertainment, and restaurants. The hotel, a former Holiday Inn, has 325 rooms, a modest health facility, a large banquet hall, and a reliable restaurant, 1313 Cafe. The airy lobby and many of the rooms were recently remodeled. Ask for a room overlooking Nicollet Mall. Skyway connected. ♿ (Downtown Minneapolis)

WHITNEY HYATT HOTEL
150 Portland Ave.
Minneapolis
612/339-9300 or 800/248-1879
$$$$
Downtown's other celebrity destination, the Whitney is an intimate (40 rooms and suites) getaway in a renovated brick factory on the banks of the Mississippi River. This European-style hotel is full of luxurious touches, a reliable restaurant (the Whitney Grille), individually appointed rooms, and handsome public spaces. Be sure to ask for a room facing the Mississippi, or you'll end up with a view of a parking lot. ♿ (Downtown Minneapolis)

DOWNTOWN ST. PAUL

EMBASSY SUITES SAINT PAUL
175 E. 10th St.
St. Paul
651/224-5400 or 800/443-4600
$$$
In this sensitively designed hotel that wouldn't be out of place on the Côte d'Azur, 210 big, comfortable suites cluster around a sunny, plant-filled atrium. Complimentary breakfast is served in the atrium, and on-site Wooley's is a pretty decent restaurant. Amenities include a large indoor pool and a free airport shuttle. The Minnesota State Capitol is six blocks away. ♿ (Downtown St. Paul)

KELLY INN STATE CAPITOL
161 St. Anthony

Jacuzzi Suite at the Nicollet Inn, p. 33

Nicollet Island Inn

St. Paul
651/227-8711 or 800/528-1234
$$

Lots of politicos stay at the Kelly for its convenient location (the Minnesota State Capitol and surrounding buildings are three blocks away), low prices, and clean, newly remodeled rooms. This Best Western outlet also has a pool and a family-style restaurant, Benjamin's. Ask for a room on the quieter north side, and you'll get the added bonus of a Capitol dome view. ♿ (Downtown St. Paul)

RADISSON HOTEL ST. PAUL
11 E. Kellogg Blvd.
St. Paul
651/291-1900 or 800/333-3333
$$$$

This 22-story, 1960s-era hotel offers lovely vistas of the Mississippi River Valley from many of its 475 recently renovated rooms. Its gorgeous, newly completed ballroom is the city's largest. A number of suites and cabana-style rooms overlook a large pool. The hotel's kitschy top-floor rotating restaurant, Le Carousel, offers panoramic views that are much better than the food. Skyway connected. ♿ (Downtown St. Paul)

RADISSON INN
411 Minnesota St.
St. Paul
651/291-8800
$$$

Radisson rescued this property from oblivion in 1996, reopening it as a more affordable alternative to its glitzier hotel a few blocks south. Located in the Town Square office and retail complex downtown, this modern hotel got a nominal facelift after five years of dormancy, and its 250 rooms are attractive and quiet. Guests receive a complimentary breakfast. Capital City Marketcafe & Bar, the hotel's cafeteria-style restaurant, serves inexpensive breakfasts, lunches, and dinners. Skyway connected. ♿ Downtown St. Paul)

SAINT PAUL HOTEL
350 Market St.
St. Paul
651/292-9292 or 800/292-9292
$$$$

Minneapolis may have a bevy of gleaming new skyscraper hotels, but those blandly contemporary towers cannot match this grand turn-of-the-century hotel's Old World sophistication. Its 250 deluxe rooms are outfitted for comfort, the two restaurants (the St. Paul Grill and The Cafe) are among the city's best, and the superb Rice Park location can't be beat. The ballroom and meeting facilities are excellent, and the concierge service is top-notch. The St. Paul is the state's only Mobil four-star diamond hotel. ♿ (Downtown St. Paul)

MINNEAPOLIS

Hotels

BEST WESTERN UNIVERSITY INN
2600 University Ave. S.E.
Minneapolis
612/379-2313 or 800/528-1234
$$

The pick of the litter among a small collection of inexpensive motels (including Days Inn University, 612/623-3999, and the Econo Lodge, 612/331-6000), the Best Western offers clean and affordable digs about six blocks east of the university campus. It is particularly convenient to the U's hockey and basketball arenas. The hotel offers free shuttle service

MINNEAPOLIS

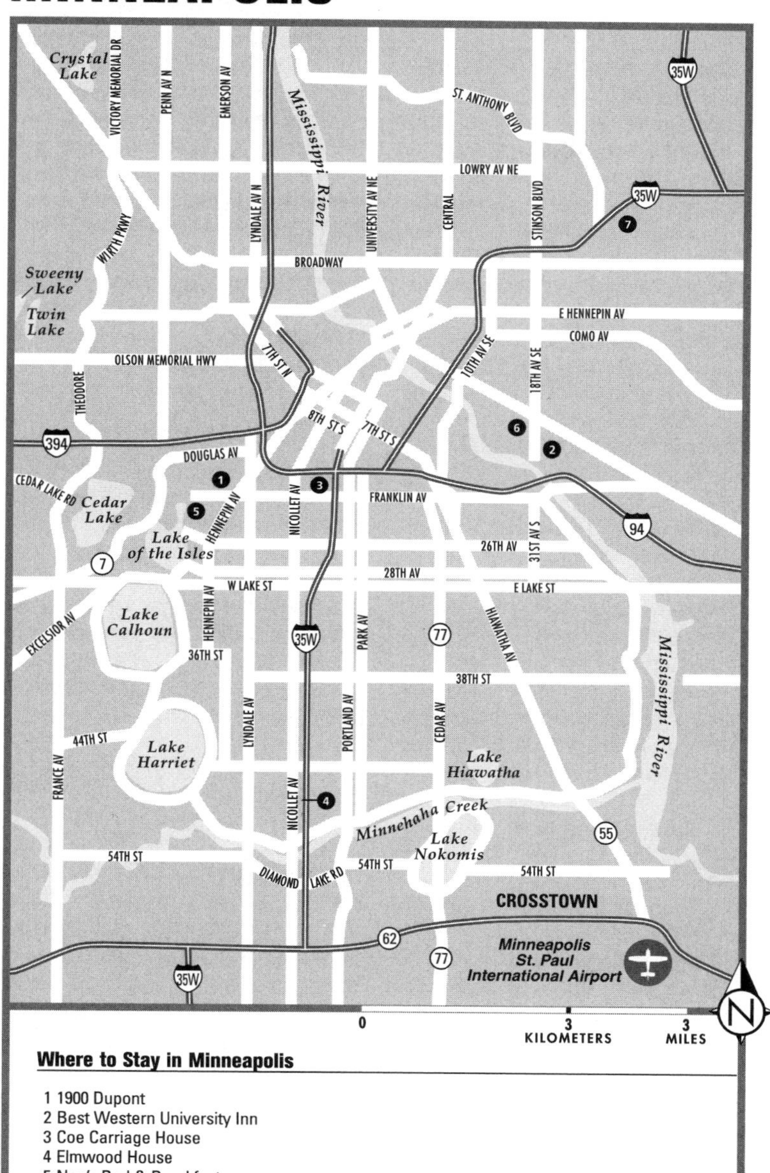

Where to Stay in Minneapolis

1 1900 Dupont
2 Best Western University Inn
3 Coe Carriage House
4 Elmwood House
5 Nan's Bed & Breakfast
6 Radisson Hotel Metrodome
7 Sheraton Metrodome Minneapolis

to the U of M Hospital and Clinic. ♿ (Minneapolis)

RADISSON HOTEL METRODOME
615 Washington Ave. S.E.
Minneapolis
612/379-8888 or 800/333-3333
$$$

This attractive, modern hotel's recent name change is somewhat misleading. Situated across the street from the U of M's medical complex, it's actually more than two miles east of the Metrodome. Misnomers aside, the 304-room hotel is full of amenities and offers two good restaurants: The Meadows, a clubby steak and wildfowl joint, and McCormick's, a lively deli. (Minneapolis)

SHERATON METRODOME MINNEAPOLIS
1330 Industrial Blvd.
Minneapolis
612/331-1900
$$

Why it's called the Sheraton Metrodome is a puzzle, since this former Hilton property is located several miles north of the stadium. However, this 250-room hotel is convenient to Rosedale, as well as to U of M's St. Paul campus and the state fairgrounds. The rooms are comfortable and clean, and kids will enjoy the large indoor swimming pool. The Anchorage, the hotel's seafood restaurant, isn't what it used to be. ♿ (Minneapolis)

1900 Dupont

1900 Dupont

Bed-and-Breakfasts

1900 DUPONT
1900 Dupont Ave. S.
Minneapolis
612/374-1973
$$

This B&B has four rooms with private baths in a three-story, 102-year-old home on Lowry Hill, just a few blocks south of the Guthrie Theater, Walker Art Center, and the Minneapolis Sculpture Garden. Pass away a rainy afternoon in the cozy second-floor library and enjoy a complimentary breakfast in the grand dining room. Rates escalate on the weekend. (Minneapolis)

COE CARRIAGE HOUSE
1700 Third Ave. S.
Minneapolis
612/871-4249
$$$$

While conveniently located just two blocks south of the Minneapolis Convention Center (and a five-minute walk to the Minneapolis Institute of Arts), this hotel borders an increasingly marginal neighborhood. But the house itself (rented as a single unit) is a stunner: a very private, deluxe three-bedroom unit in a converted 1880s carriage house, with a Jacuzzi, kitchen, fine furnishings, and cable TV. Rates are based on the number of guests. (Minneapolis)

TIP

To learn more about Gopher State B&Bs, call the Minnesota Department of Tourism, 612/296-5029 or 800/657-3700, and order *Explore Minnesota Bed and Breakfasts and Historic Inns*, an annually updated guide.

ELMWOOD HOUSE
1 E. Elmwood Pl.
Minneapolis
612/822-4558 or 888/822-4558
$$
In this comfortable 1887 house you'll find three rooms, one with a private screened porch, that share a bath. An additional third-floor suite contains two bedrooms and a bath. Designed by Henry Wild Jones (architect of Butler Square) for his family, Elmwood House sits in the charming Tangletown neighborhood, 10 minutes from both downtown and Mall of America. Pretty Minnehaha Creek and its walking and bike paths lie one block to the south. (Minneapolis)

NAN'S BED & BREAKFAST
2304 Fremont Ave. S.
Minneapolis
612/377-5118 or 800/214-5118
$
This inexpensive ($60 per night) B&B offers three rooms with shared bath in a great south Minneapolis location. It's across the street from Temple Israel, the city's largest synagogue; just six blocks east of picturesque Lake of the Isles; and a 10-minute walk to Uptown's shops, restaurants, and movie theaters. Breakfast is included, and the house is a block from four bus lines. (Minneapolis)

ST. PAUL

Hotels

RAMADA HOTEL ST. PAUL
1870 Old Hudson Rd.
St. Paul
651/735-2330 or 800/228-2828
$$
The best features of this amiable 200-room hotel are its proximity to the huge corporate campus of 3M, comfortable rooms, and big indoor swimming pool and lounge. ♿ (St. Paul)

SHERATON INN MIDWAY
400 Hamline Ave. N.
St. Paul
651/642-1234
$$
A smart choice for families, this well-maintained, 200-room hotel in St. Paul's Midway district is convenient to both downtowns (via I-94), the Minnesota State Fairgrounds, and the adjacent Midway shopping area. The hotel recently opened a new restaurant, the Cities Grill. Kids will love the Nintendo games, while parents will appreciate the free newspapers and in-room coffeemakers. ♿ (St. Paul)

Bed-and-Breakfasts

COMO VILLA BED AND BREAKFAST
1371 W. Nebraska Ave.

ST. PAUL

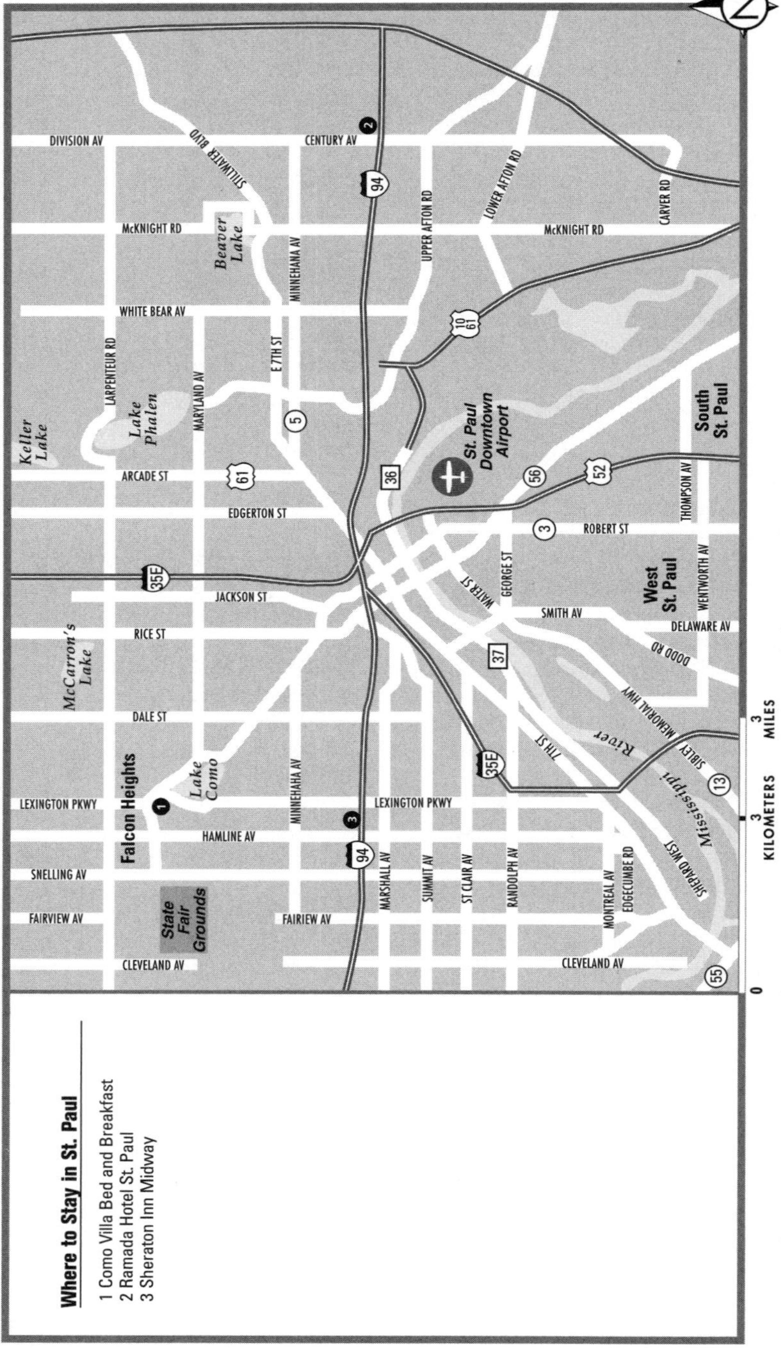

Where to Stay in St. Paul

1 Como Villa Bed and Breakfast
2 Ramada Hotel St. Paul
3 Sheraton Inn Midway

St. Paul
651/647-0471
$$
This 1870s Victorian home is just two blocks from St. Paul's Como Park and six blocks from the Minnesota State Fairgrounds. Its three rooms with private baths are furnished in tons of Victoriana, with big windows overlooking a pretty shaded yard. (St. Paul)

GREATER TWIN CITIES

Hotels and Motels

AFTON HOUSE INN
3291 S. St. Croix Trail
Afton
651/436-8883
$$$
Dating to 1867, this small, charming hotel is on the National Register of Historic Places. Many of its 15 rooms have fireplaces and Jacuzzis. Ask for a St. Croix River view. ♿ (Greater Twin Cities)

BEST WESTERN AMERICAN INN
3924 Excelsior Blvd.
Minneapolis
612/927-7731 or 800/528-1234
$
Just one mile west of Lake Calhoun, this unassuming and inexpensive suburban motel is a little-known and conveniently located gem to remember when accommodating out-of-town guests on a budget. The rooms are comfortable, in a 1970s kind of way, and clean, but the chief attractions here are the low prices and handy address. (Greater Twin Cities)

BEST WESTERN CANTERBURY INN
1244 Canterbury Rd.
Shakopee
612/445-3644 or 800/528-1234
$
A comfortable, 175-room choice for suburban lodging, close to the fun of Valleyfair amusement park, the horse races at Canterbury Park, and the gambling at Mystic Lake Casino. ♿ (Greater Twin Cities)

BEST WESTERN SEVILLE PLAZA HOTEL
8151 Bridge Rd.
Bloomington
612/830-1300 or 800/528-1234
$$
The cheesy mock-Spanish decor can be easily overlooked because the value is pretty good at this 250-room hotel located about five minutes west of Mall of America. The hotel offers free shuttle service to the mall and the airport and has an indoor pool. Rooms are plain but comfortable; those on the upper floors have nice views of Normandale Park. (Greater Twin Cities)

COUNTRY INN & SUITES BY CARLSON
2221 Killebrew Dr.
Bloomington
612/854-5555 or 800/456-4000
$$
This new hotel features 85 standard rooms and 55 suites, including 10 with whirlpools. Carlson Companies (owners of the Radisson chain) put a little extra dough into this high-profile location, so the hotel (across the street from Mall of America) is less spartan than its metro-area compatriots. A TGIFriday's restaurant is located next door. Additional locations: 2905 Snelling Ave. N., Roseville; 4940 Hwy. 61, White Bear Lake; 6003 Hudson Rd., Woodbury. ♿ (Greater Twin Cities)

GREATER TWIN CITIES

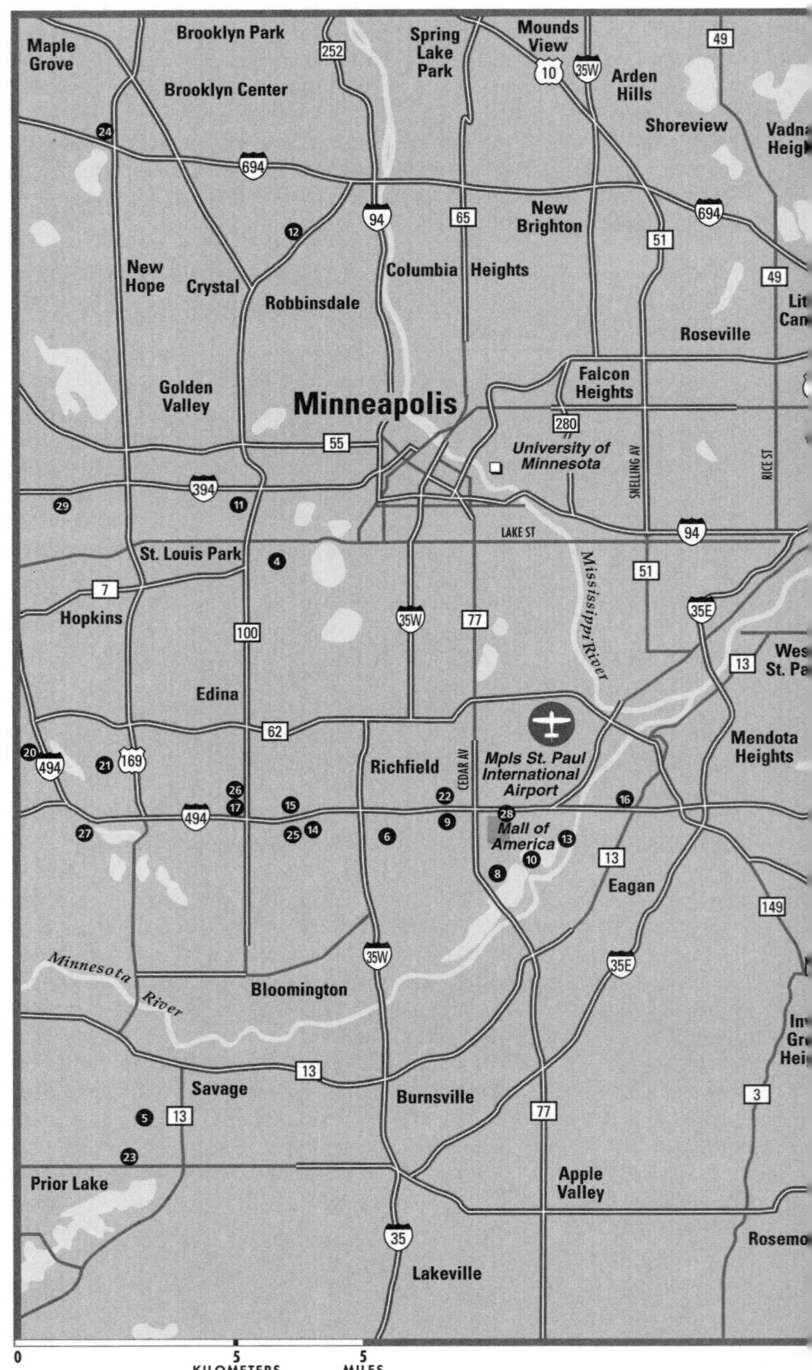

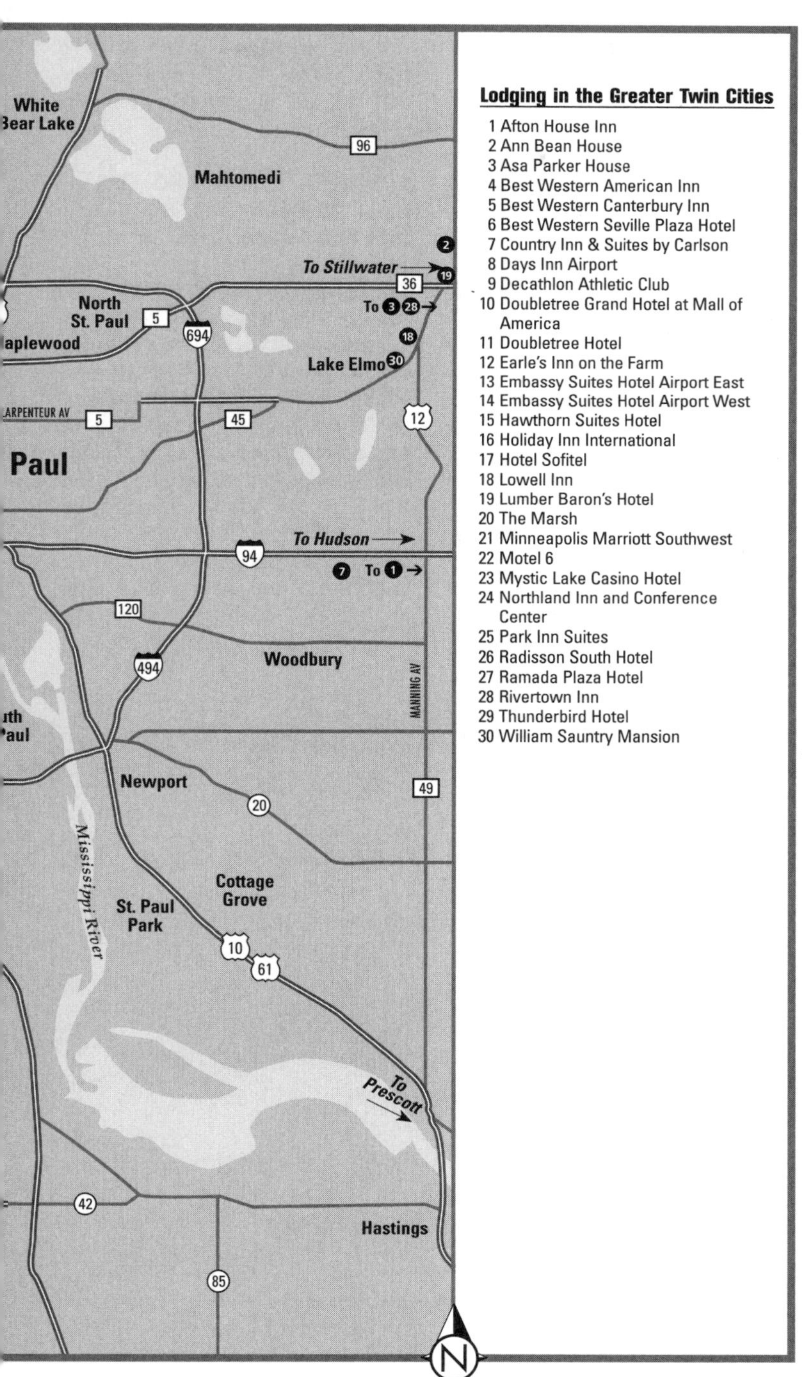

Lodging in the Greater Twin Cities

1 Afton House Inn
2 Ann Bean House
3 Asa Parker House
4 Best Western American Inn
5 Best Western Canterbury Inn
6 Best Western Seville Plaza Hotel
7 Country Inn & Suites by Carlson
8 Days Inn Airport
9 Decathlon Athletic Club
10 Doubletree Grand Hotel at Mall of America
11 Doubletree Hotel
12 Earle's Inn on the Farm
13 Embassy Suites Hotel Airport East
14 Embassy Suites Hotel Airport West
15 Hawthorn Suites Hotel
16 Holiday Inn International
17 Hotel Sofitel
18 Lowell Inn
19 Lumber Baron's Hotel
20 The Marsh
21 Minneapolis Marriott Southwest
22 Motel 6
23 Mystic Lake Casino Hotel
24 Northland Inn and Conference Center
25 Park Inn Suites
26 Radisson South Hotel
27 Ramada Plaza Hotel
28 Rivertown Inn
29 Thunderbird Hotel
30 William Sauntry Mansion

DAYS INN AIRPORT
1901 Killebrew Dr.
Bloomington
612/854-8400
$$

With a convenient Mall of America location (directly across the street from Macy's), this 207-room hotel is a cut above the usual Days Inn facility, with attractive rooms, a big indoor swimming pool, and a full-service restaurant. Free shuttle to the mall and airport. ♿ (Greater Twin Cities)

DECATHLON ATHLETIC CLUB
1700 E. 79th St.
Bloomington
612/854-7777
$$

This deluxe health club and spa, two minutes west of Mall of America, contains extensive sports and fitness facilities and also operates a well-kept secret: a small hotel of single rooms and suites at remarkably low prices. You'll receive attentive service, the run of the club and its dining facilities, plus free shuttle service to the mall and airport. (Greater Twin Cities)

DOUBLETREE GRAND HOTEL AT MALL OF AMERICA
7901 24th Ave. S.
Bloomington
612/854-2244 or 800/222-8733
$$$

Located directly across the street from Mall of America, this 320-room quasi-luxury hotel (a recent renovation of the Registry Hotel) is a great choice for those immersing themselves in the mall experience. If you feel like going all out, book a room on the Concierge Floors, which offer a free happy hour and breakfast. The hotel's Nine Mile Grill, named for a meandering Bloomington creek, isn't bad. Free mall and

Top Ten Mall of America Hotel Bargains

1. **Homewood Suites**, 2261 Killebrew Dr., Bloomington; 612/854-0900
2. **Country Inn & Suites**, 2221 Killebrew Dr., Bloomington; 612/854-5555
3. **Days Inn**, 1901 Killebrew Dr., Bloomington; 612/854-8400
4. **Motel 6**, 7640 Cedar Ave. S., Richfield; 612/861-4491
5. **Friendly Host Palm Plaza**, 1225 E. 78 St., Bloomington; 612/854-3322
6. **Exel Inn**, 2701 E. 78 St., Bloomington; 612/854-7200
7. **Comfort Inn Bloomington**, 1321 E. 78 St., Bloomington; 612/854-3400
8. **Budgetel Inn**, 7815 Nicollet Ave. S., Bloomington; 612/881-7311
9. **Super 8**, 7800 Second Ave. S., Bloomington; 612/888-8800
10. **Fairfield Inn**, 2401 E. 80 St., Bloomington; 612/858-8475

airport shuttle service. ♿ (Greater Twin Cities)

DOUBLETREE HOTEL
5555 Wayzata Blvd.
St. Louis Park
612/542-8600 or 800/542-5566
$$

Just five minutes west of downtown Minneapolis via I-394, this attractive, 300-room suburban hotel has a huge indoor swimming pool and extensive meeting and banquet facilities. Its casual restaurant's only real thrill is its great bakery, but a number of passable meals can be had within walking distance. One of the Twin Cities' largest health clubs, Northwest Athletic Club (612/546-5474), is a five-minute walk away as well. Day passes are available for $6. ♿ (Greater Twin Cities)

EMBASSY SUITES HOTEL AIRPORT EAST
7901 34th Ave. S.
Bloomington
612/854-1000 or 800/362-2779
$$$
EMBASSY SUITES HOTEL AIRPORT WEST
2800 W. 80th St.
Bloomington
612/884-4811 or 800/362-2779
$$$

These two branches of the all-suites hotel chain are organized around lushly landscaped indoor atriums. The spacious two-room suites are comfortable and quiet, and both hotels serve complimentary breakfast. The Airport West location is near Southdale (about four minutes west of Mall of America). Airport East is two minutes from both the airport and the mall and within a stone's throw of the gorgeous Minnesota Valley National Wildlife Refuge. Both hotels offer free airport/mall shuttle service. ♿ (Greater Twin Cities)

HAWTHORN SUITES HOTEL
3400 Edinborough Way
Edina
612/893-9300
$$

Comprised of 140 two-room suites with kitchenettes, this hotel offers complimentary breakfast daily and happy hour Monday through Thursday. Guests have free access to adjacent Edinborough Park, a large indoor park complete with gardens, a swimming pool, skating rink, and a children's playground, which is a winter favorite. ♿ (Greater Twin Cities)

HOLIDAY INN INTERNATIONAL
3 Appletree Square
Bloomington
612/854-9000 or 800/465-4329
$$

Located two minutes from the airport, this fancy (for a Holiday Inn) 13-story hotel has 430 rooms and an Olympic-size swimming pool. A free shuttle runs to the airport and Mall of America, both about two minutes away. Ask for a room with a southern view, and you'll look over the Minnesota Valley National Wildlife Refuge, just a five-minute walk away. ♿ (Greater Twin Cities)

HOTEL SOFITEL
5601 W. 78th St.
Bloomington
612/835-1900 or 800/763-4835
$$$

It's all très French (or at least a Midwesterner's idea of France) at this congenial and well-appointed getaway, probably the most comfortable hotel in the I-494 area. Nearly 300 rooms (all recently remodeled) are stacked around a lovely interior atrium court, along with a pool and a fairly plush health spa. The Sofitel also has three decent restaurants: Chez Collette, for casual bistro fare; La Terrasse, for quick snacks; and Le Cafe Royal, for more formal dining. ♿ (Greater Twin Cities)

LOWELL INN
102 N. Second St.
Stillwater
651/439-1100
$$$$

Expensive and romantic, this 21-room inn (built in 1930) was designed to resemble Mount Vernon. The inn is a particular favorite with honeymooners and couples celebrating anniversaries. Skip its three overpriced, underwhelming dining rooms and walk a few blocks to La Belle Vie or The Harvest instead (see Chapter 4, Where to Eat). (Greater Twin Cities)

Lowell Inn

Lowell Inn

LUMBER BARONS HOTEL
127 S. Water St.
Stillwater
651/439-6000
$$$$

This attractive 36-room hotel (partially housed in a vintage 1890 commercial building) sits in the center of Stillwater. The rooms are large and comfortably appointed, and the superior staff aims to please. The hotel boasts fabulous trompe l'oeil paintings in the dining rooms and lobby, a great bar, and a large patio and terrace overlooking the St. Croix River. ♿ (Greater Twin Cities)

MINNEAPOLIS AIRPORT MARRIOTT BLOOMINGTON
2020 E. 79th St.
Bloomington
612/854-7441 or 800/228-9290
$$$

This standard Marriott has a superb location, across a parking lot from Mall of America. This sprawling hotel has nearly 500 rooms, a large indoor pool, and an airport/mall shuttle. ♿ (Greater Twin Cities)

MINNEAPOLIS MARRIOTT SOUTHWEST
5801 Opus Pkwy.
Minnetonka
612/935-5500
$$$

This big, 325-room suburban hotel is set in a campuslike office park about five minutes west of Southdale and just north of the intersection of Highways 62 and 169. Athletes will enjoy the large on-site fitness center as well as access to miles of jogging and bike paths. ♿ (Greater Twin Cities)

MOTEL 6
7640 CEDAR AVE. S.
RICHFIELD
612/861-4491 OR 800/466-8356
$

Here you'll find clean, cheap (around $40 per night), basic accommoda-

Camping in the Twin Cities

Campsites are few and far between in the seven-county metropolitan area, but you can still find a quiet place to spend a night in a tent (or under the stars).

Hennepin County operates a number of camping facilities, including a 210-site location on beautiful Lake Independence in ***Baker Park****, about 15 miles west of downtown Minneapolis. Rates are $12 per night. The county also offers 54 sites ($9 per night) at Lake Auburn in* ***Carver Park****, about 20 miles southwest of downtown Minneapolis. Call 612/559-6700 for reservations.*

Backpackers will find two dozen year-round campsites at ***Afton State Park*** *in Hastings, about 20 minutes southeast of downtown St. Paul. Campsites cost $8 per night—a bargain for such stunning views of the St. Croix River. Call 612/922-9000 or 800/246-2267 to reserve.*

Bunker Hill Regional Park *in Anoka, 30 minutes north of downtown Minneapolis, offers 26 sites for a mere 50 cents per night. A central restroom has running water, but there are no showers or electricity. Call 612/757-3920 for reservations.*

The Minnesota Alliance of Campground Operators publishes an annually updated roster of private and public campgrounds across the state. For a free copy of Minnesota Campground and RV Parks, call the Minnesota Department of Tourism at 651/296-5029 or 800/657-3700.

tions, with Mall of America just across the confusing I-494/Highway 77 interchange. Be sure to ask at the desk for a map to the mall, or you'll never find it. The best way to get there is to follow the I-494 frontage road west to 12th Avenue. Turn south and go three blocks to 79th Street. Turn east and follow 79th Street under Highway 77 to the mall. (Greater Twin Cities)

MYSTIC LAKE CASINO HOTEL
2400 Mystic Lake Blvd.
Prior Lake
612/445-9000 or 800/262-7799
$$

Located 30 minutes southwest of downtown Minneapolis, this is the only hotel at the state's largest, most lavish casino (and the nation's second largest Native American–owned gaming operation). The comfortable

220-room suburban hotel is constantly booked solid, so call ahead for reservations. ♿ (Greater Twin Cities)

NORTHLAND INN AND CONFERENCE CENTER
7025 Northland Dr. N.
Brooklyn Park
612/536-8300 or 800/441-4622
$$$

More than 200 deluxe two- and three-room suites are arranged around a sunny, eight-story atrium at this popular destination for business travelers, 20 minutes northwest of downtown Minneapolis. The suburban hotel has extensive conference facilities, two on-site restaurants, and a lavishly appointed exercise facility. ♿ (Greater Twin Cities)

PARK INN SUITES
7770 Johnson Ave.
Bloomington
612/893-9999 or 800/528-1234
$$

Small and affordable, this no-frills hotel has 125 larger-than-usual rooms, all with refrigerators. It sits at the intersection of I-494 and France Avenue, about four minutes west of Mall of America and one mile south of Southdale. The hotel has an indoor swimming pool and whirlpool and offers complimentary breakfast and shuttle service to the mall. (Greater Twin Cities)

RADISSON SOUTH HOTEL
7800 Normandale Blvd.
Bloomington
612/835-7800 or 800/333-3333
$$$$

Bloomington's largest hotel (575 large rooms) is also a popular meeting and convention facility. It's located at the intersection of I-494 and Highway 100, about five minutes west of the mall. Request a room around the big indoor pool for a private balcony. Shipside, the hotel's seafood restaurant, isn't thrilling, but the more informal Cafe Stuga does a pretty good job with Scandinavian-themed fare. Better yet, dine across

Marquette Hotel, p. 32

Marquette Hotel

the street at one of Hotel Sofitel's restaurants. ♿ (Greater Twin Cities)

RAMADA PLAZA HOTEL
12201 Ridgedale Dr.
Minnetonka
612/593-0000 or 800/228-2828
$$$
This is a popular stop for business travelers working in the western suburbs (General Mills headquarters is two miles east on I-394). For a suburban chain hotel, this one is unusually attractive and is nicely sited on the edge of a wetlands preserve. To avoid a view of the shopping center parking lot, ask for a room overlooking the park. ♿ (Greater Twin Cities)

THUNDERBIRD HOTEL
2201 E. 78th St.
Bloomington
612/854-3411 or 800/528-1234
$$
This Best Western property is in a class all its own; it's worth checking out even if you don't intend to stay. Every square inch of Chez Thunderbird seems to be covered in Native American art and artifacts (some of it of dubious origin), and what isn't extraordinarily beautiful is supremely tacky. The faux Native American motif continues in the guest rooms. The Totem Pole Dining Room has forgettable food but an equally unforgettable atmosphere. The hotel boasts three swimming pools (indoor, outdoor, and kiddie) and a small workout area. Shuttle service runs to both Mall of America (across the street) and the airport. (Greater Twin Cities)

Bed-and-Breakfasts

ANN BEAN HOUSE
319 W. Pine St.
Stillwater
651/430-0355
$$$
This four-story, 1870s mansion contains five rooms (all with private baths), each adorned with oak woodwork and elaborate fireplaces. They come equipped with extras such as whirlpools, romantic sleigh beds, and great views. (Greater Twin Cities)

ASA PARKER HOUSE
17500 N. St. Croix Trail
Marine on St. Croix
651/433-5248
$$$$
Here you'll find five guest rooms, all with private baths, in a picture-perfect 1850s house. (Greater Twin Cities)

EARLE'S INN ON THE FARM
6150 Summit Dr. N.
Brooklyn Center
612/569-6330 or 800/428-8382
$$$
Earle's has 11 wonderfully decorated

Radisson Hotel St. Paul, p. 36

Radisson Hotel

rooms (all with private baths) housed in restored, turn-of-the-century buildings on the old Earle Brown Farm, estate of the Minnesota Highway Patrol founder. The gardens are lovely, too. The inn is located 10 minutes north of downtown Minneapolis. ♿ (Greater Twin Cities)

THE MARSH
15000 Minnetonka Blvd.
Minnetonka
612/935-2202
$$$
This soothing and luxurious health and wellness facility sports a half-dozen comfortable rooms. Guests have full access to a wide range of classes (yoga, aerobics, and Pilates), as well as a fully equipped training center. The Marsh also has a full-service spa and a well-run café. Adults only. Smoke-free. ♿ (Greater Twin Cities)

RIVERTOWN INN
306 W. Olive St.
Stillwater
651/430-2955
$$$
A lumber fortune built this 1882 Victorian mansion, and many of its eight rooms have dazzling views of the St. Croix River Valley. (Greater Twin Cities)

WILLIAM SAUNTRY MANSION
626 N. Fourth St.
Stillwater
651/430-2653
$$$
This glorious 1890 Queen Anne mansion has five antique-filled rooms with private baths and fireplaces. The smoke-free home is just up the hill from historic downtown Stillwater, and its rooms boast picture-perfect views of town and the St. Croix River Valley. (Greater Twin Cities)

Auriga

4
WHERE TO EAT

As recently as 15 years ago, the Twin Cities were strictly meat-and-potatoes towns. Eating "ethnic" meant grabbing egg rolls and chop suey at the local chow mein house, and French toast was about as nouvelle as it got.

But the area's restaurant renaissance has been remarkable, not only for its range—nearly every cuisine can be found—but also for the sheer number of new and interesting eating establishments. Today you'll find a restaurant for every taste and pocketbook, and enjoying the Twin Cities' gastronomical fare is as fun as exploring the parks, cultural institutions, and sights.

East listing contains a price rating symbol that indicates the cost per person of one meal (appetizer and entree). Price-rating symbols:

Price-rating symbols:

$	**Under $10**
$$	**$11 to $20**
$$$	**$21 and up**

All restaurants listed accept major credit cards unless otherwise noted. All Minnesota restaurants are required to provide a nonsmoking section; many ban smoking altogether.

Breakfasts
Continental Pantry and House of Fine Cakes (SP), p. 73

Cafeterias
Cafe Latte (SP), p. 71
Capital City Marketcafe & Bar (DSP), p. 64

Casual
Auriga (MP), p. 65
California Cafe (GTC), p. 80
Campiello (MP), p. 67
Chet's Taverna (SP), p. 73
D'Amico & Sons (MP), p. 67
Eat This (DMP), p. 56
Linguini & Bob (DMP), p. 57

Lucia's Restaurant (MP), p. 69
Monte Carlo Bar & Cafe (DMP), p. 58
No Wake Cafe (DSP), p. 64
Oak Grill (DMP), p. 59
128 Cafe (SP), p. 74
Palomino (DMP), p. 59
River Room (DSP), p. 64
Tavern on Grand (SP), p. 78
Twin City Grill (GTC), p. 82
The Vintage (SP), p. 78
W. A. Frost & Co. (SP), p. 78
Zander Cafe (SP), p. 78

Ethnic

Babani's Kurdish Restaurant (DSP), p. 62
The Barbary Fig (SP), p. 70
Brit's Pub & Eating Establishment (DMP), p. 53
Cafe Havana (DMP), p. 55
Cheng Heng Restaurant (SP), p. 73
Chez Bananas (DMP), p. 55
Gardens of Salonica (MP), p. 67
Lord Fletcher's on the Lake (GTC), p. 81
Nye's Polonaise Room (DMP), p. 59
Origami (DMP), p. 59
Rainbow Chinese Restaurant (MP), p. 69
Ruam Mit Thai Cafe (DSP), p. 64
Sakura (DSP), p. 65
Shilla (SP), p. 75
Shuang Cheng (MP), p. 70
Singapore Chinese Cuisine (GTC), p. 82
Taco Morelos (MP), p. 70
Tejas (GTC), p. 82

Fine Dining

Aquavit (DMP), p. 53
Bayport Cookery (GTC), p. 78
Bobino Cafe & Wine Bar (DMP), p. 53
Cafe Un Deux Trois (DMP), p. 55
D'Amico Cucina (DMP), p. 56
510 Restaurant (DMP), p. 57
Forepaugh's (DSP), p. 73
Goodfellow's (DMP), p. 57
Gustino's (DMP), p. 57
Kincaid's Steak Chop & Fish House (GTC), p. 80
La Belle Vie (GTC), p. 80
The Local (DMP), p. 57
Loring Cafe and Bar (DMP), p. 67
Lowell Inn (GTC), p. 81
New French Cafe and Bar (DMP), p. 58
St. Paul Grill (DSP), p. 65
Sophia (DMP), p. 61
Table of Contents (DMP, SP), p. 62, 75

Inexpensive

Birchwood Cafe (MP), p. 65
Convention Grill (GTC), p. 80
Highland Grill (SP), p. 73
Modern Cafe (MP), p. 69
Peter's Grill (DMP), p. 61
Punch Woodfire Pizza (SP), p. 74

Italian

Buca de Beppo (DMP), p. 55
Ciao Bella (GTC), p. 80
Giorgio (MP), p. 67
Pazzaluna (DSP), p. 64
Ristorante Luci (SP), p. 75

Novelty

Cafe Odyssey (GTC), p. 79
Minnesota Zephyr (GTC), p. 81
Planet Hollywood (GTC), p. 81
Rainforest Cafe (GTC), p. 82

Ribs

Market Bar-B-Que (MP), p. 69

Seafood

Blue Point Restaurant & Oyster Bar (GTC), p. 79
Oceanaire Seafood Room (DMP), p. 59

Vegetarian

Cafe Brenda (DMP), p. 55

DOWNTOWN MINNEAPOLIS

AQUAVIT
75 S. Seventh St.
Minneapolis
612/343-3333
$$$

This new branch of the critically acclaimed New York City restaurant is arguably the best (and most ambitious) eating spot in the Twin Cities. It's certainly one of the most attractive. The menu is Swedish with a contemporary twist, which translates into such temptations as venison loin with Arctic berry chutney and lingonberry sauce or black sea bass with dill-flavored broth. If you don't feel like wiping out the kids' college fund for dinner, then park it at the lower priced café, which offers less complicated—but no less delicious—fare. The bar features two dozen house-blended aquavits, similar to vodkas but much more potent.

BOBINO CAFE & WINE BAR
222 E. Hennepin Ave.
Minneapolis
612/623-3301
$$$

Charming and intimate, this 50-seat restaurant draws a hip crowd with its romantic surroundings and good food. The diminutive menu changes weekly, usually featuring three or four well-prepared entrees, a few salads, lots of tapas, and wonderful house-baked breads and desserts. The cozy wine bar is a chummy place in which to nurse a good merlot. Reservations recommended; lunch Tue–Sat, dinner Tue–Sun. ♿ (Downtown Minneapolis)

BRIT'S PUB AND EATING ESTABLISHMENT
1110 Nicollet Mall
Minneapolis
612/332-3908
$$

This quaint and popular place serves traditional (but often disappointing) English pub fare, as well as a long list of Brit beers, ales, and teas. Patrons enjoy lots of British pastimes, too, including darts, cribbage, and backgammon. The kitchen serves a fine high tea every afternoon, and there's

Brit's Pub and Eating Establishment

Greater Minneapolis CVA

DOWNTOWN MINNEAPOLIS

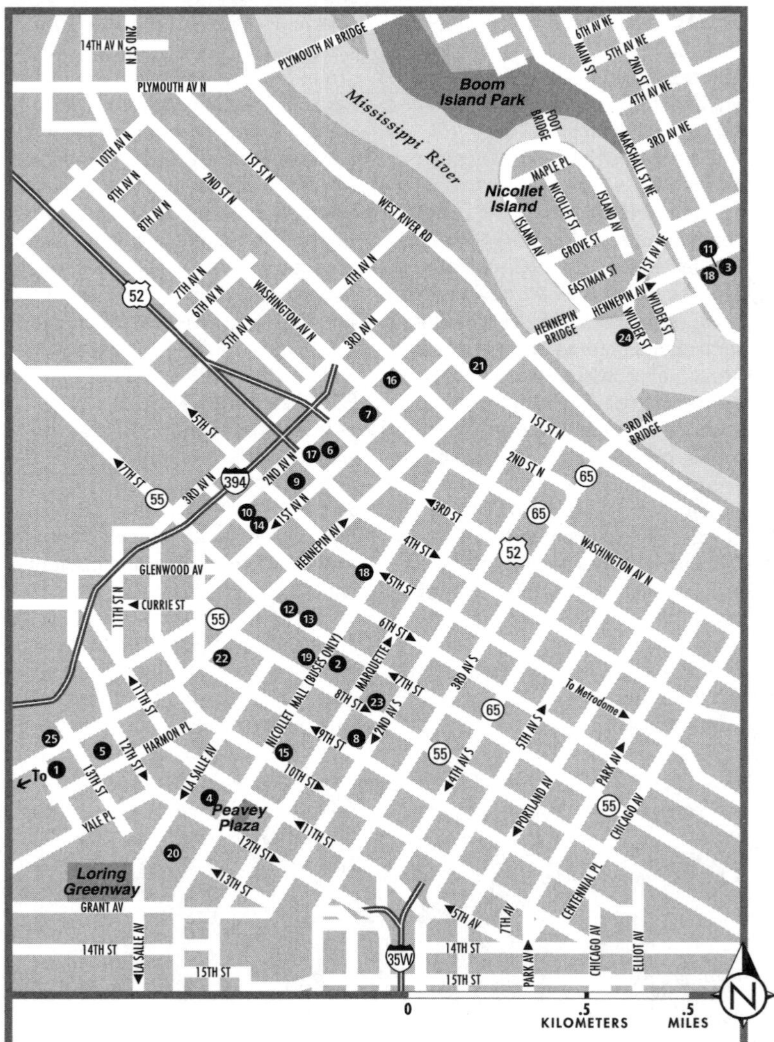

Where to Eat in Downtown Minneapolis

1 510 Restaurant
2 Aquavit
3 Bobino Cafe & Wine Bar
4 Brit's Pub and Eating Establishment
5 Buca di Beppo
6 Cafe Brenda
7 Cafe Havana
8 Cafe Un Deux Trois
9 Chez Bananas
10 D'Amico Cucina
11 Eat This
12 Goodfellow's
13 Gustino's
14 Linguini & Bob
15 The Local
16 Monte Carlo Bar & Cafe
17 New French Cafe and Bar
18 Nye's Polonaise Room
19 Oak Grill
20 Oceanaire Seafood Room
21 Origami
22 Palomino
23 Peter's Grill
24 Sophia
25 Table of Contents

no beating the big sidewalk café and stunning rooftop garden, complete with lawn-bowling green. Spotty service and forgettable food are the sore points here. No reservations; lunch and dinner daily. ♿ (Downtown Minneapolis)

BUCA DI BEPPO
11 S. 12th St.
Minneapolis
612/638-2225
$$

A series of amusingly overdecorated rooms hold this loud red-sauce house. The portions have *abbondanza* written all over them (to encourage sharing). The garlicky food isn't bad but doesn't stray from the Italian American mode of cooking. There's almost always a line, so be prepared to kill time in the tiny bar. You'll need reservations for parties of eight or more and for the family-style table in the kitchen. Three other area locations. Dinner daily. ♿ (Downtown Minneapolis)

CAFE BRENDA
300 First Ave. N.
Minneapolis
612/342-9230
$$$

Brenda's is a serene and stylish getaway for vegetarians and fish lovers. Brenda Langton's nouvelle cuisine showcases organic ingredients and eschews red meat in favor of chicken, freshwater fish, and an occasional seafood selection. The sugar-free desserts sound awful but aren't. The restaurant features a small bar and pleasant views of the city's warehouse district through the dining room's huge plate-glass windows. Reservations recommended; lunch Mon–Fri, dinner Mon–Sat. Smoke-free. ♿ (Downtown Minneapolis)

CAFE HAVANA
119 Washington Ave. N.
Minneapolis
612/338-8484
$$

Here you'll get home cooking, Cuban style. It's all about the crowd at Havana, which loves a good cigar and dresses for the swank, see-and-be-seen scene. The food's not bad, although it's often more Minnesotan than Cuban. Don't leave without ordering a piece of apple cake. Reservations accepted; dinner Mon–Sat. ♿ (Downtown Minneapolis)

CAFE UN DEUX TROIS
114 S. Ninth St.
Minneapolis
612/673-0686
$$$

This is where much of downtown Minneapolis does business over lunch, although dinner can draw a heady crowd, too. Power brokers and their well-dressed circles come for the Twin Cities' best seafood, as well as fine French bistro fare (steak frites, roast duck, *tarte tatin,* all courtesy of chef Vincent Francoual), attentive service, and chic (acres of trompe l'oeil) atmosphere. The small bar is a great spot in which to wolf down the excellent Caesar salad or nurse a fine chardonnay. You know you've arrived if owner/host Michael Morse snubs you. Reservations recommended; lunch Mon–Fri, dinner daily. ♿ (Downtown Minneapolis)

CHEZ BANANAS
119 N. Fourth St.
Minneapolis
612/340-0032
$$

Chez Bananas serves hot-hot Caribbean food in quirky surroundings. Longstanding hits include jerk chicken and jerk pork. The adventurous daily specials usually include something intriguing (and spicy). Kill time between courses with your table's Etch-a-Sketch or Crazy 8 Ball. There's a sweet little nook of a bar, too. No reservations; lunch Mon–Fri, dinner Mon–Sat. ♿ (Downtown Minneapolis)

D'AMICO CUCINA
100 N. Sixth St.
Minneapolis
612/338-2401
$$$

Elegant, understated, and very expensive, this crown jewel of the D'Amico Brothers' restaurant empire serves contemporary northern Italian cuisine in luxurious surroundings. The large menu changes seasonally and the wine cellar is nothing short of fabulous. Reservations recommended; dinner daily. ♿ (Downtown Minneapolis)

EAT THIS
212 E. Hennepin Ave.
Minneapolis
612/623-7999
$

This small restaurant has a limited menu—four vegetarian thick-crust

Let Them Eat Steak

Downtown Minneapolis is the upper Midwest's steakhouse epicenter, with six of the pricey places within an eight-block area. All follow the usual format: huge portions and expense-account prices. Blind taste tests between all six would probably stump all but the most discerning palates.

The oldest is ***Murray's Restaurant & Cocktail Lounge*** *(26 S. Sixth St., 612/339-0909) a kitschy pink palace and Minneapolis institution since 1946. Three national chains have set up shop in the past few years, drawing legions of adoring fans. The newest is the clubby and altogether wonderful* ***Capital Grille*** *(801 Hennepin Ave., 612/692-9000). Two from the old boys' club genre are* ***Morton's*** *(555 Nicollet Mall, 612/673-9700), a subdued, dark-wood dining room with top-notch service, and* ***Ruth's Chris*** *(920 Second Ave. S., 612/672-9000). Downtown's blandest beef palace is* ***Carver's*** *(1001 Marquette Ave., 612/397-4827), tucked into a corner of the hugely impersonal Hilton Hotel. Finally, there's* ***Manny's Steakhouse*** *(1300 Nicollet Mall, 612/339-9900), which for many remains the city's best. Its skilled servers ply monster portions in low-key surroundings that include a great cigar-friendly bar.*

pizzas and tossed salad (all sold by the pound), plus ice cream, brownies, and beer and wine. Everything is fresh, cheap, and delicious. Pizza combos change every so often, but could include carmelized onions, roasted garlic parmesan and fontina or Portobello mushrooms, red bell peppers, and provolone. No reservations; lunch and dinner Mon–Sat. ♿ (Downtown Minneapolis)

510 RESTAURANT
510 Groveland Ave.
Minneapolis
612/874-6440
$$$

A place tailor-made for special events, the 510 serves well-prepared American cuisine in an imposing, still-regal 1920s luxury apartment hotel. The two fixed-priced dinner packages (three courses at $29 or the pretheater special at $19) are two of the Twin Cities' best dining bargains. The wine list is extensive, appealing, and reasonably priced. Reservations recommended; dinner Mon–Sat. ♿ (Downtown Minneapolis)

GOODFELLOW'S
40 S. Seventh St.
Minneapolis
612/332-4800
$$$

Foodies argue over Goodfellow's supremacy on the Twin Cities dining scene, but one thing is certain: the restaurant's drop-dead gorgeous digs—the 1924 art deco showplace that was once the Forum Cafeteria—have no equal. The food is American regional cuisine, and while it can be quite good, dinner is very expensive. At lunch you can get smaller versions of the evening menu for about half the price—one of the best values in town. The bar is a treat, too, as is the huge wine list. Reservations recommended; lunch Mon–Fri, dinner Mon–Sat. ♿ (Downtown Minneapolis)

GUSTINO'S
30 S. Seventh St.
Minneapolis
612/349-4075
$$$

The talented singing servers are the main draw to this tired Marriott City Center Hotel restaurant. Gustino's attracts people out celebrating anniversaries or birthdays, and they tend to dress up for their big night out. Unfortunately, the food is the low note here. With luck, you'll be so enchanted by the light opera and Broadway tunes that you won't notice how mediocre—and expensive—your dinner is. Reservations recommended; dinner Mon–Sat. ♿ (Downtown Minneapolis)

LINGUINI & BOB
100 N. Sixth St.
Minneapolis
612/332-1600
$$$

This is a less formal version of the D'Amico empire's neighboring D'Amico Cucina. The attractive decor is very Pottery Barn, and the pastas, pizzas, and salads are reliable if a little overpriced. The comfortable bar can be something of a see-and-be-seen kind of place. No reservations; dinner only Mon–Sat. ♿ (Downtown Minneapolis)

THE LOCAL
921 Nicollet Mall
Minneapolis
612/904-1000
$$$

This ambitious restaurant and pub has an Irish accent. The kitchen is at

Top Ten Breakfast Spots

1. **Al's Breakfast**, 413 14th Ave. S.E., Minneapolis; 612/331-9991
2. **Bryant Lake Bowl**, 810 W. Lake St., Minneapolis; 612/825-3737
3. **Day by Day Cafe**, 477 W. Seventh St., St. Paul; 651/227-0654
4. **Sidney's Pizza Café** (five Twin Cities locations, including 2120 Hennepin Ave. S., Minneapolis; 612/870-7000)
5. **Key's Cafe** (nine Twin Cities locations, including 767 Raymond Ave., St. Paul; 651/646-5756)
6. **Ruby's Cafe**, 1614 Harmon Place, Minneapolis; 612/338-2089
7. **New French Cafe**, 128 N. Fourth St., Minneapolis; 612/338-3790
8. **No Wake Cafe**, 100 Yacht Club Rd., St. Paul; 651/292-1411
9. **Original Pancake House** (two Twin Cities locations, including 3501 W. 70 St., Edina; 612/920-4444)
10. **Serlin's Cafe**, 1124 Payne Ave., St. Paul; 651/776-9003

its best with appetizers and simple dishes, but doesn't always excel when things get complicated—although everything is pretty and often adventurous. The pub is a mob scene after work, when downtown professionals descend for a drink and deafeningly loud conversation. Located in what was once Bjorkman's, a legendary Midwestern furrier, The Local is one of downtown Minneapolis's prettiest restaurants, particularly at night, with high ceilings, huge windows, and stylish furniture. Reservations recommended; lunch and dinner daily. ♿ (Downtown Minneapolis)

MONTE CARLO BAR & CAFE
219 Third Ave. N.
Minneapolis
612/333-5900
$$

Loud, busy, and dark, this Warehouse District standby features well-prepared American standards: meat loaf, burgers, chops, and an outstanding steak sandwich. Be sure to sit in the main dining room, not in the small, secluded rooms in the front or back. The beautiful bar alone is worth a visit. Reservations recommended; lunch Mon–Sat, brunch Sun, dinner daily. ♿ (Downtown Minneapolis)

NEW FRENCH CAFE AND BAR
128 N. Fourth St.
Minneapolis
612/338-3790
$$$

This 22-year-old Warehouse District landmark sparked the neighborhood's revival, and the kitchen's sense of adventure and obvious love of good cooking spawned a new generation of Twin Cities foodies. A recent dining room makeover and a new attentiveness in the kitchen is returning the New French to its rightful place as one of the area's most appealing restaurants. It is Minneapolis's number-one spot for a weekend breakfast. The adjacent bar has its own simple menu and attracts a people-to-watch crowd. Reservations recommended; breakfast and dinner daily, lunch Mon–Fri. ♿ (Downtown Minneapolis)

NYE'S POLONAISE ROOM
112 E. Hennepin Ave.
Minneapolis
612/379-2021
$$$

The indifferent supper-club food isn't the draw here. Instead, people flock to Nye's for the 1960s time-warp atmosphere (comfy gold vinyl booths, wood paneling, and funky lighting), great service, and jumbo drinks. But top billing belongs to chanteuse/civic treasure Lou Snider, who has reigned over Nye's friendly piano bar for a quarter-century. Nye's is also home to a rip-roaring polka dance hall that has to be seen to be believed. Reservations recommended; lunch Mon–Sat, dinner daily. (Downtown Minneapolis)

OAK GRILL
700 on the Mall
Minneapolis
612/375-2200
$$

Lucky for everyone, nothing much has changed at Dayton's main restaurant since it opened in 1947—not the dark oak paneling, the red leather chairs, the centuries-old Tudor fireplace, or the great little bar's blood-red walls. And the food is pretty good, too. Try the Mandarin chicken salad or the meat loaf with Yukon gold mashed potatoes. The kitchen also pops out a mean popover and tempts with a large dessert tray. No reservations; lunch Mon–Sat, dinner Mon–Fri (closes at 7). ♿ (Downtown Minneapolis)

OCEANAIRE SEAFOOD ROOM
1300 Nicollet Mall
Minneapolis
612/333-2277
$$$

A standout among a recent crop of new downtown restaurants, this attractive and spacious place is owned by the folks behind Manny's (arguably the Twin Cities' top steakhouse, located across the hall). The Oceanaire specializes in fresh seafood—big surprise—and the selection and service are both first rate. Reservations recommended; dinner daily. ♿ (Downtown Minneapolis)

ORIGAMI
30 N. First St.
Minneapolis
612/333-8430
$$

Origami features French-Japanese fusion food, along with a decent sushi bar and a pleasant second-floor saki bar. It is housed in one of the city's last remaining late-nineteenth-century storefronts, a stone's throw from the Mississippi River. No reservations; lunch Mon–Fri, dinner daily. (Downtown Minneapolis)

PALOMINO
825 Hennepin Ave.
Minneapolis
612/339-3800
$$$

Java Jive

The Twin Cities' caffeine scene is dominated by seemingly countless Starbucks and Caribou Coffee outlets (15 and 32 locations respectively—and counting). But if cookie-cutter surroundings aren't your cup of joe, a number of one-of-a-kind joints exist to meet your sipping, reading, chatting, or crowd-scoping needs.

In South Minneapolis, grungers hang at ***Muddy Waters*** *(2401 Lyndale Ave. S., 612/870-9508), famous for its quirky menu of Rice Krispies bars, Spaghettios, and other TV-land treats. Motorcyclists congregate down the street at* ***Bob's Java Hut*** *(2649 Lyndale Ave. S., 612/871-4485).* ***Cyber X*** *(3001 Lyndale Ave. S., 612/824-3558) merges two hot trends—coffee and computers. Tops in the style department is* ***Anodyne @ 43rd*** *(4301 Nicollet Ave. S., 612/824-4300).*

Uptown's most popular joints include ***Cafe Wyrd*** *(1600 W. Lake St., 612/827-5710), which attracts a young gay and lesbian crowd, romantic* ***Uncommon Grounds*** *(2809 Hennepin Ave. S., 612/872-4811), and Calhoun Square's intimate* ***Cravings Uptown (BF)*** *(3001 Hennepin Ave. S., 612/825-9707).*

Best bets in downtown Minneapolis include mellow ***Moose & Sadie's*** *(212 Third Ave. N., 612/371-0464) and sunny* ***Espresso Royale Caffe*** *(1229 Hennepin Ave., 612/333-8882). In the Dinkytown neighborhood near the U of M, young scholars rip apart Proust over cappuccino at the* ***Purple Onion*** *(326 14th Ave. S.E., 612/378-7763) and another* ***Espresso Royale Caffe*** *(411 14th Ave. S.E., 612/623-8127).*

Downtown St. Paul's most comfortable spot is the sprawling ***Black Dog Cafe*** *(308 Prince St., 651/228-9275). In other parts of the city, check out* ***Nina's*** *(165 Western Ave. N., 651/292-9816), located in an 1880s luxury apartment house; busy* ***Black Bear Crossings*** *(831 Como Ave., 651/488-4327); and* ***Gingko Coffeehouse*** *(721 Snelling Ave. N., 651/645-2647), specializing in live music.*

Always packed and pulsing with energy, this large and wildly overdecorated chain restaurant is downtown's top pre-theater destination. The spit-roasted garlic chicken is always a good bet, as are the pastas and thin-crust pizzas. The adjacent bar is downtown's most sophisticated (but hardly understated) pickup joint. Reservations recommended; lunch Mon–Sat, dinner daily. Smoke-free. ♿ (Downtown Minneapolis)

PETER'S GRILL
114 S. Eighth St.
Minneapolis
612/333-1981
$

Peter's has been a downtown home-cooking destination since 1919. Lunch (roast turkey with mashed potatoes, club sandwiches, chef's salad, and other standards) is big business here, and it's hard to leave without a slice of one of Peter's legendary pies. (President Clinton couldn't resist). The big but not terribly comfortable wooden booths date from the original Peter's Grill on Ninth Street, as do many of the no-nonsense waitresses. Wednesday evening's quarter-chicken dinner—priced to move at $3.25—is the Twin Cities' best blue-plate special. No reservations; no credit cards; no liquor; breakfast and lunch Mon–Sat; dinner Mon–Fri. ♿ (Downtown Minneapolis)

SOPHIA
65 S.E. Main St.
Minneapolis
612/379-1111
$$$

Dimly lit and bewitchingly romantic in a swanky, 1930s nightclub kind of way, Sophia serves continental American favorites to an older, well-heeled, and rather dressy crowd. Live music, a small dance floor, and a swell bar add to the allure, as do vistas of the downtown skyline. The service is polished. Reservations recommended; lunch Mon–Sat, dinner daily. ♿ (Downtown Minneapolis)

Outdoor dining at Sophia

J. Bruch

Top Ten Outdoor Dining Spots

Twin Citians take any chance they can get to break bread under the open sky. Here are 10 particularly noteworthy places in which to enjoy a pleasant warm-weather day.

1. **Black Forest Inn**, 1 E. 26th St., Minneapolis; 612/872-0812
2. **Brit's Pub and Eating Establishment**, 1110 Nicollet Mall, Minneapolis; 612/332-3908
3. **Loring Cafe and Bar**, 1624 Harmon Place, Minneapolis; 612/332-1617
4. **Lord Fletcher's on Lake Minnetonka**, 3746 Sunset Dr., Spring Park; 612/471-8613
5. **Sidney's Pizza Cafe**, 3510 W. 70th St. (Galleria Shopping Center), Edina; 612/925-2002
6. **The Vintage**, 572 Selby Ave., St. Paul; 651/222-7000
7. **Backstage@Bravo**, 900 Hennepin Ave., Minneapolis; 612/338-0062
8. **W. A. Frost**, 374 Selby Ave., St. Paul; 651/224-5715
9. **Gallery 8**, 725 Vineland Place (Walker Art Center), Minneapolis; 612/375-7600
10. **Joe's Garage**, 1610 Harmon Place, Minneapolis; 612/904-1163

TABLE OF CONTENTS
1310 Hennepin Ave.
Minneapolis
612/339-1133
$$$

This offspring of a popular St. Paul restaurant has style to burn, and the food is as chic and sophisticated as the surroundings. The menu changes often but might include a terrific cracker-crust pizza, tuna tartar, or a peppery lamb shank. Lunch is a great value, and the soigné bar features a naughty—and very popular—martini menu. Sunday brunch is affordable and delicious. Reservations recommended; lunch Mon–Fri, brunch Sun, dinner daily. ♿ (Downtown Minneapolis)

DOWNTOWN ST. PAUL

BABANI'S KURDISH RESTAURANT
544 St. Peter St.
St. Paul
651/602-9964
$

Billed as "America's first Kurdish restaurant," Babani's serves simple and wonderfully aromatic food that emphasizes fresh vegetables, herbs, and spices. Prices are reasonable and portions are enormous. You can't go wrong with just about any of the menu's rice dishes or stir frys. Be sure to try the *dowjic* (Kurdish chicken soup), the fragrant tabbouleh, and the delicious *naska nan wa paneer*, the restaurant's addict-

DOWNTOWN ST. PAUL

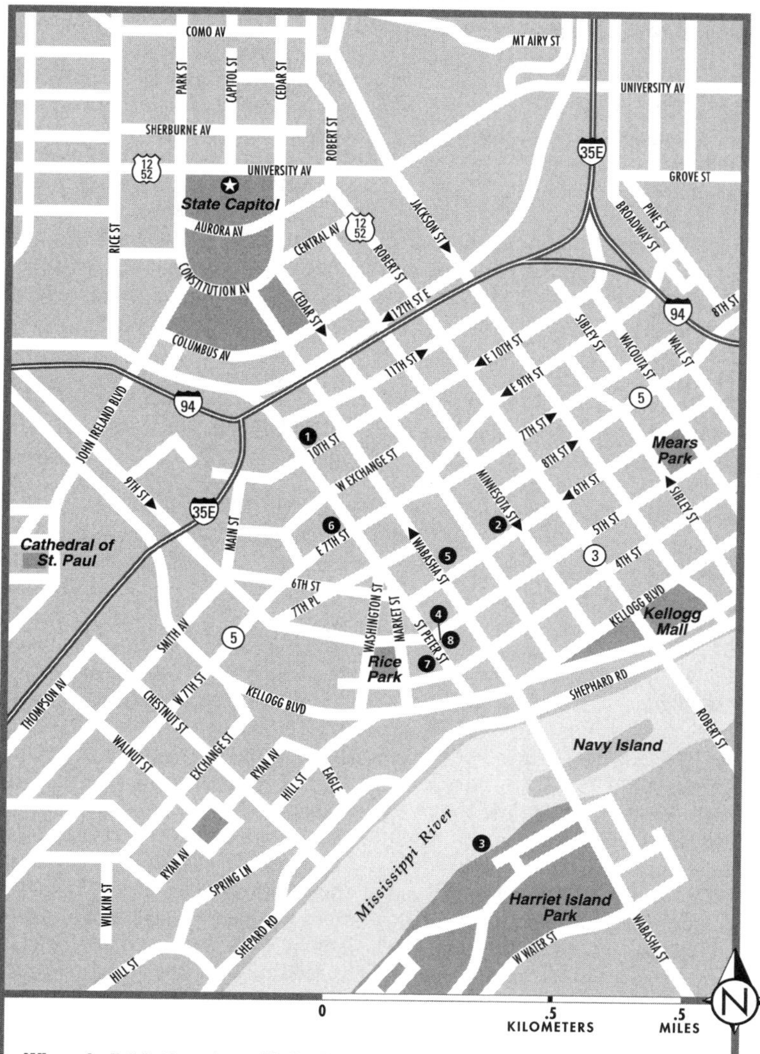

Where to Eat in Downtown St. Paul

1 Babani's Kurdish Restaurant
2 Capital City Marketcafe & Bar
3 No Wake Cafe
4 Pazzaluna
5 River Room
6 Ruam Mit Thai Cafe
7 St. Paul Grill
8 Sakura

ing house-baked bread. Reservations recommended; lunch and dinner Mon–Sat. ♿ (Downtown St. Paul)

CAPITAL CITY MARKETCAFE & BAR
411 Minnesota St.
St. Paul
651/222-8383
$

This cafeteria-style restaurant, located on the second floor of the Radisson Inn, is a quick, inexpensive alternative to the surrounding food courts. Several fresh soups accompany a changing roster of hot entrees, decent gourmet pizzas by the slice, big rich desserts, and a so-so continental breakfast. No reservations; breakfast, lunch, and dinner daily. ♿ (Downtown St. Paul)

NO WAKE CAFE
100 Yacht Club Rd.
St. Paul
651/292-1411
$

If breaking bread on a boat on the Mississippi is what you seek, head over to Harriet Island (opposite downtown St. Paul via the Wabasha Street Bridge) to this tiny (15-table) and delightful floating restaurant, located on a 1946 tugboat. The food is home cooking at its best, the kind you would have grown up on if Sheila Lukens had been your mother. The café also has irresistible desserts, stunning downtown views, and a nice wine list. Reservations are recommended. Open March 21 through mid-November for lunch Wed–Fri, brunch Sat–Sun, dinner Wed–Sun. ♿ (Downtown St. Paul)

PAZZALUNA
360 St. Peter St.
St. Paul
651/223-7000
$$$

This gorgeous new Italian trattoria is the most ambitious restaurant to open in downtown St. Paul in nearly a decade. Pazzaluna is Italian for crazy moon, and that sense of fun permeates the place, from the swank decor to the open kitchen to the antipasto bar. The food, another standout, is by Mario Maggi and Tina Raniolo, an Italian couple with a resume a mile long, including a decade-long stint opening branches of the fabled Bice chain in Tokyo, Seoul, Milan, Istanbul, and New York City. Reservations recommended; dinner Tue–Sat. ♿ (Downtown St. Paul)

RIVER ROOM
411 Cedar St.
St. Paul
651/292-5174
$$

This debonair restaurant (black lacquered walls, mirrors, pink tablecloths, and massive crystal chandeliers) on the second floor of Dayton's dowdy downtown St. Paul store is a smart choice for a quiet, secluded lunch or pre-Ordway dinner. The menu features department-store favorites like chicken pot pie, pork chops, and the signature Mandarin chicken salad, along with an excellent wild-rice soup and warm, flaky popovers. Try the Frango mint cheesecake for dessert. Reservations recommended; lunch Mon–Sat, dinner Mon–Fri (closes at 7). ♿ (Downtown St. Paul)

RUAM MIT THAI CAFE
473 St. Peter St.
St. Paul
651/290-0067
$

The surroundings aren't so special, but you won't notice once your food arrives. Ruam Mit is arguably the Twin Cities' best Thai restaurant, with a large but not overwhelming menu that includes all the Thai classics and some surprises, with temperatures that range from merely hot to scorching. The *rad na*, *pad Thai*, and deep-fried trout are particularly popular. No reservations; lunch and dinner daily. ♿ (Downtown St. Paul)

ST. PAUL GRILL
350 Market St.
St. Paul
651/224-7455

This is the first place that pops into people's heads when they want a meal in downtown St. Paul. The classic grill fare (steaks, chops, salads) is the draw, along with the handsome, comfortable surroundings. The dark clubby bar lures a heady mix of state politico types and business leaders. The Grill is also the number one pre–Ordway Music Theatre destination, and its big windows offer stunning views of the Rice Park area. Reservations recommended; lunch Mon–Sat, brunch Sun, dinner daily, late-night bar menu (until midnight) daily. ♿ (Downtown St. Paul)

SAKURA
350 St. Peter St.
St. Paul
651/224-0185
$$

Consistently the Twin Cities' best sushi house, Sakura also serves tempura, donburi, teriyaki, and many Japanese noodle dishes. But most people come for the sushi, which is classically prepared, reasonably priced, and occasionally exotic, at least by Minnesota standards. The surroundings, which include a small saki bar, are sunny and comfortable, with an emphasis on blond wood. Reservations recommended; lunch and dinner daily. ♿ (Downtown St. Paul)

MINNEAPOLIS

AURIGA
1934 Hennepin Ave. S.
Minneapolis
612/871-0777
$$$

Named for a constellation, this starry restaurant with a pleasant wine bar has some of the most flattering lighting in town and a menu to match. The four chef/owners roll their menu over every few weeks, but it usually features hard-to-beat pizzas and salads, plus beautifully presented beef, seafood, and game. The polenta appetizer, served with a scrambled egg, is amazing, and the desserts aren't too shabby, either. Reservations recommended; lunch Tue–Fri, dinner Tue–Sun. ♿ (Minneapolis)

BIRCHWOOD CAFE
3311 E. 25th St.
Minneapolis
612/722-4474
$

Tasty, inexpensive, and full of surprises, this cheerful neighborhood café draws fans from all over the Twin Cities for its mostly vegetarian and often organic sandwiches, soups, pizzas, and prepared salads. The homey desserts are noteworthy, the house-baked bread is equally fine, and the kitchen whips up a great weekend breakfast. Owners Susan Muskat and Tracy Singleton also run the terrific Emerald Cafe (329 Cedar Ave., Minneapolis, 612/338-6824), a great lunch and dinner

MINNEAPOLIS

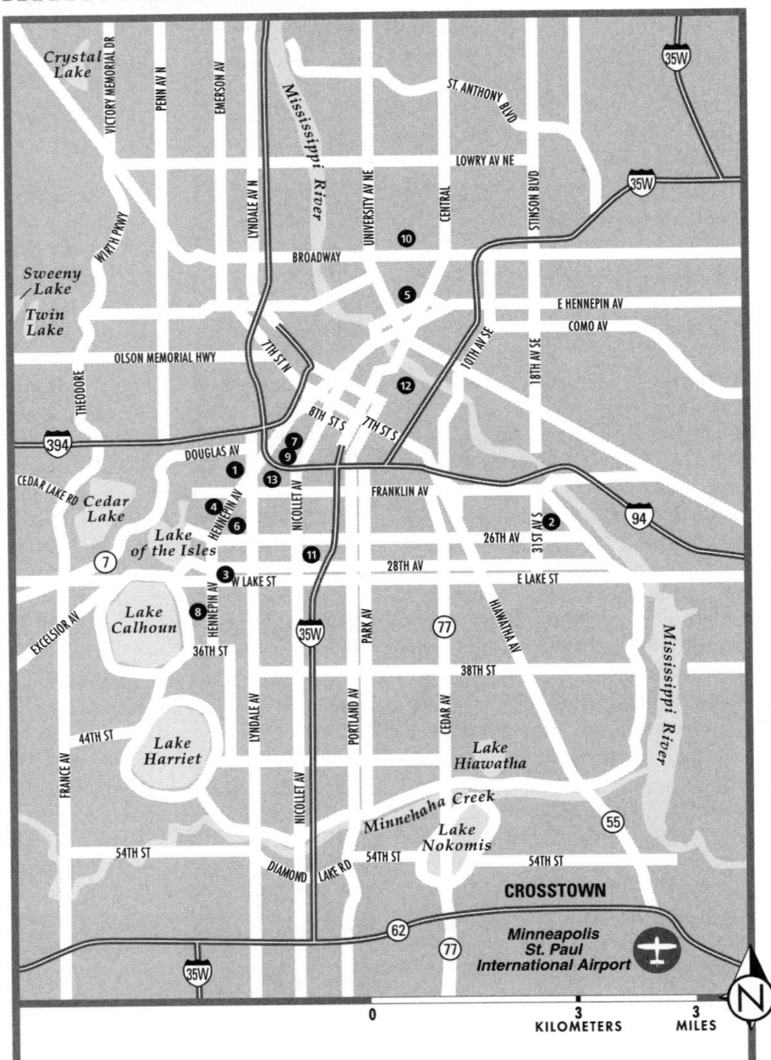

Where to Eat in Minneapolis

1 Auriga
2 Birchwood Cafe
3 Campiello
4 D'Amico & Sons
5 Gardens of Salonica
6 Giorgio
7 Loring Cafe and Bar
8 Lucia's Restaurant
9 Market Bar-B-Que
10 Modern Cafe
11 Rainbow Chinese Restaurant
12 Shuang Cheng
13 Taco Morelos

spot near the university's West Bank campus. No reservations; no credit cards; no liquor. Breakfast Sat–Sun, lunch and dinner Tue–Sat. ♿ (Minneapolis)

CAMPIELLO
1320 W. Lake St.
Minneapolis
612/825-2222
$$$

Uptown's snazziest restaurant—part of the D'Amico empire—specializes in smooth service and pastas, pizzas, poultry, and salads. The eye-catching food is a treat to eat. The animated but often noisy dining room is flanked by a popular martini bar and an open kitchen, but sit there anyway; avoid the back room, which has all the appeal of a conference room at a second-rate law firm. The no-reservation policy is a drag (the restaurant is forever busy), but you can call ahead and put your name on the waiting list. Also at 6411 City West Pkwy., Eden Prairie; 612/941-6868. Sunday brunch, dinner daily. ♿ (Minneapolis)

D'AMICO & SONS
2210 Hennepin Ave. S.
Minneapolis
612/374-1858
$

The D'Amico brothers' successful chain of quick-serve restaurants offers prepared sandwiches and salads, as well as pastas and thin-crust designer pizzas. The bakery does great things with Italian breads, and the cookies and chocolate torte are especially tasty. Most of the chain's 11 spiffy locations serve beer and wine. Don't miss the great weekend brunch. No reservations; lunch and dinner daily, brunch Sat–Sun. ♿ (Minneapolis)

GARDENS OF SALONICA
19 Fifth St. N.E.
Minneapolis
612/378-0611
$

This appealing Greek café specializes in boughatsas, tempting triangles of phyllo dough stuffed with savory ingredients. Or try the pita-crust "pitzas" and large selection of fresh Greek spreads served with pita bread. The chalkboard menu always includes an appealing soup or two, plus inexpensive and imaginative entrees. Vegetarians will find a lot here, and Salonica also offers a small to-go deli counter. No reservations; no credit cards; lunch and dinner Mon–Sat. (Minneapolis)

GIORGIO
2451 Hennepin Ave. S.
Minneapolis
612/374-5131
$$

Small and cluttered—but in a good way—this storefront operation is the place for rustic Tuscan food with a kick. The kitchen is particularly adept at pasta and roasted meats, and the dessert tray rarely disappoints. Owner Giorgio Cherubini owns two other popular places: Giorgio's on Lake (1601 W. Lake St., Minneapolis; 612/822-7071) and Locanda di Giorgio (4924 France Ave. S., Edina; 612/928-0323), but the original Giorgio remains his best effort. No reservations; no credit cards; lunch Tue–Fri, dinner Tue–Sun. ♿ (Minneapolis)

LORING CAFE AND BAR
1624 Harmon Place
Minneapolis
612/332-1617
$$$

A little slice of Montemarte in the heart of Minneapolis. The Loring's

Night Owls

The Twin Cities aren't exactly late-night towns, but a few restaurants do outstay the 10 o'clock news.

Cheap, delicious eats, a great beer and wine selection, bowling on six lanes, and a busy cabaret make ***Bryant Lake Bowl*** *(810 W. Lake St., 612/825-3737) a South Minneapolis hot spot. No reservations; open until 1 a.m. daily.*

Caffe Solo *(123 N. Third St., Minneapolis; 612/332-7108) serves tasty pasta and pizza in an animated warehouse space. You'll find a good wine list and fab breakfasts, too. Open Sunday through Thursday until 11 p.m., Friday and Saturday until 1 a.m.*

The open kitchen at ***Figlio*** *(3001 Hennepin Ave. S., Minneapolis; 612/822-1688) prepares vaguely Italian fare, including pastas, salads, sandwiches, and pretty good wood-fired pizzas for a young and fashionable crowd. Open until 1 a.m. Sunday through Thursday, until 2 a.m. Friday and Saturday.*

Pizza Luce *(119 N. Fourth St., Minneapolis; 612/333-7359) throws the Twin Cities' best pizza, bar none, with chewy, hearty, herby crusts and fresh homemade toppings. Open until 2 a.m. Thursday, until 3 a.m. Friday and Saturday.*

Something's always worth watching—and eating—at the ***Mpls. Cafe*** *(1110 Hennepin Ave., Minneapolis; 612/672-9100). Served in a lively atmosphere, the Mediterranean menu features beautiful salads, seafood, and pizzas. Open Sunday and Monday until 11 p.m., Tuesday through Thursday to 1 a.m., and Friday and Saturday to 2 a.m.*

Downtown St. Paul's sole late-night option is venerable ***Mickey's Diner*** *(36 W. Seventh St., 651/222-5633), sited in a 1938 railroad dining car. You can order the Mulligan stew and a cup of the rocket-fuel coffee 24 hours a day.*

Stockmen's *(501 Farwell Ave., South St. Paul; 651/455-9719) is a home-cooking truck stop and smoker's paradise. It is open 24 hours.*

inspired food focuses on regionally grown ingredients and stunning presentation, and the candlelit, La Bohème atmosphere is utterly romantic. If you can handle the waitstaff'syou-should-be-thrilled-that-I'm-serving-you attitude, you'll develop a love affair with this place. The sprawling bar features its own abbreviated menu, live music, and hordes of Prada-wearing yuppies. The enchanting summertime patio seating in the back alley is unequaled in its whimsy. Reservations recommended; lunch and dinner daily. (Minneapolis)

LUCIA'S RESTAURANT
1432 W. 31 St.
Minneapolis
612/825-1572
$$

This is one of the Twin Cities' most consistently appealing restaurants. For more than a decade, owner Lucia Watson has been making the most of area farms' abundance in her unpretentious storefront restaurant. The small and surprisingly affordable menu changes weekly, but there's always something for fish and beef lovers, as well as for vegetarians. Weekend brunches are a distinct pleasure, desserts are dreamy, and the candlelit wine bar next door is Uptown's best getaway for tasty, inexpensive fare and great people-watching. Reservations recommended; smoke-free; lunch Tue–Fri, brunch Sat–Sun, dinner Tue–Sun. ♿ (Minneapolis)

MARKET BAR-B-QUE
1414 Nicollet Ave. S.
Minneapolis
612/872-1111
$$

This 52-year Minneapolis institution specializes in smoky, St. Louis–style spare ribs; you add the sauce. The side dishes can be uneven (except for the always fabulous baked beans), but with ribs this good and a fun 1940s atmosphere, nobody notices. Also at 1532 Wayzata Blvd., Minnetonka; 612/475-1770. Reservations recommended; lunch and dinner daily. ♿ (Minneapolis)

MODERN CAFE
337 13th Ave. N.E.
Minneapolis
612/378-9882
$

A neighborhood joint with a citywide draw, specializing in contemporary comfort food. Twenty- and thirty-somethings flock to the Modern for the outstanding New England pot roast with root vegetables and horseradish, the meat loaf or pan-roasted chicken breasts with garlic mashed potatoes, or the BLT with garlic mayonnaise. Mondo weekend breakfasts include fluffy buttermilk pancakes, "pampered" eggs, and heaping platters of huevos rancheros. Sunday dinner is served family-style, and it's a great value. No reservations; breakfast Sat–Sun, lunch Tue–Fri, dinner Tue–Sun. ♿ (Minneapolis)

RAINBOW CHINESE RESTAURANT
2739 Nicollet Ave. S.
Minneapolis
612/870-7084
$$

There are Chinese restaurants, and then there's the Rainbow. Seafood is one of owner Tammy Wong's specialties, but she does a lot for vegetarians, too. Devoted Rainbow fans sing the praises of Wong's sesame noodles, whole-fish preparations, delicious dumplings, roast beef with mustard greens, tempura-style prawns with broccoli and red curry sauce, and her

TIP

Too tired to cook or go out? For a $7 fee (tip not included), Gourmet Express (612/922-3463) will deliver just about anything from several dozen restaurants in Minneapolis and its southern and western suburbs directly to your door.

many noodle soups. Now in a fabulous new location, the House of Wong is the Twin Cities' most attractive Chinese restaurant and one of the few to offer a full bar. Reservations recommended; lunch and dinner daily. ♿ (Minneapolis)

SHUANG CHENG
1320 Fourth St. S.E.
Minneapolis
612/378-0208
$$

Even better than the Rainbow is this eight-year-old gem, located in the Dinkytown neighborhood near the University of Minnesota campus. Owner Daniel Lam runs one of the state's best seafood restaurants, and it's certainly one of the most affordable. Ocean-fresh lobster, crab, shrimp, and sole are menu staples, but the daily specials board usually lists a few exotic items, along with house specialties such as beef with orange peel, salmon with black-bean sauce, and a heavenly Peking duck. The deceptively modest dining room is always jammed. The service is outstanding. No reservations; lunch Mon–Sat, dinner daily. ♿ (Minneapolis)

Goodfellows, p. 57

Greg Page

TACO MORELOS
14 W. 26 St.
Minneapolis
612/870-0053
$

You know it's authentic Mexican when everyone behind the counter—and most of the customers—are speaking Spanish. Try the tamales, the sopas, the gorditas, or the wonderful corn-tortilla tacos. You'll also find a blistering salsa and tons of fresh cilantro, along with a fun selection of south-of-the-border soft drinks. No reservations; no credit cards; no liquor; lunch and dinner daily. ♿ (Minneapolis)

ST. PAUL

THE BARBARY FIG
720 Grand Ave.
St. Paul

651/290-2085
$$
The flavors of North Africa are the focus of this couscous restaurant, which also has a way with Moroccan stews. The kitchen offers a lot for vegetarians (it has quite a way with eggplant), and the surroundings are attractively low-key. No reservations; lunch Mon and Wed–Sat, dinner Mon and Wed–Sun. ♿ (St. Paul)

CAFE LATTE
850 Grand Ave.
St. Paul
651/224-5687
$
The Twin Cities' most popular cafeteria serves soups, sandwiches, and hot entrees along with a large selection of baked goods (the Turtle Cake is legendary). The large, two-story dining room is a little on the late-1980s side, but it's sunny and genial. Latte does a big to-go bakery business, and a wine bar—with a separate food menu—sits in the back. The restaurant also operates a smart sandwich shop called Bread and

Grease Is the Word

A few authentic drive-ins from the 1950s and 1960s remain in the Twin Cities. For nearly 20 years, ***Wagner's*** *(7000 W. Broadway, Brooklyn Park; 612/533-8262) has drawn a devoted clientele to its modest carports by serving tasty burgers, crisp fried chicken, and eight flavors of creamy malt. .*

Family-owned ***Dari-Ette*** *(1440 Minnehaha Ave., St. Paul; 651/776-3470) fries up a mean hamburger in addition to its ho-hum Italian fare. The wide-ranging sundae and malt selections include fun flavors like black raspberry and creme de menthe.*

The ***Minnetonka Drive-In*** *(4658 Shoreline Dr., Spring Park; 612/471-9383) features a big menu of all the hot-dog and burger standards (try the giant "Minnetonka Twins" burger), plus barbecued ribs, fried chicken, and fish and chips. Families will enjoy the large kids' menu.*

Porky's *(1890 University Ave., St. Paul; 651/644-1790) isn't a drive-in per se, but it still rates if you're into car culture. The fried chicken, thick malts, and battered catfish are pretty darned good, but Porky's biggest draw is the impromptu classic car show that materializes in the parking lot (spilling over to University Avenue) every warm Friday and Saturday night.*

ST. PAUL

Where to Eat in St. Paul

1 128 Cafe
2 The Barbary Fig
3 Cafe Latte
4 Cheng Heng Restaurant
5 Chet's Taverna
6 Continental Pantry and House of Fine Cakes
7 Forepaugh's
8 Highland Grill
9 Punch Woodfire Pizza
10 Ristorante Luci
11 Shilla
12 Table of Contents
13 Tavern on Grand
14 The Vintage
15 W. A. Frost & Co.
16 Zander Cafe

Chocolate across the street (867 Grand Ave., 651/228-1017). No reservations; smoke-free; breakfast Mon–Fri, brunch Sat– Sun, lunch and dinner daily. ♿ (St. Paul)

CHENG HENG RESTAURANT
448 University Ave. W.
St. Paul
651/222-5577
$

The Twin Cities' only Cambodian restaurant has a modest decor and extremely low prices. The kitchen does wonderful things with beef, and its noodle soups and sweet-and-sour dishes are pretty special, too. Don't leave without ordering a few out-of-this-world spring rolls. No reservations, lunch and dinner daily. (St. Paul)

CHET'S TAVERNA
791 Raymond Ave.
St. Paul
651/646-2655
$$

Casual and eclectic, this charming new storefront café is one of the Twin Cities' best neighborhood restaurants. The owners are the people behind Northeast Minneapolis's wonderful Modern Café, and this time around they're trying their hand at Mediterranean fare, with terrific results. The menu changes seasonally, but you can't go wrong with the inventive pastas, the tasty pizzas, and the homey desserts. No reservations; lunch Tue–Fri, dinner Tue–Sat, brunch Sun. ♿ (St. Paul)

CONTINENTAL PANTRY AND HOUSE OF FINE CAKES
381 Michigan St.
St. Paul
651/291-8757
$

German American cuisine is the specialty of the house, along with terrific breakfasts (the light-as-air pancakes are a special treat). And the house is something else: a dining room filled with more tchotchkes than Miss Havisham's bedroom and presided over by co-owner Ray Granda, whose lippy attitude amuses some and offends others. The restaurant's lobby showcases the Fine Cakes portion of the Continental Pantry, and chef Joe O'Brien's extravagant but affordable triple layer cakes taste as good as they look. No credit cards; breakfast, lunch, and dinner Tue–Sun. (St. Paul)

FOREPAUGH'S
276 S. Exchange St.
St. Paul
651/224-5606
$$$

This special-event destination is housed in a restored Victorian mansion on the edge of historic Irvine Park. The house is the primary lure here because the overpriced, quasi-French food is uneven at best. Still, Forepaugh's has its devoted fans, who come for the surroundings and the fawning service. Reservations recommended; lunch Mon–Fri, brunch Sun, dinner daily. ♿ (St. Paul)

HIGHLAND GRILL
771 Cleveland Ave.
St. Paul
651/690-1173
$

A friendly neighborhood joint with flair. You won't notice the modest decor (the grill is housed in an old Haagen-Dazs franchise) once you've dug into the huge servings of simple fare, the kind Martha Stewart would serve on a limited budget. Breakfasts

Sweet Tooth

A number of tempting bakeries sugarcoat the Twin Cities. Here are few worth visiting:

***French Meadow Bakery & Cafe** (2610 Lyndale Ave. S., Minneapolis; 612/870-7855) is organic and sourdough central, and the adjoining counter-service café specializes in healthful salads, soups, sandwiches, and exasperating service.*

***New French Bakery** (122 N. Fourth St., Minneapolis; 612/341-9083) whips up some of the Twin Cities' tastiest breads, along with a tempting array of cakes and cookies. Also at 2609 26th Ave. S., Minneapolis, 612/728-0193.*

***Blackey Bakeries** (639 22nd Ave. N.E., Minneapolis; 612/789-5326) specializes in spectacular Danish and Polish breads.*

***Jerebek Bakeries** (61 W. Winifred St., St. Paul; 651/228-1245) reprises the kind of baked goods (including terrific layer cakes) your grandmother used to make.*

***Isles Bun & Coffee Co.** (1422 W. 28 St., Minneapolis; 612/870-4466) serves up the Twin Cities' most addicting sweet rolls.*

***Turtle Bread Company** (3415 W. 44 St., Minneapolis; 612/924-6013) sells more than a dozen kinds of bread, marvelous cookies, killer pies, and wonderful cupcakes.*

are particularly hearty, and service is with a smile. No reservations; breakfast, lunch, and dinner daily. ♿ (St. Paul)

128 CAFE
128 Cleveland Ave.
St. Paul
651/645-4128
$$

Fine seasonal fare from the hands of a youthful and talented kitchen staff, served in a pair of wood-paneled dining rooms near the campus of the University of St. Thomas. Specialties include a Fred Flintstone–sized rack of tangy barbecue ribs, a pretty platter of grilled vegetables, and a juicy beef tenderloin. You'll also find wonderful service and a pleasant Sunday brunch. Reservations recommended; brunch Sun, dinner Mon–Sat. (St. Paul)

PUNCH WOODFIRE PIZZA
704 Cleveland Ave.
St. Paul
651/696-1066
$

This stylish little open-kitchen café

serves classic Neapolitan pizza. The menu offers more than two dozen varieties, large enough for two but designed to serve one. The crusts are thin and full of fresh herbs, and the toppings include top-notch ingredients such as imported Italian tomatoes and picholine olives. Salads are fab, too. No reservations; lunch and dinner Mon–Sat. ♿ (St. Paul)

RISTORANTE LUCI
470 Cleveland Ave. S.
St. Paul
651/699-8258
$$$

This intimate, family-owned place specializes in tasty Italian food. The four-course fixed-price option is a steal, but the no-reservations policy only exacerbates problems in the cramped, no-nonsense dining room. Luci's sister restaurant, Luci Ancora (2060 Randolph Ave., St. Paul; 651/698-6889), is strictly a second-best alternative. No reservations; dinner daily. ♿ (St. Paul)

SHILLA
694 Snelling Ave. N.
St. Paul
651/645-0006
$$

If you're in the mood for Korean food, don't be fooled by this place's gussied-up VFW hall atmosphere. Menu winners include *bi bim bop* (vegetable salad with a snappy sauce and a boiled egg), *man do* (pork and vegetable dumplings), *bul go gi* (tender sliced beef), *jungal* (seafood gumbo), and *chop chae* (cold vermicelli noodles in a red-pepper sesame sauce). Get the most out of the experience by ordering many different dishes and sharing them with your fellow diners. Plan a visit for Sunday afternoon, when the place is packed with post-church Koreans. No reservations; no credit cards; lunch and dinner daily. ♿ (St. Paul)

TABLE OF CONTENTS
1648 Grand Ave.
St. Paul
651/699-6595

Outdoor dining at W. A. Frost & Co., p. 78

Thomas K. Perry

GREATER TWIN CITIES

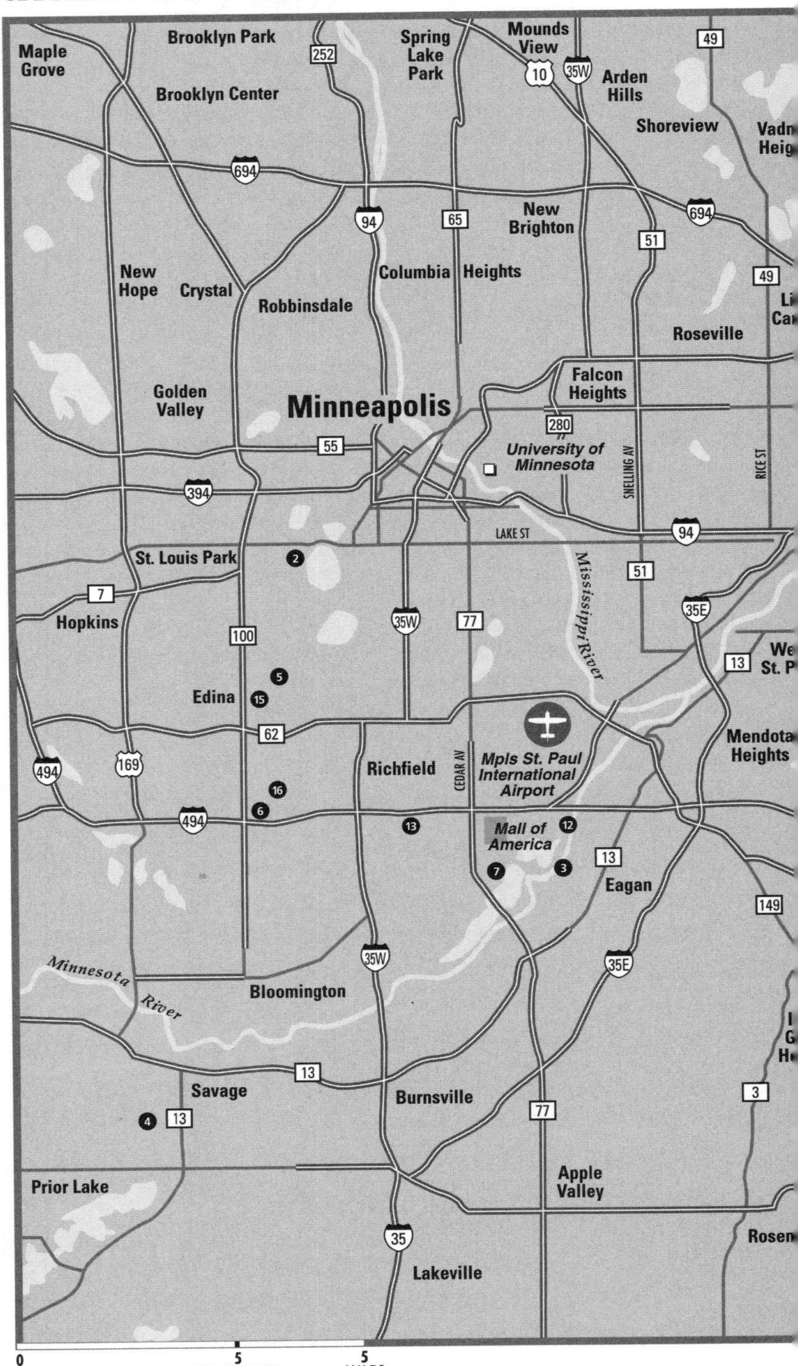

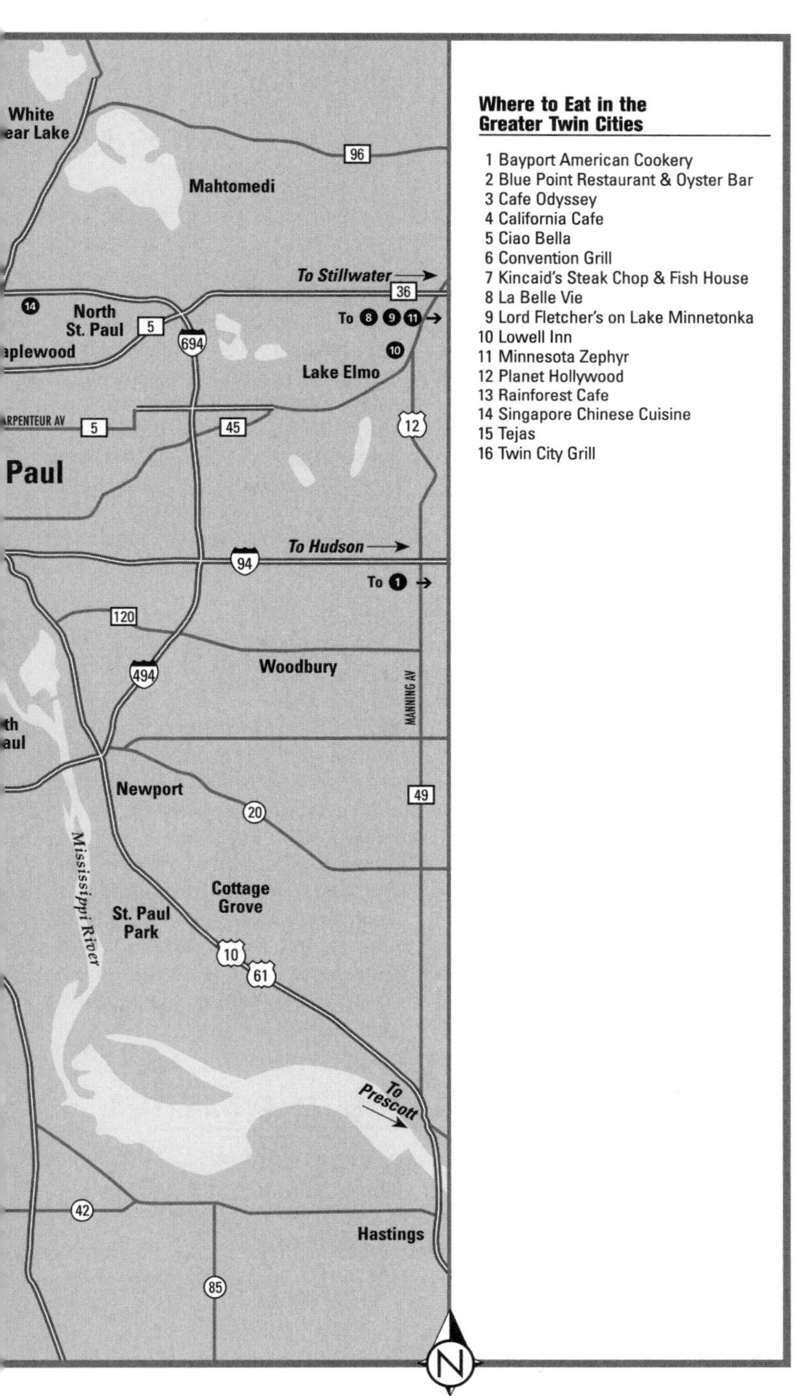

Where to Eat in the Greater Twin Cities
1 Bayport American Cookery
2 Blue Point Restaurant & Oyster Bar
3 Cafe Odyssey
4 California Cafe
5 Ciao Bella
6 Convention Grill
7 Kincaid's Steak Chop & Fish House
8 La Belle Vie
9 Lord Fletcher's on Lake Minnetonka
10 Lowell Inn
11 Minnesota Zephyr
12 Planet Hollywood
13 Rainforest Cafe
14 Singapore Chinese Cuisine
15 Tejas
16 Twin City Grill
White
Mahtomedi
96
To Stillwater
36
North St. Paul
5
694
To 8 9 11
10
Lake Elmo
5
45
12
Paul
To Hudson
94
To 1
120
494
Woodbury
MANNING AV
Newport
20
49
Mississippi River
Cottage Grove
St. Paul Park
10
61
To Prescott
42
Hastings
85
N

$$$
This restaurant serves sly, adventurous food in intimate surroundings. Named for its proximity to the Hungry Mind bookstore, the Table is known for contemporary American cuisine with occasional Asian accents. The cracker-crust pizzas can be perfection, and entrees such as grilled duck and pork tenderloin get the star treatment. The one faltering step is the kitchen's signature dessert, a scary deep-fried pound cake. Reservations recommended; smoke-free; lunch Mon–Fri, brunch Sun, dinner daily. ♿ (St. Paul)

TAVERN ON GRAND
656 Grand Ave.
St. Paul
651/228-9030
$$
In the lake-cabin atmosphere of "walleye-lovers' central," the kitchen serves more walleye than any other restaurant in the state, if not the world. It's heaps of fun, and the food ain't bad, either. No reservations; lunch and dinner daily. ♿ (St. Paul)

THE VINTAGE
579 Selby Ave.
St. Paul
651/222-7000
$$
This pretty restaurant and wine bar is set inside a beautifully restored 1890s mansion with several fireplaces and acres of warm woodwork. Stick with the many fine appetizers and salads; when the kitchen tries something complicated, it can disappoint. The enormous wine list has the largest by-the-glass selection in the Twin Cities, and cigar smokers will not feel like second-class citizens. Reservations recommended; lunch Mon–Fri, dinner daily. ♿ (St. Paul)

W. A. FROST & CO.
374 Selby Ave.
St. Paul
651/224-5715
$$$
Frost's elegant dining rooms—graced with high ceilings, French doors, ornate woodwork, and lots of antiques—make it one of the Twin Cities' most romantic restaurants. There's no better place in St. Paul to wait out a snowstorm or kill a sleepy late afternoon than Frost's beautiful bar. The shady, well-tended Victorian garden is the city's premiere outdoor dining locale in summer. A new chef—Twin Cities veteran Lenny Russo—has finally brought the menu up to the standards set by the decor and wine list. Reservations recommended; lunch Mon–Sat, brunch Sun, dinner daily. ♿ (St. Paul)

ZANDER CAFE
525 Selby Ave.
St. Paul
651/222-5224
$$
This new and wonderfully intimate café serves a handful of fresh soups, salads, and sandwiches and a few daily entrees, all reasonably priced. It has a great wine list and live jazz. Named for chef/owner Alexander Dixon, the restaurant's atmosphere leans toward small, spare, and cozy. No reservations. Lunch Tue–Fri, brunch Sun, dinner Tue–Sat. (St. Paul)

GREATER TWIN CITIES

BAYPORT COOKERY
328 Fifth Ave. N.
Bayport
651/430-1066
$$$

Lord Fletcher's on Lake Minnetonka/Thoen & Assoc.

Lord Fletcher's on Lake Minnetonka, p. 81

When chef/owner Jim Kyndberg is having a good night, this modest restaurant offers one of the most agreeable dining experiences in the Twin Cities. Kyndberg prepares a different five-course, fixed-priced dinner every evening, served at a single seating. If you don't like what's being served, you're out of luck, but Kyndberg's innovative recipes, quality ingredients, and attention to detail often make for a great evening. Be prepared to devote several hours to dinner, because service can be glacially slow. Reservations recommended; dinner Wed–Sun. ♿ (Greater Twin Cities)

BLUE POINT RESTAURANT & OYSTER BAR
739 E. Lake St.
Wayzata
612/475-3636
$$$

The menu at this faux 1940s roadhouse is all about superbly grilled, broiled, sautéed, and poached fresh seafood, a Minnesota rarity. The catch-of-the-day list usually features eight or more choices, and side dishes tend to fall into the "swell" category. Other hallmarks include excellent house-baked breads, a laudable wine list, and killer Key lime pie. The bar up front is snug and inviting. Reservations recommended; dinner daily. ♿ (Greater Twin Cities)

CAFE ODYSSEY
Mall of America
Bloomington
612/854-9400
$$

The megamall's newest and largest eatertainerie (400 seats!) has three dining rooms, each visually transporting diners to a trio of exotic locales: Macchu Picchu, the Serengheti Plain, and the mythical city of Atlantis. It's all rather silly, but the food is a cut above the quality one usually finds at such operations, with a large menu of watered-down world cuisines (Asian tacos, Spanish spring rolls, and the like) along with the standard burgers/pasta/sandwiches routine. No reservations; lunch and dinner daily. ♿ (Greater Twin Cities)

CALIFORNIA CAFE
Mall of America
Bloomington
612/854-2233
$$$

Chic and urbane in an early-90s kind of way, the megamall outlet of this West Coast chain does such a good job with pastas and pizzas that you'll forget that you're deep inside the bowels of a sinister suburban shopping mall. Standouts include the great wine list and well-trained servers. Steer clear of the deafening "outdoor" seating area, perched above the cacophony of the Knott's Camp Snoopy amusement park. Reservations recommended; lunch and dinner daily. ♿ (Greater Twin Cities)

CIAO BELLA
3501 Minnesota Dr.
Bloomington
612/841-1000
$$$

Designed to resemble an Italian villa—albeit one with a 250-seat dining room—this sprawling and comfortable suburban restaurant has tons of style and legions of followers, who come for the attentive service and the predictable (but pretty) menu staples: roasted meats (get the pork tenderloin), pastas, and wood-fired pizzas. Many come all dressed up to mingle in the handsome bar. Reservations recommended; lunch and dinner daily. ♿ (Greater Twin Cities)

CONVENTION GRILL
3912 Sunnyside Rd.
Edina
612/920-6881
$

A half-order of fries could serve a hungry family of four, the hand-formed burgers (arguably the Twin Cities' best) are thick and juicy, and each sinfully rich malt comes with the can. The grill serves decent chicken soup, too, and an addicting hot-fudge sundae. You'll find the same menu at Annie's Parlour (315 14th Ave. S.E., Minneapolis; 612/825-4455), but Annie's can't match the grill's no-nonsense atmosphere and great jukebox. No reservations; no liquor; lunch and dinner daily. ♿ (Greater Twin Cities)

KINCAID'S STEAK CHOP & FISH HOUSE
8400 Normandale Blvd.
Bloomington
612/291-2255
$$$

Here you'll enjoy nicely done steaks and chops, served in the sunny atrium of a suburban skyscraper. Preparations are straightforward, meaning the high-quality beef and seafood shine on their own merits. Thanks to its office-park location, the restaurant is a big business destination at lunch and rather clubby at dinnertime, with detail-attentive service. The large bar is a big draw. Reservations recommended; lunch Mon–Fri, brunch Sun, dinner daily. ♿ (Greater Twin Cities)

LA BELLE VIE
312 S. Main St.
Stillwater
651/430-3545
$$$

This romantic, 75-seat downtown Stillwater restaurant has an ambitious (and expensive) menu focusing on Mediterranean fare. Chef/owner Tim McKee was named one of America's most promising chefs in 1997 by *Food & Wine* magazine, and he spent a number of years running

D'Amico Cucina in downtown Minneapolis before opening his own place in early 1998. Reservations recommended; lunch Mon–Fri, brunch Sun, dinner daily. (Greater Minneapolis)

LORD FLETCHER'S ON LAKE MINNETONKA
3746 Sunset Dr.
Spring Park
612/471-8513
$$$

A superb Lake Minnetonka view is the draw here, along with tremendous people-watching and a dining room fashioned after a grandly timbered English country manor house. Fletcher's is best during summer, when its mobbed decks become ground zero for the lake's boating crowd (the restaurant has its own 70-slip marina). As for the food, it's strictly of the supper-club genre, but it works. Reservations recommended; lunch Mon–Sat, brunch Sun, dinner daily. ♿ (Greater Twin Cities)

LOWELL INN
102 N. Second St.
Stillwater
651/439-1100
$$$

A time warp. With an exterior that recalls Mount Vernon, it's no wonder that this Stillwater landmark has a pretty main dining room named for George Washington. Two other dining rooms consist of the oddly charming Garden Room and the tacky Matterhorn Room, which specializes in fondue. All three rooms serve American country club fare—dull and overpriced—and service is disconcertingly formal. Nothing has changed here in at least 40 years, and the Lowell's dowdiness will either charm the socks off you or drive you insane. Reservations recommended; breakfast, lunch, and dinner daily. ♿ (Greater Twin Cities)

MINNESOTA ZEPHYR
601 N. Main St.
Stillwater
651/430-3000 or 800/992-6100
$$$

Have dinner in a restored 1940s railroad dining car as you take a three-hour, 15-mile journey through the picturesque countryside of the St. Croix River Valley. The experience—rife with nostalgia and romance—is what you'll remember, because the hum-drum five-course dinner (around $55 per person) is on par with the average chain-hotel dining room fare. Reservations recommended; brunch Sun, dinner Wed–Sat. ♿ (Greater Twin Cities)

PLANET HOLLYWOOD
Mall of America
Bloomington
612/854-7829
$$

If tourista is what you seek, look no further than this loud local outlet of the national chain, which somehow manages to get better with age. The Minnesota version of movieland excess can be a hoot for pop-culture buffs, and kids love it. The bar is decked out like Norma Desmond's swimming pool in *Sunset Boulevard*, Dick Van Dyke's carousel horse from *Mary Poppins* hangs from the ceiling, the pots thrown by Demi Moore's character in *Ghost* are enshrined behind Lucite as if they were priceless Estruscan artifacts, and a Judy Garland dress from *Easter Parade* greets you at the front door. The food offers no surprises—burgers, sandwiches, pasta, salads, jumbo desserts, and overpriced, keep-the-glass drinks—but it's not bad. No reservations; lunch and dinner daily. ♿ (Greater Twin Cities)

RAINFOREST CAFE
Mall of America
Bloomington
612/854-7500
$$
This is the first branch of what has become a hugely popular jungle-themed chain restaurant dripping with phony ambience: a downpour is simulated every 20 minutes (lightning, thunder, water, the works), competing with a menagerie of live and fake animals, plants, and food. The most genuine element at work is the rampant commercialism, with the requisite store nearly as large as the huge dining room. If you must go, stick with the burgers (the menu doesn't feature foods indigenous to the rain forest), and visit during weekday mid-afternoons for the shortest wait. No reservations; smoke-free; lunch and dinner daily. ♿ (Greater Twin Cities)

SINGAPORE CHINESE CUISINE
1715 Beam Ave.
Maplewood
651/777-7999
$$
Singapore is where insiders go for Malaysian food. Its humble strip-mall decor belies the culinary treats that await. Don't order from the "American" menu; insist on seeing the "Chinese" menu. Call ahead and request the sea bass wrapped in banana leaves or try one of the spicy shrimp preparations. Lunch and dinner Tue–Sun. ♿ (Greater Twin Cities)

TEJAS
3910 W. 50th St.
Edina
612/926-0800
$$
Before this popular Tex-Mex joint decamped to the suburbs a few years back, it was one of downtown Minneapolis' most glamorous and adventurous restaurants—qualities that were tamed considerably after the move. Still, the food is pretty good, particularly the tortilla soup, Caesar salad, spicy corn bread, and almost every dessert. Servers are attentive, and the restaurant boasts a wonderfully urbane sidewalk patio. No reservations; smoke-free; lunch Mon–Sat, brunch Sun, dinner daily. ♿ (Greater Twin Cities)

TWIN CITY GRILL
Mall of America
Bloomington
612/854-0200
$$
This spot is Mall of America's best restaurant in terms of value and sheer food appeal. The kitchen gives American standards a fresh twist, starting with awesome flatbread appetizers. The Chinese chicken salad is a keeper, and the hearty meat loaf, pork chop, and baked chicken dinners pull the crowds in, too. Desserts are monumentally large, and the ambience recalls a sturdy 1930s-era diner. Reservations recommended; lunch and dinner daily. ♿ (Greater Twin Cities)

Greater Minneapolis CVA

5

SIGHTS AND ATTRACTIONS

To the casual observer, Minneapolis is the more modern of the Twin Cities. That's because it has a long-standing penchant for bulldozing anything in the name of progress. You'll find many more architectural links to the past in St. Paul. Still, some historic structures have managed to hang on in the raze-crazy Mill City, and some notably preserved sites can be found in downtown Minneapolis—standing shoulder-to-shoulder with numerous superb contemporary buildings. St. Paul's much greater appreciation of its heritage is reflected in the larger proportion of its late nineteenth- and early-twentieth-century architecture that remains intact. Both downtowns are relatively compact, enabling easy trips on foot.

DOWNTOWN MINNEAPOLIS

BUTLER SQUARE
100 N. Sixth St.
Minneapolis
612/339-4343

This beloved office/restaurant complex in the Warehouse District is a fine example of adaptive-reuse restoration. Designed by Harry Jones and built in 1907, the rugged, Italianate palazzo was originally a warehouse. Its brilliant renovation (done in two stages, in 1974 and 1981) carved two bright atria into the massive timbered building. The result: an underused and endangered structure became a popular urban asset, while its historic value remained uncompromised. (Downtown Minneapolis) ♿

FARMERS AND MECHANICS SAVINGS BANK
88 S. Sixth St.
Minneapolis
612/973-1111

There's no better-looking place to open a checking account than the city's last remaining grand banking hall, a two-story lobby (from 1941, by

DOWNTOWN MINNEAPOLIS

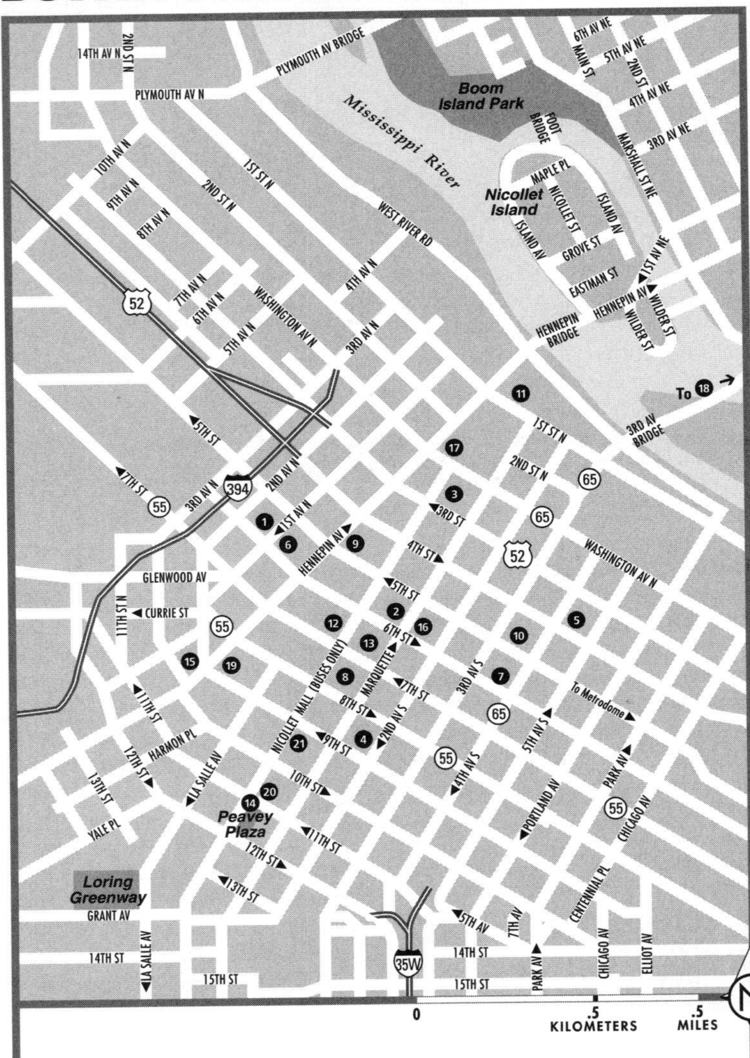

Sights in Downtown Minneapolis

1 Butler Square
2 Farmers and Mechanics Savings Bank
3 Federal Reserve Bank
4 Foshay Tower
5 Grain Exchange Building
6 Hennepin Center for the Arts
7 Hennepin County Government Center
8 IDS Center
9 Lumber Exchange Building
10 Minneapolis City Hall
11 Minneapolis Post Office
12 Nicollet Mall
13 Norwest Center
14 Orchestra Hall
15 Orpheum Theatre
16 Rand Tower
17 ReliaStar Building
18 St. Anthony Falls and the Stone Arch Bridge
19 State Theatre
20 WCCO-TV
21 Young Quinlan Building

McEnary and Kraft) with fine art deco lines, a gorgeous circular staircase, and sculpted chandeliers. (Downtown Minneapolis) ♿

FEDERAL RESERVE BANK
250 Marquette Ave.
Minneapolis

Downtown's most unusual structure, this striking landmark was home to the Fed from 1971 to 1997. It's actually two buildings: the first is a multifloor secured area buried beneath a sloping, windswept, and rather awful granite plaza; the second is literally hung above it, a la suspension bridge construction. Architect Gunnar Birkerts argued that the bank's need for unobstructed office space necessitated such engineering. His justification seems beside the point because the building is a stunner, more sculptural than architectural. However, this memorable home may be endangered, since the Fed traded it in 1997 for dull new digs a few blocks north. The Birkerts' building now sits empty until developers devise a new use for it. (Downtown Minneapolis) ♿

FOSHAY TOWER
821 Marquette Ave.
Minneapolis
612/341-2522

Plumbing magnate Wilbur Foshay built this endearing homage to the Washington Monument in 1929, although he wasn't around very long to enjoy it. Shortly after its completion, he was sent to prison for financial irregularities. After he had commissioned John Philip Sousa to write a rousing march for the tower's pompous three-day opening, his check to the composer bounced.

The 32-story obelisk (by Magney and Tusler) has such a novel design

Marc Caryl

Foshay Tower

that the architects had it patented, and Foshay's limitless ego led him to carve his name in 10-foot letters at the top. The Foshay dominated the Minneapolis skyline for more than 40 years, until it was dwarfed by the IDS Tower in 1973. The open-air public observation deck on the 31st floor (open April to September) is the only one of its kind in town, indoors or out, and on a clear day you can see for 30 miles. The art deco lobby is magical. (Downtown Minneapolis) ♿

GRAIN EXCHANGE BUILDING
400 S. Fourth St.
Minneapolis
612/321-7101

Kees and Colburn designed this lyrical gem in 1902 for the Minneapolis Chamber of Commerce, borrowing liberally from Louis Sullivan's Wainwright Building in St. Louis. Note the terra-cotta corn ears and stalks of grain on the building's facade. For tours—including a peek at the often wild trading floor—call the above phone number. (Downtown Minneapolis) ♿

HENNEPIN CENTER FOR THE ARTS
528 Hennepin Ave.
Minneapolis
612/332-4478

Built as a Masonic temple, this 1889 Richardsonian Romanesque pile was saved from the wrecking ball in the mid-1970s and reopened in 1979 as a center for the arts. It currently hosts studio, rehearsal, and performance space for a number of dance, theater, and musical organizations. (Downtown Minneapolis) ♿

HENNEPIN COUNTY GOVERNMENT CENTER
300 S. Sixth St.
Minneapolis
612/348-3000

Architect John Warneke designed this twin-tower complex, with the county courts to the east, and county administrative offices to the west. The two are connected by a vertiginous 24-story atrium, aligned to frame the City-Hall clock tower. At its opening in 1973, the center was widely judged too lavish for a Minnesota government building, with critics citing onyx boardroom panels, not-so-durable Swiss tiles on the plazas, and an astronomical heating bill for that giant atrium. But the building endures because of its fine materials, particularly the same purple-gray granite (quarried in Ortonville, Minnesota) used in City Hall. The center's two plazas—one cold and formal with a dramatic waterfall, the other grassy and inviting—are both popular destinations, serving as the town squares that downtown Minneapolis sorely lacks. (Downtown Minneapolis) ♿

IDS CENTER
80 S. Eighth St.
Minneapolis
612/376-8000

This mixed-use complex—a full-block of retail, offices, and a hotel connected by a vast interior atrium—ushered downtown Minneapolis into a new era. When this urban icon opened in 1973, its Crystal Court instantly became the vibrant indoor town square that its architect, Philip Johnson, had envisioned—something along the lines of the Galleria in Milan. Johnson carved out the center of a city block, ringing the perimeter with four blue, glass-sheathed buildings and creating an enormous public space inside. Eight stories above the pink granite floor he installed a white metal canopy and covered it with hundreds of clear Plexiglass pyramids, hence the name Crystal Court. Unfortunately, the center has gone through some hard times, thanks to several insensitive remodelings by a parade of owners, including the latest, Heitman Properties. Throughout much of the 1990s, the distinctive space was devoid of the trees, flowers, benches, and shops that had provided its joie de vivre. Much of that vitality has been recently restored, and the court again pulses with energy and life. The city's skyway system converges on the court, and thousands of pedestrians pour through it every day.

As for the IDS Tower (named for Investors Diversified Services, now American Express Financial Advisors, downtown's largest employer), it's the city's tallest building (777 feet) and one of America's finest skyscrapers. Johnson ingeniously cut back the tower's four corners, reducing its bulk on the skyline and giving the landlord an added bonus of 32 corner offices per floor. The tower's highly reflective blue glass often throws the building into a pas de deux with the sky. Its imperious lobby was subjected to a ghastly and unnecessary renovation a few years ago, hopefully not a sign of things to come for this peerless mid-century masterpiece. (Downtown Minneapolis) ♿

LUMBER EXCHANGE BUILDING
10 S. Fifth St.
Minneapolis
612/334-3011

Another Richardsonian Romanesque gem, the Lumber Exchange Building is the grand dame of Hennepin Avenue. Built of rustic Lake Superior brownstone, the city's first skyscraper has been lovingly restored to its original 1885 condition, and the lavish marble lobby is worth a peek. Minneapolis was the world's largest lumber-milling center from the 1880s until World War I, and this building served as the center for that vital trade. (Downtown Minneapolis) ♿

MINNEAPOLIS CITY HALL
350 S. Fifth St.
Minneapolis
612/673-3000

This beloved heap of purple granite encompasses an entire city block, took 16 years to build (1889–1905), and almost bankrupted the city. But when the doors finally opened, the new municipal building was an immediate stamp of legitimacy for a city emerging from infancy into adulthood. The 345-foot clock tower (its faces are larger than Big Ben's) no longer dominates the city's skyline, but city hall still exudes a solid, implacable grandeur. A series of renovations have returned parts of the building, including the grand Fourth Street entrance, to their original splendor. Just inside, in a sumptuously appointed interior court, sits the massive *Father of Waters* statue by sculptor Larkin Goldsmith Mead.

Across Fourth Street is the city's new Federal Courts Building, a $103-million monstrosity designed by Kohn Pedersen Fox Associates. The nicest thing that can be said about the building is that its hideous, user-unfriendly plaza finally allows passersby to take in City Hall's muscular facade in one appreciative glance. (Downtown Minneapolis) ♿

MINNEAPOLIS POST OFFICE
100 S. First St.
Minneapolis
612/321-5957

This broad-shouldered 1933 Moderne jewel spans two city blocks. Inside, the main concourse is a fine, if restrained, example of art deco. Outside, the monumental building unfortunately blocks the city from the Mississippi River and St. Anthony Falls. (Downtown Minneapolis)

NICOLLET MALL
Nicollet Ave. between
Washington Ave. and Grant St.

Nicollet Mall

Greater Minneapolis CVA

Scenic Drives

Parkways in both Minneapolis and St. Paul offer beautiful and relaxing drives, walks, and bike rides, full of pretty scenery and fine residential architecture. From its starting point at the Cathedral of St. Paul, ***Summit Avenue*** *winds through the capital city for five miles, terminating at the Mississippi River. Along the way, this lovely, tree-lined boulevard—the city's most prestigious residential address for more than a century—showcases the nation's longest and best-preserved span of Victorian architecture. No one architectural style dominates; you'll see wonderfully overblown examples of Gothic, Italianate, French, Greek Revival, and everything in between (F. Scott Fitzgerald, a Summit resident himself, once referred to the avenue as "a museum of architectural failures"). Summit's most famous house is the Governor's Mansion (1006 Summit Ave.), a stately Jacobean affair built originally for industrialist Horace Irvine and donated to the state in 1965. Governor Jesse Ventura and his family now reside in the grand house. The big houses are punctuated by several beautiful churches and well-tended college campuses, including the William Mitchell College of Law, Macalaster College, the University of St. Thomas, and St. Paul Seminary.*

Minneapolis

In 1967 noted San Francisco landscape architect Lawrence Halprin converted faded Nicollet Avenue (the city's principal shopping street) into one of the country's first pedestrian malls. Halprin replaced the traffic-clogged street with an undulating, 30-foot roadway for buses and taxis, then widened the sidewalks and turned them into shady, flower-filled promenades. The result was an urban design revolution that fomented in dozens of cities around the world.

Halprin's classic design ensured that Nicollet Mall would remain healthy and vibrant for years. Unfortunately, the delicate pavement proved ill-suited for Minnesota's harsh climate, and after 20 years of hard use, the mall was looking its age. Rather than simply repave the street, a number of ambitious business and civic leaders decided to rethink and rebuild the mall. The results were mediocre at best, disastrous at worst.

The new Nicollet Mall, designed by Minneapolis-based BRW and completed in 1992, is a depressing and unoriginal reworking of Halprin's

*Another fine St. Paul scenic drive is **Mississippi River Boulevard**, which starts in the city's comfortable Highland Park neighborhood and winds along the top of the river bluff to Marshall Avenue, where it connects with Minneapolis's East River Road parkway. The boulevard's east side is lined with enormous homes, including Eastcliff (176 N. Mississippi River Blvd.), the official residence of the University of Minnesota's president.*

*Minneapolis has several obvious choices, including the city's famous **Chain of Lakes** and **Minnehaha Parkway** (see Chapter 8, Parks, Gardens, and Recreation Areas). For something a little less touristy, consider two alternatives on the city's north side. The first is **Theodore Wirth Parkway**, a beautiful meander through Minneapolis's largest park. The terrain changes constantly, from woods to marshes to ponds to rolling hills. Continue north to Lowry Avenue, where you'll hit **Victory Memorial Drive**, a two-mile Beaux Arts homage to World War I veterans. The drive's 587 elms, planted in 1921, each represent a fallen Hennepin County soldier and are matched with commemorative markers. A memorial to Abraham Lincoln stands at the circle from which the drive turns east toward the Mississippi River.*

ingenious scheme. BRW flattened Halprin's sinuous roadway, replacing each block's S-curve (Halprin's "urban dance") with a flatter C-curve. The leafy honey locusts that once shaded the mall were chopped down (on Earth Day!) and replaced with Austrian pines, which quickly died. Halprin's elegant Modernist lampposts were replaced by quasi-Victorian horrors. The sturdy and handsome bus shelters were torn down and ghastly fake gazebos erected. Fountains and art were removed, never to be seen again. The list goes on and on.

Happily, some things are worth seeing on the new Nicollet Mall. BRW's granite paving is a vast improvement over Halprin's original terrazzo. The new mall is also liberally sprinkled with art, including George Morrison's intriguing pavement mosaic (in front of the IDS Center between Seventh and Eighth Streets) and Stanton Sears' Stone Boat, a curving, anthropomorphic granite bench (in front of City Center at Seventh Street). A lovely clock, remaining from the Halprin mall, holds court over Peavey Plaza at 11th Street. (Downtown Minneapolis)

NORWEST CENTER
90 S. Seventh St.
Minneapolis
612/344-1200

New York City's RCA Building was architect Cesar Pelli's inspiration for this 775-foot, 52-story tower, which became an instant landmark upon its completion in 1988. By night, when floodlights bathe it in a warm glow, Norwest becomes a beacon and one of downtown's most romantic sights. The building is sheathed in warm Kasota sandstone (quarried in nearby Mankato), which Pelli accented with white marble and gleaming bronze.

Norwest is a gracious neighbor to the IDS; together, they're the Fred and Ginger of the Minneapolis skyline. Pelli even permitted the IDS to retain its status as the city's tallest tower—by two feet. Inside, the architect skillfully incorporated elements from the site's previous occupant, the stodgy Northwestern National Bank building, which burned in a spectacular fire on Thanksgiving Day 1982. The Northwestern's ornate chandeliers, railings, and other decorative elements were later reinstalled in Norwest's understated, full-block lobby and banking rotunda. Inside the lobby, the bank displays its gorgeous, ever-changing twentieth-century decorative art collection. Norwest will soon be known as Wells Fargo Bank, following its 1998 acquisition by the San Francisco–based financial institution. (Downtown Minneapolis)

ORCHESTRA HALL
1111 Nicollet Mall
Minneapolis
612/371-5600

The building with the ocean-liner vents on the roof is Orchestra Hall, designed by Hardy, Holzman & Pfeiffer Associates and Hammel, Green and Abrahamson in 1974. This home to the Minnesota Orchestra has near-perfect acoustics, due in large part to its unique design, utilizing hundreds of plaster cubes sprayed playfully across stage and ceiling of the 2,500-seat house. Stylistically, the high-tech hall has its enemies, and with good reason. The orchestra devoted much of its money to acoustics, leaving the cramped lobby and other public spaces fairly spartan. Lively Peavey Plaza (see Chapter 8, "Parks and Gardens") is just outside. (Downtown Minneapolis)

ORPHEUM THEATRE
910 Hennepin Ave.
Minneapolis
612/339-0075

At its 1921 opening, the 2,900-seat Orpheum was the nation's second largest vaudeville house. By the mid-1980s, it was owned by singer (and Minnesota native) Bob Dylan and was falling apart. After the roaring success of the State Theatre's renovation, the city stepped up to the plate, bought the Orpheum, and pumped $9 million into its renovation, completed in 1994. The results are more subdued—but no less triumphant—than the State's. Included is a glittering dome, lined with 30,000 four-inch aluminum squares and lit by a 2,000-pound chandelier. (Downtown Minneapolis)

RAND TOWER
527 Marquette Ave.
Minneapolis
612/673-0747

Once a dominant force on the Minneapolis skyline, this 27-story art deco stunner just keeps getting better with age. The 1930s lobby is straight out of a Busby Berkeley

Greater Minneapolis CVA

Stone Arch Bridge

movie, and a recent renovation has restored its considerable luster. (Downtown Minneapolis)

RELIASTAR BUILDING
20 Washington Ave.
Minneapolis
612/372-5432

Architect Minuro Yamasaki (the man behind New York City's World Trade Center) designed this 1963 Greek-temple-as-office-building to be the crown jewel of the Gateway Center, an ambitious slum-clearance project that leveled 20 blocks in the city's oldest commercial district. Unfortunately, the bulldozers took some amazing bits of history with them, including the universally beloved Metropolitan Building. Instead, block after block of second-rate modern architecture and bland, lifeless plazas were erected, with this light-as-air building a main exception. Its striking open-air portico acts as a terminus for Nicollet Mall, and its well-tended grounds, reflecting pool, and cheerful Henry Bertoia sculpture in the lobby are just some of Yamasaki's thoughtful touches. (Downtown Minneapolis)

ST. ANTHONY FALLS
AND THE STONE ARCH BRIDGE
125 Main St. S.E.
Minneapolis
612/627-5433

The only falls on the Mississippi serve as the Twin Cities' raison d'être. The roaring 32-foot cataract that Father Louis Hennepin christened St. Anthony Falls was a sacred spot for the area's Sioux and Chippewa residents. St. Paul grew up a few miles downstream at the river's northernmost navigable landing, and Minneapolis was born around the mills that sprouted near the falls. The falls' natural beauty was destroyed in 1869, when an ill-advised tunnel project collapsed in a disastrous accident. They were saved from an unremarkable future as mere rapids by the construction of a concrete apron. By 1880, the falls area served as a nucleus of the nation's flour- and lumber-milling industries, and dozens of ugly mills

..vded the river's east and west ..nks. Today all but one are gone, but St. Anthony Falls retains its might, particularly when water levels are high in spring and early summer.

In 1883 railroad czar James J. Hill built his Stone Arch Bridge just below the falls. Modeling it after a Roman viaduct, he positioned it to provide both a majestic entry into the city and sweeping views of the powerful waterworks from his trains. Built entirely of massive limestone blocks (although it leaps across the river as if it were light as a feather), "Jim Hill's Folly" is an engineering marvel and the second-oldest bridge still spanning the Father of Waters. Its gently curving simplicity and strength also make it one of the most beautiful bridges on the river. The 2,100-foot bridge was extensively renovated in 1994 and is now open to bike and pedestrian traffic only. The views are spectacular. Guided hourlong tours of the St. Anthony Falls area, sponsored by the Minnesota Historical Society, are available May–October Wed–Sunday 12–4. $4 adults, $3 seniors, $2 children. (Downtown Minneapolis)

SKYWAY SYSTEM
Various downtown sites

On Seventh Street between Second and Marquette Avenues is the city's oldest skyway bridge. Now ubiquitous, this second-story span was revolutionary at its 1962 debut. Today the skyway system (which is predominantly privately owned) connects more than 50 downtown blocks, and it's possible to walk more than a mile without ever dealing with harsh weather. The public's love of skyways has clearly played a part in downtown Minneapolis' continued commercial vitality, but the system's influence hasn't been completely rosy. First-floor street life has declined since pedestrians moved up to the second floor, and the bridges themselves can be ugly as well as devastating to the buildings they pierce and the vistas they block. Some are worth a look, however, including the terra-cotta bridge spanning Marquette Avenue between the Norwest Center and the Firstar Bank Building, designed by Minneapolis sculptor Siah Armajani. (Downtown Minneapolis)

STATE THEATRE
805 Hennepin Ave.
Minneapolis
612/339-0075

Painstakingly restored in 1991 to its joyously overdecorated glory, the 2,200-seat State Theatre now provides a steady diet of touring musicals, plays, concerts, and lectures. Given its checkered history as a vaudeville house, movie theater, and church, this 1920 wonder is remarkably well preserved. The theater created a protracted battle among city officials, preservationists, and developers of LaSalle Plaza, which was eventually built around its outer shell. That the State was almost razed now seems unimaginable: All of its parts—from the golden proscenium arch to the glittering chandeliers, intricate murals, and rich plaster details—bring smiles to every theatergoer. (Downtown Minneapolis)

WCCO-TV
Nicollet Mall at 11th St.
Minneapolis
612/339-4444

Designed by Hardy, Holzman & Pfeiffer Associates and opened in 1981, the WCCO Television Communications Center is probably the most sensitively rendered contemporary building in downtown Minneapolis. Built of beige Kasota stone, the relatively small building exudes warmth, and the big front window news studio and the sidewalk monitors are fun touches. (Downtown Minneapolis)

YOUNG QUINLAN BUILDING
81 S. Ninth St.
Minneapolis
612/333-6128

The Young Quinlan Company was the work of Elizabeth Quinlan, a brilliant retailer who brought ready-to-wear to Minneapolis and built this gem of a store, one of the country's prettiest, in 1926. Even after she sold her business in 1945, Y-Q remained the Midwest's most elegant store for some years. (Neiman-Marcus modeled its Dallas store after Miss Quinlan's French-inspired emporium.) In its current incarnation as an office and retail complex, the six-story palace still imparts a soothing and urbane presence. Polo/Ralph Lauren now occupies most of the grand first floor. Don't miss the big Y-Q clock just inside the store's Nicollet entrance, the lanterns and iron railings on the mezzanine, or the handsome "Paris–New York–Minneapolis" bronze placard on the building's Ninth Street and Nicollet Mall facade. Miss Quinlan's elegant Lowry Hill home, bearing a striking resemblance to her store, still stands at 1711 Emerson Avenue South. (Downtown Minneapolis)

DOWNTOWN ST. PAUL

CAPITOL MALL
Constitution Ave.
St. Paul

This large, well-groomed park evolved during post–World War II urban planning, when a massive slum clearance project rid the area of dilapidated structures—plus a few historically and architecturally significant ones. In their places, state

A Capital Error

One of the biggest blunders in St. Paul city-planning history was the decision to sever downtown St. Paul from the Capitol area with I-94. Even before its 1967 completion, the freeway cut deep emotional scars, eliminating whole neighborhoods, including Rondo, the city's largest African American enclave.

In the mid-1990s, a one-mile stretch (from Western Avenue to East Seventh Street) was given an imperial makeover, complete with towering stonelike walls, iron railings, classical lamps, porticos, and other vaguely Beaux Arts touches. The impressive results have gone a long way toward restoring some of the area's long-wounded civic pride.

Landmark Center

Landmark Center, p. 97

government erected several dreary office buildings, ringing a wide greensward approach to architect Cass Gilbert's exquisite white marble Capitol.

Today Capitol Mall is a pleasant respite, dotted with statues and memorials (including a moving new one dedicated to Minnesota's Vietnam veterans). The park hosts several annual festivals, including Taste of Minnesota (July Fourth weekend) and the St. Paul Winter Carnival. The mall's green sweep ends at the understated Veterans Service Building, which is highlighted by Alonzo Hauser's graceful fountain, *The Promise of Youth*. (Downtown St. Paul)

CATHEDRAL OF ST. PAUL
239 Selby Ave.
St. Paul
651/228-1767

One of the country's largest churches presides over the city's best site: high on a hill overlooking downtown and the Mississippi River Valley, at the foot of Summit Avenue. Architect Emmanuel Masqueray was lured to Minnesota by Archbishop John Ireland to create a cathedral of sweep and grandeur, and his Renaissance-inspired design resulted in one of the state's most magnificent buildings. After nine years of construction, the $1.5 million structure opened in 1915, although extensive interior work continued for several decades. Masqueray's massive copper dome rises 300 feet from the nave's floor, and cathedral walls are covered in pale Minnesota granite. The building's Summit Avenue facade is flanked by a pair of carillon towers, and the sanctuary—one of Minnesota's most breathtaking spaces—seats 3,000 worshippers. A small basement museum contains Masqueray's original building plans. Open daily 7 to 6, with guided tours Mon, Wed, and Fri at 1. (Downtown St. Paul)

ECOLAB CENTER
320 N. Wabasha St.
St. Paul
651/293-2233

St. Paul's response to the 1960s urban-renewal juggernaut was Capital Centre, which leveled the city's charming, historic center, replacing it with block after block of dreadful modernist office towers and barren plazas. The one bright spot among the wreckage is this modestly handsome 19-story skyscraper. Clad in black granite and stainless steel, the building is set back from the street by a shallow moat and faces two plazas. The larger of the two, Osborne Plaza, was recently—and smartly—renovated. It is named for the founder of Ecolab, an international maintenance and sanitation company and an important St. Paul employer. (Downtown St. Paul)

DOWNTOWN ST. PAUL

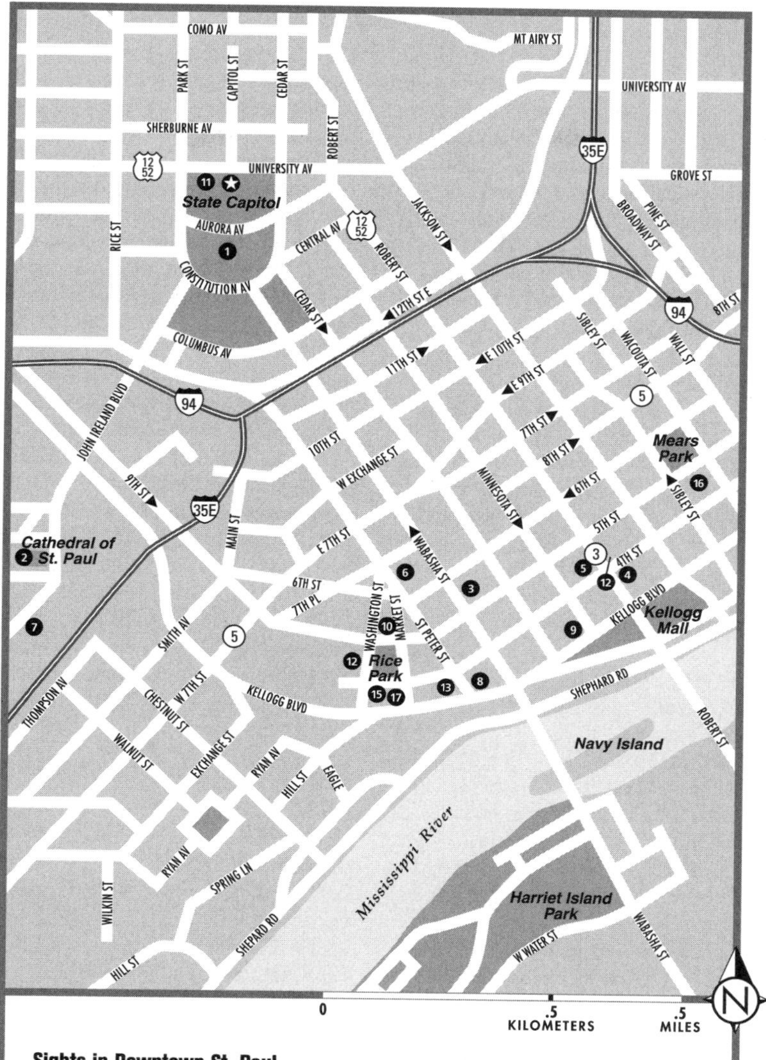

Sights in Downtown St. Paul

1 Capitol Mall
2 Cathedral of St. Paul
3 Ecolab Center
4 Endicott on Fourth Building
5 First National Bank Building
6 Hamm Building
7 James J. Hill House
8 Jemne Building
9 Kellogg Mall
10 Landmark Center
11 Minnesota State Capitol
12 Ordway Music Theater
13 Pioneer Building
14 St. Paul City Hall/Ramsey County Courthouse
15 St. Paul Public Library/James J. Hill Reference Library
16 St. Paul Union Depot
17 US West

ENDICOTT ON FOURTH BUILDING
141 E. Fourth St.
St. Paul

The Endicott, designed by James Knox Taylor and Cass Gilbert, opened in 1890, a year after the Pioneer Building. More refined than the Pioneer Building next door, it sports an Italian palazzo facade and a pretty pink marble lobby. (Downtown St. Paul)

FIRST NATIONAL BANK BUILDING
332 Minnesota St.
St. Paul
651/225-3666

When it was built in 1931, the First's gigantic neon "1st" sign atop the 31-story limestone tower became an instant symbol of the city. The red and beige marble lobby is as rich as ever, but the bank—now called US Bank—regrettably moved its teller lobby to a nondescript skyway location in the mid-1970s. (Downtown St. Paul)

HAMM BUILDING
St. Peter and Sixth Sts.
St. Paul
651/222-7463

This beloved terra-cotta building started out in 1914 as the home of the Mannheimer Brothers department store. World War I intervened, and the uncompleted building stood vacant until 1919, when brewer William Hamm converted it into an office building. Recently restored, the splendid structure has a noteworthy lobby, and its first floor once again bustles with shops and restaurants. (Downtown St. Paul)

JAMES J. HILL HOUSE
240 Summit Ave.
St. Paul
651/297-2555

The base of Summit Avenue is anchored not only by the Cathedral of St. Paul but also by James J. Hill's forbidding stone mansion. A tour through these palatial digs, now owned by the Minnesota Historical Society, provides a jaw-dropping glimpse into what astonishing wealth could buy at the turn of the century. Designed by Peabody & Stearns, the house took more than three years to build (at a cost of $1 million, an astronomical sum at the time) and first occupied in 1891. The Richardsonian Romanesque structure stretches 200 feet along one of the Twin Cities' most commanding sites. Inside, it sprawls across 36,000 square feet. With 32 rooms (including 13 bathrooms), it's the largest house in the state. Aside from its two-story art gallery (emptied briefly in 1915 to fill the vacant walls of the just-opened Minneapolis Institute of Arts), the house contains a massive pipe organ and a number of turn-of-the-century advances in domestic technology, including an ingenious central heating system and electric lights. Tours Wed–Sat 10–3:30. $4 adults. (Downtown St. Paul)

JEMNE BUILDING
305 St. Peter St.
St. Paul

Named for its architect, this refined 1931 art deco beauty, decked out in Kasota stone, once housed the St. Paul Women's City Club and later, the Minnesota Museum of American Art. Listed on the National Register of Historic Places, it's now home to Wold Architects, the firm that renovated St. Paul's city hall and county courthouse. (Downtown St. Paul)

KELLOGG MALL
Kellogg Blvd. between Robert and Wabasha Sts.
St. Paul

This recently renovated three-block esplanade was originally conceived in the 1930s to provide vistas of the Mississippi River Valley. From the mall's vantage point high atop the bluffs, it's easy to see the vital role the river played in the city's development. Several memorials dot the mall, including a spot near the intersection of Kellogg and Robert, where Father Lucien Galtier constructed the city's first building, an 1841 log cabin church named for the apostle Paul. Both mall and boulevard are named for Frank B. Kellogg, a St. Paul native and Nobel Peace Prize–winning diplomat. (Downtown St. Paul)

LANDMARK CENTER
75 W. Fifth St.
St. Paul
651/292-3225

Rice Park's anchor is pile of French-accen ite, red tile roofs, turrets, tower, gables, and other whimsical details. Dedicated in 1902 and designed by Willoughby J. Edbrooke as a federal courts building and post office, this Victorian gem was nearly razed in the late 1960s, until an enterprising group of preservationists fought for its survival. The federal government sold it to the city for $1 in 1972, and after six years of painstaking renovation, it reopened as Landmark Center. It has been a focal point of city life ever since.

The opulence continues inside, with a soaring five-story skylit courtyard and lavishly appointed rooms

Native Son

St. Paul's Cathedral Hill neighborhood was the home of author F. Scott Fitzgerald, and a number of addresses bear his history. Fitzgerald was born at 481 Laurel Avenue. As a child he lived in the splendid row house at 294 Laurel Avenue and also at 509 and 514 Holly Avenue.

He wrote his first published novel, This Side of Paradise, *while living at 599 Summit Avenue. He penned* The Beautiful and the Damned *while living at 626 Goodrich Avenue, which was also his first home with wife, Zelda. The couple's last St. Paul residence was the Commodore Hotel (79 Western Avenue), where Fitzgerald wrote* Winter Dreams.

The Fitzgeralds left St. Paul in 1922, never to return. Fitzgerald wasn't crazy about his hometown, but the city is fond of its native son. He's memorialized by a statue in Rice Park, and the theater from which Garrison Keillor broadcasts A Prairie Home Companion *also bears his name.*

Tim Rummelhoff

James J. Hill House, p. 96

with 20-foot ceilings, Vermont marble fireplaces, and exquisitely carved mahogany and marble details. The breathtaking cortile and four major courtrooms are now used for public receptions. The rest of the building is devoted to office space for arts organizations and exhibition space for the Minnesota Museum of American Art, the Ramsey County Historical Society, and the Schubert Club. Other features include a 200-seat basement auditorium and a fine lunch spot, Taste of Scandinavia, on the first floor. Free tours Thu at 11, Sun at 1. (Downtown St. Paul)

MINNESOTA STATE CAPITOL
Park and Aurora Sts.
St. Paul
651/296-2881

The Capitol crowns one of two hills that dominate old St. Paul (the other is topped by the mighty Cathedral of St. Paul). The two imposing buildings—secular and state—stare one another down from opposite ends of John Ireland Boulevard. The Capitol—the state's third—took six years to build, cost $4 million, and opened in 1904. The first, a modest brick and wood structure, burned to the ground in 1881. The second, a Victorian horror, was outdated before it opened and was razed in the 1930s.

As for the existing building, St. Paul architect Cass Gilbert beat out 40 competitors to win the commission, and he modeled his winning entry—particularly its stunning, unsupported 220-foot marble dome—on St. Peter's in Rome. The building is considered by many to be the nation's most beautiful state capitol, and with good reason: The interior is palatially (some might say grossly) detailed, and the building's materials, scale, and sweep could never be replicated today. Climb the front steps for a breathtaking view of downtown St. Paul, the cathedral, and the Mississippi River Valley. Perched above the main entrance is *Quadriga*, a recently restored gilded statue by Daniel Chester French and Edward Potter.

The legislature convenes for the first three to four months every year,

Irvine Park

Irvine Park, the focal point of St. Paul high society in the 1880s, had fallen into serious decline by the 1970s. A restoration of this green Victorian square and its enclave of homes (some of the oldest in the state) reversed that slide, and today the area is one of the city's most charming districts. The park is located two blocks south of the West Seventh and Walnut Street intersection.

The neighborhood's best-known landmark is the Alexander Ramsey House (265 S. Exchange St.), a 1872 Second Empire mansion built for the state's first governor, now owned by the Minnesota Historical Society. Tours May–Dec Tue–Sat 10–3. $4 adults, $3 seniors, $2 children. Crowds are particularly heavy before Christmas, when the house is done up with period decorations. Reservations recommended; call 651/296-8760.

and when the House and Senate are in session, all galleries and hearing rooms are open to the public. The Minnesota Historical Society offers free tours every hour from 9 to 3 weekdays, 10–3 Sat, and 1–3 Sun. (Downtown St. Paul)

ORDWAY MUSIC THEATER
345 Washington St.
St. Paul
651/282-3000

Designed by St. Paul native Benjamin Thompson, the Ordway has been a city hub since it opened in 1984 to great acclaim (*Time* magazine called it a "jewel on the Mississippi"). That's exactly the role that 3M heiress Sally Irvine had in mind when she donated $10 million in her father's name to create a performing arts center for sleepy downtown St. Paul. Laid out in the manner of a European opera house, the main theater, grand lobby, and 300-seat McKnight Theater are distinguished by handsome contemporary details. The popular building is the principal home of the St. Paul Chamber Orchestra, Minnesota Opera, and Schubert Club. A variety of theatrical and dance performances take place here, including long runs of Broadway touring companies. (Downtown St. Paul)

PIONEER BUILDING
336 Robert St.
St. Paul

Built in 1889 and named for its original tenant, the St. Paul Pioneer Press, the Pioneer was St. Paul's first skyscraper. Its red brick and granite exterior (by architect Solon Beman) remains as handsome as ever. Duck inside for a peek at the dizzying 15-story light court, equipped with manually operated glass elevators and a crazy circular manually operated staircase. (Downtown St. Paul)

ST. PAUL CITY HALL/
RAMSEY COUNTY COURTHOUSE
15 Kellogg Blvd.
St. Paul
651/226-8023

Many Minnesotans consider this 20-story structure the state's finest public building. The 1932 masterpiece is a study in contrasts. Its restrained, monochromatic limestone exterior belies the madcap goings-on of its jazzy, ornate, Zigzag Moderne interior. Designed by Holabird and Root and Ellerbe Architects, this landmark was given a magnificent $48 million restoration and expansion in 1993 by Wold Architects and Architectural Alliance.

The entire building is a study in exquisite detailing (the $4-million, Depression-era budget went a long, long way) and deserves serious exploration. Memorial Hall, the building's lobby, has few rivals for sheer drama. It offers a three-story sweep of blue/Black Belgian marble excess worthy of any opera stage, culminating in *Vision of Peace*, Carl Milles's stunning 36-foot statue of an Indian god, carved in Mexican white onyx. The 60-ton statue pivots 130 degrees every two and a half hours. The building boasts 25 different types of wood, more than a dozen varieties of stone, and 50,000-plus feet of gold leaf. The third-floor city council chambers are dominated by four giant WPA Moderne–style murals by John Norton. (Downtown St. Paul)

ST. PAUL PUBLIC LIBRARY/JAMES J. HILL REFERENCE LIBRARY
90 W. Fourth St.
St. Paul
651/292-6311

This subdued, Northern Italian Renaissance palace for the people was designed by Electus Litchfield in 1916. Railroad baron James J. Hill commissioned the building to house his extensive private collection and to serve as the city's public library. Modeled after the Morgan Library in New York City, the exterior is clad in pink Tennessee marble. The interior is slathered in tons of carved sandstone cut from the Kettle River in northern Minnesota. Portions of the public library side have been sadly neglected for years but are now undergoing a much-needed renovation.

The building's crown jewel is the Hill Library's stately reading room, which occupies the entire east wing. One of the Twin Cities' most appealing rooms, this carefully maintained three-story vault looks just like a library should: classical, dark, and serious. An excellent business research library, it is a repository for the James J. and Louis B. Hill papers, and a pot of free coffee (caffeinated, of course) is always on. (Downtown St. Paul)

ST. PAUL UNION DEPOT
214 E. Fourth St.
St. Paul

During its heyday, this severe limestone structure, built in 1923 by architect Charles Frost, was one of the country's busiest passenger terminals. The depot's no-nonsense exterior (highlighted by an imposing row of 10 huge Doric columns) belies its vast interior spaces, which were restored in 1983 and realigned for a number of restaurant tenants. (Downtown St. Paul)

US WEST
70 W. Fourth St.
St. Paul
651/344-5569

A trio of buildings houses telecommunications giant US West, with each structure representing a different generation in twentieth-century commercial architecture. The finest is the earliest: the Tri-State Telephone Building at the corner of Fourth and Market Streets, designed by Clarence Johnston Jr. in 1937. The splendid lobby of this restrained art deco tower was restored in 1986. It now houses the fascinating Pioneer Telephone Museum, which chronicles the history of the telephone and is managed by the Telephone Pioneers of America. Free tours by appointment only. (Downtown St. Paul)

MINNEAPOLIS

BASILICA OF ST. MARY

88 N. 17th St.
Minneapolis
612/333-1381

Even a series of ill-placed freeways couldn't obliterate this grand Beaux Arts church. The nation's first basilica, it is another work of Cathedral of St. Paul architect Emmanuel Masqueray. This enormous white marble structure is currently undergoing a multiyear, much-needed restoration that has revealed long-overlooked marvels both inside and out. (Minneapolis)

CHRIST LUTHERAN CHURCH

3233 34th Ave. S.
Minneapolis
612/721-6611

The final work (1949) of Finnish architect Eliel Saarinen truly fashions something out of nothing. In a lesser architect's hands, the modest materials and forgettable site would have been entirely undistinguished, but Saarinen skillfully imbues both with timeless dignity and stature. Eliel's son Eero Saarinen designed the building's education wing in 1962. (Minneapolis)

GUTHRIE THEATER

725 Vineland Pl.
Minneapolis
612/347-1100

The Guthrie Theater

Michal Daniel

MINNEAPOLIS

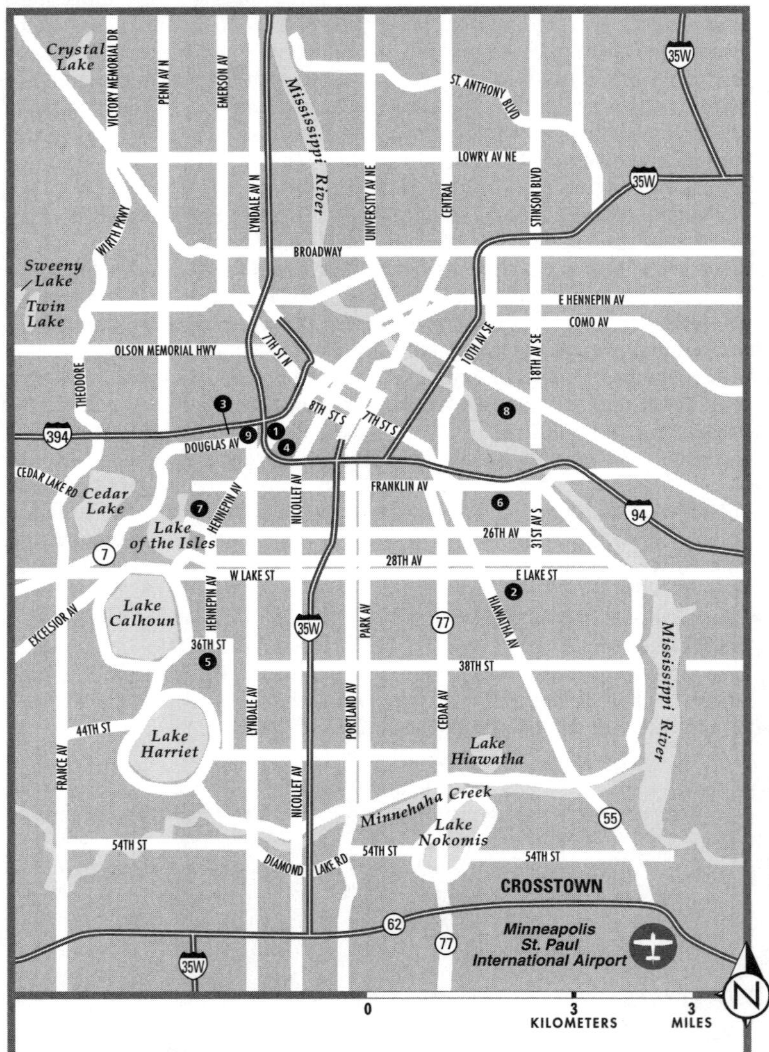

Sights and Attractions in Minneapolis

1 Basilica of St. Mary
2 Christ Lutheran Church
3 Guthrie Theater
4 Irene Hixon Whitney Bridge
5 Lakewood Cemetery
6 Milwaukee Avenue
7 Purcell-Cutts House
8 University of Minnesota
9 Walker Art Center and Minneapolis Sculpture Garden

When director Sir Tyrone Guthrie announced his intention to establish a permanent repertory acting company outside of Broadway's difficult commercial environment, Minneapolis' civic, business, and academic leaders lured him here (the promise of a new theater, built to his specifications, didn't hurt). The American regional theater movement was born on May 7, 1963, when the venue opened with a modern-dress production of Hamlet, directed by Guthrie, starring George Grizzard and Jessica Tandy.

Designed by Minnesota architect Ralph Rapson, the theater rejected the traditional proscenium for a thrust design, with the audience wrapped around a minimalist stage. The building's original distinctive facade was a lively pastiche of large windows behind a cubist frame of plaster panels. But lousy construction led to the facade's demise within a decade, and a 1993 renovation did away with it entirely, replacing it with a blandly smooth glass wall facing the Minneapolis Sculpture Garden. The interior has also been tweaked over the years—seats with poor sightlines were removed, and the stage was enlarged—but the auditorium remains recognizably the same. (Minneapolis)

IRENE HIXON WHITNEY BRIDGE
Loring Park
Minneapolis

This dynamic yellow and blue pedestrian bridge is the work of Minneapolis sculptor Siah Armajani. Leaping across 16 terrifying lanes of traffic, the bridge acts as a psychological and physical link between downtown, Loring Park, and the Lowry Hill neighborhood, which were severed by the construction of I-94 in the late 1960s. Like most of Armajani's works, the Whitney Bridge incorporates the written word—in this case, a poem by John Ashberry. (Minneapolis)

LAKEWOOD CEMETERY
3600 Hennepin Ave. S.
Minneapolis
612/822-2171

The city's largest cemetery is full of treasures. Memorial Chapel, designed by Harry Wild Jones and built in 1908, is an exquisite Byzantine wonder, recently restored and filled with eye-popping mosaics and a series of stained-glass windows that double as a sundial. Opened in 1871, the grounds, overlooking Lake Calhoun, are a restorative escape. Hubert H. Humphrey is buried here, as are Minneapolis park system designer Horace Cleveland and Emil Oberhoffer, the first musical director of the Minneapolis Symphony. Other permanent residents include such well-known families as the Walkers, Lorings, and Blaisdells. Open 8–dusk daily; chapel open weekdays 8–4:30. Free. (Minneapolis)

MILWAUKEE AVENUE
24th Ave. S. and Franklin Ave.
Minneapolis

This two-block street of modest homes, largely built in the 1880s for working-class immigrants, was restored during the 1970s. This compact neighborhood, listed on the National Register of Historic Places, is a living monument not only to the workers who shaped the city, but also to a people determined to preserve their history. The avenue is located about a mile west of the Mississippi River. (Minneapolis)

PURCELL-CUTTS HOUSE
2328 Lake Pl.

Minneapolis
612/870-3131
This 1913 Prairie School house is owned by the Minneapolis Institute of Arts. It was built by Purcell and Elmslie for Purcell's family, bequeathed to the institute by Anson Cutts Jr., then restored in 1991. The house's intricate and delicate decorative touches, including colorful stencils, 80 art-glass windows, and original furniture, make it a treat to explore. Second Sat of each month 10–4:30. Reservations required. Free. (Minneapolis)

UNIVERSITY OF MINNESOTA
612/626-8687
The Minneapolis campus of the U of M is one of the nation's largest, and its jumble of architectural styles makes for a varied, if somewhat discordant, academic environment. But a handful of buildings do have genuine merit. Besides the thrilling new Frederick R. Weisman Art Museum (333 E. River Rd.), highlights include Cass Gilbert's stately mall, patterned after Thomas Jefferson's Roman Romanum design at the University of Virginia. It is presided over by monumental Northrop Auditorium (84 Church St. S.E.) and Coffman Memorial Union (300 Washington Ave.). Other notable buildings are Pillsbury Hall (310 Pillsbury Dr. S.E.), a massive 1890 Richardsonian Romanesque fortress designed by L. S. Buffington; Williamson Hall (231 Pillsbury Dr. S.E.) and Civil/Mineral Engineering (500 Pillsbury Dr. S.E.), both examples of 1970s submerged structures designed by BRW; the Knoll (Church St. and Pillsbury Dr. S.E.), the school's original campus and a charming enclave of historic buildings; and the Law Center (229 19th Ave. S.), a spacious and gracious 1970s structure designed by Minnesota resident Leonard Parker. Free tours are available; call for information. (Minneapolis)

WALKER ART CENTER AND MINNEAPOLIS SCULPTURE GARDEN
725 Vineland Pl.
Minneapolis
612/375-7600
This contemporary art museum and 11-acre garden combine to create one of the country's great urban wonderlands. Perhaps the most superb piece in the garden is the Walker itself, a magnificent minimalist object looming above its outdoor galleries.

The museum building dates from 1972 and is the second gallery to occupy the site. Lumber baron T. B. Walker moved his odd collection of paintings, Japanese porcelain, and ceramics to this address in 1921. Over the ensuing years, the Walker turned its attention to contemporary art, and in 1972 it christened a new building, designed by Edward Larabee Barnes, more suited to its modern collections. The minute the doors opened, the Walker became one of the city's most popular places.

Its accompanying Sculpture Garden, a 1988 joint effort of the Walker and the Minneapolis Parks and Recreation Department, is the city's most-visited attraction—and with good reason. Its artwork, ever-changing landscape, and intriguing design make it a year-round delight. For more information, see Chapter 7, "Museums and Art Galleries." (Minneapolis)

Don Wong—Weisman Art Museum

6

MUSEUMS AND ART GALLERIES

Minneapolis and St. Paul are serious museum towns. Minneapolis is home to the Walker Art Center, an internationally renowned contemporary art museum on the southern edge of downtown, as well as the University of Minnesota's acclaimed Frederick R. Weisman Art Museum, housed in a striking building by architect Frank Gehry. In between, you can explore the encyclopedic European, Asian, and American art collections at the splendid Minneapolis Institute of Arts.

In St. Paul, you can uncover the Gopher State's rich past at the Minnesota Historical Society's fascinating Minnesota History Center. Children can throw themselves into the complexities of nature at the Science Museum of Minnesota, explore why things work at the delightful Minnesota Children's Museum, or learn about the harsh realities of life on an early-nineteenth-century frontier army post at historic Fort Snelling.

ART MUSEUMS

FREDERICK R. WEISMAN ART MUSEUM
333 E. River Rd.
Minneapolis
612/625-9494
hudson.acad.umn.edu/wamhome.html

Frank Gehry's flamboyant 1993 building is perhaps the most stunning piece in the museum's collection and the most talked-about structure in the Twin Cities. "The Fred" faces the Mississippi River with an undulating and dramatic facade covered in polished stainless steel, and it's particularly ravishing at sunset.

For all the goofy drama on the outside, the interior is surprisingly understated, and the modestly scaled and wonderfully lit galleries are so attractive that the *New York Times* called

TRIVIA

The most extensive collection of works by American painter Marsden Hartley has its home at the Frederick R. Weisman Art Museum at the University of Minnesota. The paintings were acquired by Hudson Walker, the University Art Museum's first director. Walker was a Hartley aficionado and the grandson of Walker Art Center founder T. B. Walker.

them "possibly the five best rooms for viewing art in the world."

The museum's mostly twentieth-century collection contains the world's largest assemblage of works by Marsden Hartley and Alfred Maurer, as well as paintings and prints by Georgia O'Keeffe, Arthur Dove, and Robert Motherwell, among others. The entrance is dominated by Roy Lichtenstein's *World's Fair Mural*. Be sure to take in the river view from the tiny balcony, located one floor above the galleries. And don't miss the museum shop, full of affordable baubles and amusing Gehry-related merchandise. Parking is available in a garage under the galleries. Tue, Wed, and Fri 10–5, Thu 10–8, Sat and Sun 11–5. Free. ♿ (Minneapolis)

MINNEAPOLIS INSTITUTE OF ARTS
2400 Third Ave. S.
Minneapolis
612/870-3131
612/870-3132 TDD
www.artsmia.org

With a collection of more than 85,000 objects, the MIA is one of the country's top art museums. Housed in a grand 1915 white marble Beaux Arts building by McKim, Mead and White (and a 1974 addition by Kenzo Tange), the museum's galleries have been undergoing renovations and reinstallations over the past few years, and its permanent collection has never looked better. Unlike many big-city art museums, which have a tendency to overwhelm, the manageable MIA is easily explored in a few hours.

Must-sees include the small but exceptional gallery of French Impressionist paintings, including works by Monet, Degas, Bonnard, and van Gogh; the exquisite Asian collection; *Lucretia*, considered by art historians to be the best Rembrandt in the country; the astounding, muscular *Doryphoros*, one of the finest Roman copies of the well-known but no longer existing Greek statue; and works by old masters such as Titian, El Greco, and Poussin. The museum also houses significant works by a laundry list of nineteenth- and twentieth-century American and European artists, including Picasso, Kandinsky, Matisse, Rodin, Rouault, Millet, Stella, and Klee.

The MIA is chock-full of smaller delights, too. The period rooms are fascinating, the tapestry collection is a wonder, and the newly opened photography and print galleries rotate appealing exhibitions culled from the museum's enormous collections. The Minnesota Gallery constantly introduces the work of new and emerging local artists. In addition, several major touring shows hang each year in MIA's large Dayton Hudson Gallery on the second floor.

The museum's second-floor cafeteria is always a smart choice for a delicious, inexpensive lunch. A large but not particularly compelling gift shop sits just inside the lobby. Tue, Wed, Fri, Sat 10–5; Thu 10–9; Sun 12–5. Admission is free; special exhibitions $5 adults, $3.75 students over 11 and seniors. Call 612/870-3200 for 24-hour exhibition information. ♿ (Minneapolis)

MINNESOTA MUSEUM OF AMERICAN ART
75 W. Fifth St.
St. Paul
651/292-4355

After spending much of the 1990s on the brink of financial disaster, this small museum resurfaced in 1998 with fine new galleries on Landmark Center's second floor. Here the museum has adequate breathing room to show off its fine collection of 10,000 paintings, drawings, and prints. Tue, Wed, Fri, Sat 11–4; Thu 11–7:30; Sun 1–5. Free. ♿ (Downtown St. Paul)

WALKER ART CENTER/ MINNEAPOLIS SCULPTURE GARDEN
725 Vineland Pl.
Minneapolis
612/375-7600
612/375-7585 TDD/TTY
www.walkerart.org

The Walker is o
best contempora
a center of Twin
The nine stark,
offer glimpses
large collection
tures, prints, drawings, and multimedia works, as well as a steady diet of traveling exhibitions. The permanent collection includes important works by a veritable Who's Who of contemporary art, including Willem de Kooning, Mark Rothko, Franz Marc, Stuart Davis, Andy Warhol, Joan Mitchell, Roy Lichtenstein, Donald Judd, Sol LeWitt, Chuck Close, and Dan Flavin. The museum is also the repository for Tyler Graphics. In addition, the Walker hosts a schedule of innovative theater, music, dance, film, video, and performance programs, as well as a never-ending series of classes, workshops, and lectures.

The Walker Book Shop sells a variety of gifts, artist-designed jewelry, toys, and museum-related items and has the city's top selection of art books and periodicals. Gallery 8, the museum's cafeteria, offers inexpensive and delicious fare. Spend a few moments in the Information Room for an excellent multimedia introduction to the Walker and its current exhibitions. On the second Friday of every month, the museum hosts Walker After Hours, the Twin Cities' hottest

TRIVIA

The Minneapolis Institute of Arts houses the country's most significant Chinese jade collection, much of it bequeathed to the museum by the Pillsbury and Walker families. Of special significance is *Jade Mountain*, a spectacular sixteenth-century sculpture carved from a single 640-pound piece of jade. One of four sculptures by Emperor Ch-ien Lung, it's the largest piece of historic jade in the Western Hemisphere.

TRIVIA

The Walker Art Center got its start in 1879, when lumber baron T. B. Walker opened a gallery in his spacious home at Eighth Street and Hennepin Avenue. The house was razed in the early 1920s to make way for the State Theatre, and the gallery moved to its much larger present site opposite Loring Park.

see-and-be-seen cocktail party. Families enjoy the first Saturday of every month, when the museum schedules free kids-oriented events and activities. Tue, Wed, Fri, Sat 10–5; Thu 10–8; Sun 11–5. Guided tours Thu at 2 and 6, Sun at 2. $4 adults, $3 seniors and students; free Thu and first Sat of each month. Call 612/375-7577 for 24-hour exhibition information.

The 11-acre Minneapolis Sculpture Garden is a year-round showcase for more than 40 works of art, including major sculptures by George Segal, Isamu Noguchi, Ellsworth Kelly, Richard Serra, Jenny Holzer, Alexander Calder, Henry Moore, Scott Burton, Franz Lipschitz, and Mark di Suvero. The garden's most famous (and beloved) symbol is the amusing *Spoonbridge and Cherry,* a 55-foot spoon topped by a 15-foot red Bing cherry, designed by Claes Oldenburg and Coosje van Bruggen. The garden's entrance is flanked by Ampersand, a pair of monumental granite columns by Martin Puryear. Its north end is dominated by a 300-foot stainless-steel arbor, planted with a colorful variety of blooming plants and flowers during summer.

Constantly in use, the garden is one of the most popular places in the city, even during the harshest of winter days. The Cowles Conservatory is a perfect gloomy-weather respite, with a changing display of blooming plants as well as a palm court dominated by Frank Gehry's *Standing Glass Fish.* Daily 6 a.m.–midnight. Ad-

Big Names at the Walker

Besides maintaining its permanent collection, which prospered under the stewardship of Milton Friedman for more than three decades and is now overseen by Kathy Halbreich, the Walker Art Center has either originated or lured a number of critically acclaimed exhibitions, including Picasso: Selections from the Musee Picasso *in 1980,* Tokyo: Form and Spirit *in 1985,* Hockney Paints the Stage *in 1987, and major retrospectives for Jeff Koons (1993), Robert Ryman (1994), Bruce Naumann (1995), and Willem de Kooning (1997).*

mission is free. Free tours (starting in the Walker lobby) Sat and Sun at 1. ♿ (Minneapolis)

SCIENCE AND HISTORY MUSEUMS

JAMES FORD BELL MUSEUM OF NATURAL HISTORY

10 S.E. Church St.
Minneapolis
612/624-7083

Here on the East Bank of the U of M campus, more than 100 species of Minnesota animals and birds exist in their native habitats. The kid-scaled Touch and See Room is a favorite. Tue–Fri 9–5, Sat 10–5, Sun 12–5. $3 adults, $2 seniors and ages 3–16; free to U of M students and children under 3, free Thu. (Minneapolis)

MINNESOTA HISTORY CENTER

345 Kellogg Blvd. W.
St. Paul
651/296-6126

The nation's largest state historical society now has a proper home, and it's a must for tourists and residents alike. The imposing but comfortable building is worth a visit itself. Designed by Hammel, Green and Abrahamson and completed in 1992, the 427,000-square-foot facility admirably frames St. Paul's two most important buildings, the Cathedral of St. Paul and the Minnesota State Capitol. It also manages to stand on its own as a distinctive, almost heroic work of architecture. Unfortunately, the building is surrounded by freeways, keeping it somewhat isolated from the city.

The center's permanent exhibits include the Smithsonian-inspired Minnesota A to Z, an ingenious depiction of various aspects of Minnesota life over the past 150 years. A new show nods to multicultural Minnesota families past and present. In another exhibit, visitors can learn how a grain silo operates and how native Minnesotans harvest wild rice.

Much of the building is devoted to research, and the warehouse areas are as large as three football fields, housing the society's collection of 100,000 objects and 500,000 documents. The center also features a comfortable auditorium, a teeming gift shop, and a popular cafeteria. Tue, Wed, Fri, Sat 10–5; Thu 10–9; Sun 12–5. Free. ♿ (Downtown St. Paul)

MINNESOTA TRANSPORTATION MUSEUM

Various sites
651/228-0263

Learn about the history of local train, boat, streetcar, and bus travel by visiting this collection of working locomotives, steamships, train depots, roundhouses, trolleys, and motor coaches. The MTM has five exhibit sites in the Twin Cities area, visited by more than 100,000 people annually.

The most popular exhibit is the Como–Harriet Streetcar Line, a rebuilt

TRIVIA

The University of Minnesota's natural history museum is named to honor one of its greatest benefactors, the late James Ford Bell. A conservationist and naturalist, Bell brought General Mills, the milling and cereal company, to national and international stature.

TRIVIA

The Bakken Library was founded in 1975 by Earl Bakken, inventor of the portable heart pacemaker and the man behind Medtronic, a leading medical technology company based in suburban Fridley.

portion of the nation's once-largest urban rail service. Restored cars dating from 1893, 1908, 1915, and 1947–49 run a two-mile round-trip course (a fraction of the former 500-mile system) between Lakes Harriet and Calhoun in South Minneapolis. Board at the Linden Hills Station (Queen Avenue and 42nd Street, just west of the Lake Harriet Bandshell) or at the Lakewood Cemetery platform, just south of 36th Street on East Lake Calhoun Parkway. Memorial Day –Labor Day Mon–Fri 6:30 p.m.–dusk, Sat 1–dusk, Sun 12:30–dusk; Sept and Oct weekends only. Cars run every 15 minutes. $1 adults and children, under 4 free.

The museum's other big draw is the *Minnehaha*, a 1906 Lake Minnetonka steamboat, which once used to ferry streetcar passengers all over Lake Minnetonka. Today the Minnehaha plies the lake between the cities of Excelsior and Wayzata. May–Sept Wed–Fri 1–5, Sat–Sun 8–6. One-way fare $5 adults, $4 seniors, $3 ages 6 to 16; round-trip $8 adults, $7 seniors, $5 ages 6 to 16. Tickets available at the Excelsior dock, at the end of Excelsior Boulevard near the Ferris wheel. Call 612/474-4801 for departure and arrival times. (Minneapolis, St. Paul, Greater Twin Cities)

SCIENCE MUSEUM OF MINNESOTA
30 E. 10th St.
St. Paul
651/221-9488
www.sci.mus.mn.us

A fascinating, hands-on center of discovery for kids of all ages. The museum's extensive permanent collections include anthropology, paleontology, biology, and technology exhibits, plus temporary exhibits on everything from holograms to cyberoptics to the workings of the human heart. The most popular attraction is the William T. McKnight –3M Omnitheater, which screens a constantly changing repertory of films.

The state's largest reptile (outside of the state legislature, as some politicos joke) guards the museum's front door—a 40-foot steel iguana by sculptor Nick Swearer. The no-nonsense 1980 facility is beginning to show its age and inadequacies, but the crowds keep pouring in. A lavish new building, now under construction on Kellogg Boulevard, is scheduled to open in late 1999. The 10th Street facility will then become a museum dedicated to the state's industrial workers. (Mon–Wed 9:30–5, Thu–Sat 9:30–9, Sun 10:30–7. $5 adults, $4 seniors and ages 4 to 15. For Omnitheater information, call 612/221-9444. ♿ (Downtown St. Paul)

OTHER MUSEUMS

AMERICAN SWEDISH INSTITUTE
2600 Park Ave. S.
Minneapolis
612/871-4907

St. Paul CVB/Tim Rummelhoff

Minnesota History Center, p. 109

www.americanswedishinst.org
Get a glimpse into how the other half lived at the turn of the century in this palatial, 33-room French Châteauñesque limestone mansion. Four years in the making, this castle was the pride and joy of Swan Turnblad, a Swedish immigrant and self-made millionaire publisher. Upon its completion, he and his wife, Christina, found it too ostentatious for their tastes, so they lived in an apartment across the street, using the house for entertainment purposes only.

After Swan's death, his family founded the American Swedish Institute and donated the house to serve as its headquarters. Today most of the building is open for exploration, and its ornate interior has to be seen to be believed. The museum features rotating exhibits on 150 years of the Swedish immigration experience, plus an excellent gift shop, basement bookstore, and informal restaurant.

As for the neighborhood, the house was—and remains—the grandest of all the stupendous homes that once lined this section of Park Avenue. The street has seen better days, but a few of the mansions remain, in varying shades of decay, on the four-block stretch between 26th Street and Franklin Avenue. Tue and Thu–Sat 12–4, Wed 12–8, Sun 1–5. $3 adults, $2 seniors and children. (Minneapolis)

BAKKEN LIBRARY AND MUSEUM OF ELECTRICITY IN LIFE
3537 Zenith Ave. S.
Minneapolis
612/927-6508
www.bakkenmuseum.org
Housed in a beautiful Tudor-style mansion, this fascinating museum houses an extensive collection of rare books, manuscripts, gadgets, and scientific instruments—all relating to the mystery and power of electricity. The library's lush gardens feature more than 200 varieties of medicinal plants. Mon–Fri 9–5 by appointment only, Sat 9:30–4:30. $3 adults, $2 seniors and children over 8. ♿ (Minneapolis)

MINNESOTA CHILDREN'S MUSEUM
10 W. Seventh St.
St. Paul
651/225-6001
This remarkable hands-on institution is a playful adventureland for kids and families, one of the largest of its kind in the country. (See Chapter 6, Kids' Stuff) Tues–Sun 9–5. $5.95 ages 3 to adult, $3.95 ages 1–2 and seniors. (Downtown St. Paul)

PAVEK MUSEUM OF BROADCASTING
3515 Raleigh Ave. S.
St. Louis Park
612/926-8198

This museum takes you on a modest and slightly eccentric trip back through time, to when the wireless was king of mass communications. Founded by amateur radio historian Joseph Pavek, the museum includes early radio equipment, crystal sets, and other paraphernalia. Tue–Fri 10–6, Sat 9–5. $3 adults, $2 children under 13 and seniors. ♿ (Greater Twin Cities)

ART GALLERIES

BARRY THOMAS FINE ARTS
400 First Ave. N.
Minneapolis
612/338-3656

Works by local, regional, and national artists are on display here, at the most ambitious of the half-dozen galleries within the Wyman Building. Every sixth Saturday evening, this neighborhood's galleries open their doors and throw a "gallery crawl," showing off their latest exhibits and drawing an eclectic crowd. (Downtown Minneapolis)

CIRCA
1637 Hennepin Ave. S.
Minneapolis
612/332-2386

This small, sunny storefront sits around the corner from the popular Loring Cafe and Bar, at the edge of Loring Park. The gallery shows paintings, ceramics, sculpture, and prints from local, national, and international artists. (Minneapolis)

DOLLY FITERMAN FINE ARTS
100 University Ave. NE
Minneapolis
612/623-3300

This art gallery boasts what may be the Twin Cities' finest gallery space: a beautiful white marble library dating from 1904. The gallery focuses on the works of contemporary painters, sculptors, and architects. (Minneapolis)

Dolly Fiterman Fine Arts

Dolly Fiterman Fine Arts

GROVELAND GALLERY
25 Groveland Terrace
Minneapolis
612/377-7800

Located in a beautiful mansion at the foot of Lowry Hill, this handsome gallery showcases paintings, watercolors, and prints created by local and regional artists. (Minneapolis)

JON OULMAN GALLERY
400 First Ave. N.
Minneapolis
612/333-2386

Part art gallery, part hair salon, this airy space at the top of the Wyman Building is particularly adept at displaying large-canvassed works by contemporary painters. Owner Jon Oulman's dog is the largest beast in the Warehouse District, and probably the friendliest. (Downtown Minneapolis)

NORTHERN CLAY CENTER
2375 University Ave.
St. Paul
612/642-1735

This unique gallery offers a huge range of ceramics classes and also features a space showcasing work from local and national ceramic artists. (St. Paul)

THOMSON GALLERY
321 Second Ave. N.
Minneapolis
612/338-7734

The spare, two-story venue shows paintings and small-scale sculptures by local and regional artists. (Downtown Minneapolis)

Jeff Greenberg/Unicorn Stock Photos

7
KIDS' STUFF

Residents have long extolled the virtues of raising a family in the Minneapolis/St. Paul area. Both cities have much to offer in terms of family fun, whether it's instructional, recreational, or both. The Twin Cities are home to one of the country's most fascinating zoos, a brand-new children's museum, and the nation's largest and oldest children's theater company, as well as two substantial amusement parks (one indoors, one out), the country's newest aquarium, and a bevy of interesting and affordable historical sites and museums to fascinate and educate kids of all ages.

ANIMALS AND THE GREAT OUTDOORS

COMO ZOO
Midway Pkwy. and Kaufman Dr.
St. Paul
651/488-5571

More than 300 animals can be seen at this small zoo, a St. Paul draw for nearly a century. Its exhibits are fashioned after natural habitats. Crowd favorites include the primate house and Sparky the sea lion's show. Zoodale, the gift shop, has lots of inexpensive trinkets. Call for hours. Free. (St. Paul)

MINNESOTA ZOO
13000 Zoo Blvd.
Apple Valley
651/432-9000 or 800/366-7811
612/297-5353 TTY
www.mnzoo.org

These 500 acres about 20 minutes south of either downtown contain five separate habitat trails (Ocean, Tropics, Minnesota, Northern, and Discovery), meriting extensive exploration. On the Northern Trail, visitors ride an overhead monorail for treetop views of wolves, moose, musk oxen, caribou, red pandas, Siberian tigers, trumpeter swans, bison, and Asian

Siberian tigers at the Minnesota Zoo

wild horses. On the Tropics Trail, sights include Komodo dragons, leopards, gibbons, sharks, and exotic tropical fish. Ocean Trail visitors see dolphins and a host of other sea creatures.

The zoo has an excellent gift shop, bookstore, concession stands, and picnic areas. The Weesner Family Amphitheater hosts family-oriented entertainment. Come winter, the groomed cross-country ski trails are tops. The zoo's $8 million 600-seat 3-D movie theater presents a constantly changing film schedule. Daily 9–4. $8 adults, $5 seniors, $4 ages 3–12. (Greater Twin Cities)

UNDERWATER WORLD
First floor, East Broadway
Mall of America
Bloomington
888/DIVETIME

One of Mall of America's biggest attractions is this $26 million aquarium. More than 15,000 saltwater and freshwater fish call Underwater World home. The ingenious facility features a meandering 400-foot acrylic tunnel simulating a scuba-dive experience in four different habitats: the Gulf of Mexico, a coral reef, the Mississippi River, and a frozen Minnesota lake. The moving walkway tour (complete with audio) takes about 35 minutes. Call for hours. $8.95 adults, $6.95 seniors, $4.95 ages 3–12. Tours begin every 15 minutes. Reservations suggested. (Greater Twin Cities)

MUSEUMS

FORT SNELLING
Highways 5 and 55
St. Paul
612/726-1711

Built at the strategic confluence of the Mississippi and Minnesota Rivers, Fort Snelling has been completely restored as a living-history museum that depicts the harsh realities of frontier life. Sponsored by the Minnesota Historical Society, this 1821 limestone fort comes to life with soldiers, servants, cooks, wives, officers, and laundresses, who reenact life at the post, circa 1827. May–Oct Mon–Sat 10–5, Sun 12–5. $4 adults, $3 seniors, $2 ages 6–15. (Greater Twin Cities)

GIBBS' FARM MUSEUM
2097 W. Larpenteur
Falcon Heights
612/646-8629

Get a peek at life on a turn-of-the-century farm at one of the few remaining farmsteads in the area. Owned and operated by the Ramsey County Historical Society, the site includes the Gibbs' fully furnished 1854 farmhouse, two barns, a one-room school, working gardens, and farm animals, all presided over by costumed guides. May–Oct Tue–Fri 10–4,

Sat and Sun 12–4. $3 adults, $2.50 seniors, $1.50 children (St. Paul)

MINNEAPOLIS PLANETARIUM
300 Nicollet Mall
Minneapolis
612/372-6644
Three generations of Twin Cities schoolchildren are veterans of this popular attraction, located downtown at the Minneapolis Public Library. The half-hour show changes about every 10 weeks, and includes an animated whirl through the current sky, vividly reproduced on a domed ceiling, and a spin through varied astronomical topics. Call for daily show times. $4 adults, $2.50 ages 3–12. Laser rock-music shows Fri and Sat. (Downtown Minneapolis)

MINNESOTA CHILDREN'S MUSEUM
10 W. Seventh St.
St. Paul
651/225-6001
651/225-6057 TDD
Kids under 10 will love this colorful, playful place. Housed in a large, cheerful new facility in downtown St. Paul, the museum has five exhibition areas as well as space for several touring shows. Possibilities include Habitot, scaled for infants and toddlers, and World Works, designed for inventors ages 3 to 7. Nature-conscious 4- to 8-year-olds will enjoy exploring Earth World's four different Minnesota animal habitats. One World takes 6- to 10-year-olds on a journey through several international communities. Changing World and World of Wonder house traveling shows from children's museums around the world.

A Day at the Farm

Although apple- and berry-picking farms abound around the Twin Cities area, ***Rush River Produce*** *(W4098 200th Ave., Maiden Rock, Wisconsin; 715/594-3648) is the friendliest and least commercial. You and the kids can pick blueberries, raspberries, lingonberries, and gooseberries, plus garden produce and red, black, and white currants. The farm, an hour southeast of the Twin Cities, boasts beautiful views of Lake Pepin, lovely flower gardens, and a picnic ground. Prime picking time is July through September. Open 8–dusk.*

Other popular area orchards include ***Aamodt's Apple Farm*** *in Stillwater (651/439-3127),* ***Afton Apple Orchard*** *in Afton (651/436-8385),* ***Emma Krumbee's*** *in Belle Plaine (612/873-4334),* ***Pine Tree Orchards*** *in White Bear Lake (651/429-7202), and* ***Sponsel's*** *in Jordan (651/492-2785).*

At *Grand Slam Sports & Entertainment* (3984 Sibley Memorial Dr., Eagan; 651/452-6569), kids can go crazy over minigolf, video games, bumper cars, Space Ball, batting cages, laser tag, a play zone, and more. The huge indoor center, which caters to kids ages 6 to 13, also has a decent snack bar. Adults are not required to accompany their children.

The best day for families is the first Tuesday of every month, when groups are not allowed. Creative Kidstuff, an innovative toy shop and bookstore, is located in the lobby, and an intimate, 150-seat theater schedules performances and readings for children. The museum is a terrific place to throw a kid's birthday party; call 651/225-6036 for b-day bash details. Tue–Sun 9–5; also open Mon 9–5 Memorial Day–Labor Day. $5.95 ages 3 to adult, $3.95 seniors and ages 1–2. All children must be accompanied by an adult. (Downtown St. Paul)

MURPHY'S LANDING
2187 E. Hwy. 101
Shakopee
612/445-6900

A unique living-history museum, Murphy's Landing is a collection of 40 different period buildings on an 88-acre wooded site along the Minnesota River. A fur-trading post, two farmsteads, a country schoolhouse, shops, and homes, as well as costumed interpreters and craftspeople, provide a fascinating glimpse into nineteenth-century immigrant life in rural Minnesota. Located one mile west of Valleyfair, about 35 minutes southwest of downtown Minneapolis. Memorial Day–Labor Day daily 10–5, Sept–Dec weekends only. $7 adults, $6 seniors and students, $5 groups, $4 student groups, free to children under 6. (Greater Twin Cities)

SCIENCE MUSEUM OF MINNESOTA
30 E. 10th St.
St. Paul
651/221-9488
www.sci.mus.mn.us

An exploratorium for kids of all ages, designed to stimulate an interest in science. Constantly changing exhibits complement the museum's extensive permanent collections, which include several dramatic dinosaur fossils. The museum's most popular attraction is the William T. McKnight 3M Omnitheater. Mon–Sat 9:30–9, Sun 10–9. $5 adults, $4 seniors and ages 4–15. For Omnitheater information, including hours and ticket prices, call 612/221-9444. (Downtown St. Paul)

TRAINS AT BANDANA
1021 Bandana Blvd.
St. Paul
651/647-9628

Model O-scale replicas of trains from the 1930s, 1940s, and 1950s whir around meticulously landscaped settings in this fun museum, the handiwork of the Twin Cities Model Railroad Club. Fri 10–8, Sat 10–6, Sun 12–5. Free. (St. Paul)

WALKER ART CENTER
725 Vineland Pl.
Minneapolis
612/375-7600
612/375-7685 TDD
www.walkerart.org

The first Saturday of every month, the Walker sponsors Free First Saturday, a daylong activity series that introduces children and their parents to the worlds of art, music, theater, and performance. Kids also love the 11-acre Minneapolis Sculpture Garden just outside the museum. Tue, Wed, Fri, and Sat 10–5; Thu 10–8; Sun 11–5. $4 adults, $3 seniors and students; free Thu and first Sat each month. Sculpture Garden open daily 6–midnight. Free. (Minneapolis)

THEATER AND ENTERTAINMENT

THE AMAZING SPACE
Second floor, West Market
Mall of America
Bloomington
612/851-0000

You'll feel good about dropping the kids at this exploratory, instructive play space while you shop. Mon–Sat 10–9:30, Sun 11–7. $5.50 adults and children over 3, $3 ages 2–3. (Greater Twin Cities)

CHILDREN'S THEATRE COMPANY
2400 Third Ave. S.
Minneapolis
612/874-0400
www.childrenstheatre.org

At the nation's largest professional children's theater, the talented company of children and young-at-heart adults produces imaginative adaptations of classic children's works.

Come to the Fair

*The two-week **Minnesota State Fair** (1265 Snelling Ave., St. Paul; 651/642-2200 or 651/642-2372 TTY) is the nation's largest. It attracts more than 1.5 million people, who enjoy everything from agricultural competitions to stock-car races to Grandstand concerts to Midway rides and games to pie-baking contests. Kids can get their first up-close glimpse of cows, pigs, sheep, and horses in the 4-H animal barns or can take in their small counterparts at the fair's popular petting zoo. Another big attraction is the great fair food: Pronto Pups, cheese curds, walleye-on-a-stick, malts, foot-long hot dogs, cotton candy, and countless other once-a-year delicacies, sold by more than 350 concessionaires. You'll see a true cross section of Minnesota in all its diverse glory.*

Save yourself a headache (and a few bucks) and park at one of Metro Transit's distant lots and take the bus in. Open the 12 days before Labor Day 6 a.m.–midnight. $5 adults, $4 seniors and ages 5–12, free for children under 5.

Ramsey Country Historical Society

Gibbs Farm Museum, p. 115

Productions have included *The Story of Babar, The Reluctant Dragon, The Hobbit, Cinderella, Little Women, Not Without Laughter, A Wrinkle in Time, The 500 Hats of Bartholomew Cubbins, How the Grinch Stole Christmas,* and dozens more, as well as new plays commissioned for the company. Adults appreciate the superb production values, while kids are entranced by the storytelling. The 750-seat auditorium has extra-wide aisles for fidgety kids, and there isn't a bad seat in the house. The September through June season usually features seven to nine productions. Ticket prices vary but usually run $8 to $25; deeply discounted rush tickets are available 15 minutes before curtain. (Minneapolis)

CHILD'S PLAY THEATRE COMPANY
1111 Mainstreet
Hopkins
612/979-1111

This more modest alternative to the CTC performs at a handsome new theater on the edge of downtown Hopkins, a western suburb. Ticket prices are affordable, and the casts of nearly every play—including reworked fairy tales and other children's stories—consist almost entirely of kids. The season runs October through July. Ticket prices vary but average $8 adults, $6 seniors and children ages 3–16. (Greater Twin Cities)

HOLIDAZZLE
Nicollet Mall
Minneapolis
612/338-3807

Thousands of families line the sidewalks of Nicollet Mall (from 12th to 5th Streets) every night from Thanksgiving to Christmas to take in the spectacle of a dazzling winter parade, complete with a bevy of storybook characters, floats, marching bands, choirs, a grand marshal, and, of course, Santa Claus. Bundle up and have a ball. Carol singalongs take place Saturday and Sunday evenings in the IDS Crystal Court before the parade. Daily Nov 24–Dec 30 6:30 p.m. Free. (Downtown Minneapolis)

LEGO IMAGINATION CENTER
First floor, South Avenue
Mall of America
Bloomington
612/858-8949

LEGO aficionados of all persuasions will fall head-over-heels in love with this savvy play area. Everywhere you look, there's a LEGO statue or a LEGO object, each more fanciful than the last. Lots of regularly scheduled events and activities involve a full complement of LEGO products in a selection that even Toys 'R' Us can't match. Hours vary by season. Free. (Greater Twin Cities)

STORES KIDS LOVE

CREATIVE KIDSTUFF
4313 Upton Ave. S.
Minneapolis
651/927-0653
Colorful, creative toys, games, and doodads. Two locations in St. Paul: 1074 Grand Ave., 612/222-2472; 10 W. 7th St., 651/225-6606. One location in the greater Minneapolis area: 13019 Ridgedale Dr., Minnetonka; 612/540-0022. (Minneapolis)

THE GREAT BIG TOY BOX
7525 France Ave. S.
Edina
612/835-2627
Here you'll find a huge selection of educational toys that still manage to be fun. (Greater Twin Cities)

RED BALLOON BOOKSHOP
891 Grand Ave.
St. Paul
651/224-8320
This delightful children's bookstore with more than 20,000 titles is located less than a block from the Victoria Crossing shopping area. (St. Paul)

WILD RUMPUS CHILDREN'S BOOKSTORE
2720 W. 43rd St.
Minneapolis
612/920-5005
Designed for maximum kid accessibility, this enchanting store seeks to ignite children's interest in reading. (Minneapolis)

RESTAURANTS KIDS LOVE

CONVENTION GRILL & FOUNTAIN
3912 Sunnyside Rd.
Edina
612/920-6881
This is a genuine diner with a family-oriented dining room in back. Its kids' menu will please the finnickiest of eaters, with the thickest, juiciest burgers in the Twin Cities and superlative malts. (Greater Twin Cities)

HEARTTHROB CAFE
30 E. Seventh St.
(World Trade Center)
St. Paul
651/224-2783
Very popular with teenagers, the Heartthrob's atmosphere shouts vintage 1950s rock 'n' roll: loud, colorful, and slightly obnoxious. Servers glide around on roller skates and perform choreographed song-and-dance rou-

Dinner and a Movie

Take the kids to dinner and the movies—in one stop—at the ***Cinema Cafe*** *or the* ***Cinema Grill****. Both offer lots of family-oriented titles, low admission prices, and the kinds of food (burgers, pizza, snacks) that kids and parents love. Cinema Cafe has three suburban locations (Burnsville, New Hope, and Woodbury; call 612/894-8810), and the Cinema Grill (612/841-8419) is located a half-mile south of Southdale in Edina.*

Greater Minneapolis CVA

Knott's Camp Snoopy

tines. Birthday celebrations are particularly entertaining. The affordable food includes burgers, malts, and the like, and it's pretty good. (Downtown St. Paul)

PLANET HOLLYWOOD
Mall of America
Bloomington
612/854-7827

Kids love the brash surroundings, and everyone gets a kick out of the movieland memorabilia at this popular chain restaurant. The menu features burgers, pizzas, sandwiches, and salads, and the desserts are huge. No reservations; lunch and dinner daily. (Greater Twin Cities)

RAINFOREST CAFE
Mall of America
Bloomington
612/854-7500

The wait may kill you, but kids eat up the fake rain-forest decor, live animals, simulated rainstorm (with thunder and lightning, no less), and obligatory gift shop. Food is standard theme-restaurant fare. Lines are shortest midweek late in the afternoon; otherwise, expect to wait, sometimes up to two hours. No reservations; lunch and dinner daily; smoke-free. (Greater Twin Cities)

THEME PARKS

KNOTT'S CAMP SNOOPY
Mall of America
Bloomington
612/883-8600

The mall's biggest entertainment attraction is Knott's Camp Snoopy, a seven-acre indoor amusement park loaded with more than two-dozen fun rides appealing to kids of all ages. Attractions include a roller coaster, log flume (expect to get a little wet), Ferris wheel, and bumper cars, as well as games, food stalls, and shops. During the day the park can be bright and obnoxious, but at night the skylights darken, and thousands of twinkly lights bring Knott's Camp Snoopy to life. Peanuts fans will get a kick out of all the Charlie Brown, Snoopy, and Woodstock touches. Hours vary by season. Attractions operate on a point system, with rides costing one to six points. Points are 60 cents each, and super-saver packages include 110 points for $50, 60 points for $30, 38 points for $20, and 18 points for $10. (Greater Twin Cities)

VALLEYFAIR
1 Valleyfair Dr.
Shakopee
612/445-7600
The Upper Midwest's largest theme park boasts 75 scream-inducing rides (including four roller coasters), a refreshing water park, an IMAX theater, live entertainment, and lots of food, games, and shops. Kids under five will enjoy Berenstain Bear Country, Half-Pint Park, and Tot Town. The park's 90 acres are lavishly landscaped, and the staff is hyperfriendly. Valleyfair is about 35 minutes southwest of downtown Minneapolis. Memorial Day–Labor Day daily 10–10, May and Sept weekends only. $20.95 adults and children over 3, $4.95 seniors and children under 3. (Greater Twin Cities)

Minnesota Office of Tourism

8

PARKS, GARDENS, AND RECREATION AREAS

The Twin Cities area is blessed with some of the most extensive and attractive urban parkland in the country. Residents today are grateful to the farsighted Twin City planners, who set aside significant amounts of land for public use in the late nineteenth century.

Minneapolis, in particular, has one of the nation's most extensive—and enchanting—park systems. In total, the city maintains more than 6,000 parkland acres at 170 different sites. Unlike most cities, Minneapolis governs its park system though an independently elected board, removing it from volatile city-hall politics.

Of the 22 lakes within city limits, almost all are surrounded by public parklands. Many lakes are connected by a 55-mile series of "Grand Rounds" parkways that thread throughout the city. Minneapolis is now reclaiming the St. Anthony Falls area as a recreational destination, and the river gorge from the University of Minnesota to Fort Snelling is one of the most pristine urban waterways in America.

St. Paul has its share of delightful parks, and the surrounding suburbs also host extensive park systems. Hennepin County planners wisely set aside a number of large parks along its western and southern borders.

RES PARK

ust of the Southdale Shopping Center on 70th Street, this formal garden comes as a surprise in this suburban setting. The park's grounds include a charming gazebo as well as a number of formal blooming beds, all maintained by the Edina Garden Club. (Greater Twin Cities)

COMO CONSERVATORY

Como Park
1325 Aida Pl.
St. Paul
651/489-1740

A splendid 1993 renovation has restored this delicate Victorian palace to its original 1915 luster. The building's north wing houses tropical plants, and its south wing features a small fern room. But its most dazzling attraction is the soaring Palm Court. Now on the National Register of Historic Places, the conservatory is a lifeline for weather-battered Minnesotans, seeking injections of floral color and fragrance year-round. The conservatory attracts 300,000 annual visitors, who come for the springtime tulips and the seemingly endless poinsettia blooms each December.

On spring and summer weekends, the conservatory and its surrounding gardens are flooded with bridal parties; many couples are married here, but most come just to be photographed in front of all the blooming bounty. The Ordway Japanese Garden is not to be missed, and it hosts a number of fancy summer-time teas. Oct–May daily 10–4, Apr–Sept daily 10–6. 50 cents adults, 25 cents seniors and ages 11 to 16. (St. Paul)

COMO PARK

Hamline and West Jessamine Aves.
St. Paul
651/266-6400

This grand Victorian park is the Twin Cities' most popular urban outdoor destination. Como's 450 very active acres overlooking pretty Lake Como are packed with attractions, including a concert pavilion,

Como Park Conservatory

Como Park Conservatory

Top Ten Picnic Spots

1. **Como Park**, Lexington and Como Ave., St. Paul
2. **Minnehaha Park**, Hwy. 55 and Minnehaha Pkwy., Minneapolis
3. **Beards Plaisance**, W. Lake Harriet Pkwy. at 48th St., Minneapolis
4. **East Bank Flats**, East River Rd. below University Heart Hospital, Minneapolis
5. **Fort Snelling State Park**, Hwy. 5 and Post Rd., St. Paul
6. **Irvine Park**, Walnut St. and Ryan Ave., St. Paul
7. **Kenwood Park**, 2101 W. Franklin Ave., Minneapolis
8. **Lyndale Park Gardens**, King's Hwy. at 41st St. S., Minneapolis
9. **Mears Park**, Fifth and Sibley Sts., St. Paul
10. **Theodore Wirth Park**, Glenwood Ave. at Wirth Pkwy., Minneapolis

picnic areas, a marvelous turn-of-the-century carousel, and bike and paddleboat rentals (651/489-9311). You'll also find an 18-hole golf course complete with restaurant and pro shop (651/488-9673), a small amusement park with a collection of Midway rides (651/488-4771), an Olympic-size outdoor pool (651/489-2811), a large athletic field, walking and biking trails, and more. Sunrise–11 p.m. daily; hours for attractions vary. (St. Paul)

COMO ZOO
Como Park
Midway Pkwy. and Kaufman Dr.
St. Paul
651/488-5571

Young children will particularly enjoy this small, accessible zoo. Como Zoo was once one of those depressing prisons where animals were kept behind bars. Thankfully, that has all changed (although some of the empty cages remain), but it is still difficult to see nonnative animals, particularly such noble creatures as lions and giraffes, living in cramped, seminatural habitats. One thing that hasn't changed is the free Sparky the Sea Lion show, which has delighted kids for decades. Hours vary by season. Free. (St. Paul)

EDINBOROUGH PARK
7700 York Ave. S.
Edina
612/893-9890

A city park that's entirely indoors is a godsend during Minnesota's sometimes seemingly endless winter. Managed by Edina Parks and Recreation, Edinborough contains a bubbling brook surrounded by paths, trees, and seasonal flowering plants, as well as a skating rink, running track, swimming pool, small health club, and children's play area. Sun–Thu 9–9, Fri–Sat 9–5. Admis-

Cass Gilbert Memorial Park

On the east side of the Capitol, just north of the Cedar and University intersection, is tiny Cass Gilbert Memorial Park. It's really nothing more than a lookout—but what a view! The entire Mississippi River Valley yawns below, and it's quite a sight indeed.

sion: $3, but kids' play area is free. (Greater Twin Cities)

HENNEPIN PARKS
612/559-9000

Hennepin County operates 14 large parks within its borders, as well as in Scott and Carver Counties. A few highlights are listed here. Baker Park Reserve (3800 County Rd. 24, Maple Plain; 612/476-4666) offers swimming and boating on three lakes, including lovely Lake Independence, as well as camping, picnicking, golfing, hiking, and biking. Carver Park Reserve (7025 Victoria Dr., Victoria; 612/559-6700) has camping, fishing, and boating on four lakes, hiking and biking trails, and the Lowry Nature Center. Murphy-Hanrehan Park Reserve (15501 Murphy Lake Rd., Savage; 612/941-7922) maintains hiking/biking and horseback riding trails. Hyland Lake Park Reserve (10145 E. Bush Lake Rd., Bloomington; 612/941-4362) has hiking and biking trails, fishing, boating, and the Richardson Nature Center. Just up the street is the downhill Hyland Hills Ski Area (8800 Chalet Dr., Bloomington; 612/835-4604). Daily parking at Hennepin parks $5 (or $25 for annual parking). Call 612/559-9000 for detailed information. (Greater Twin Cities)

LORING PARK
15th St. at Hennepin Ave.
Minneapolis

Loring Park dates to 1883, when the city bought the land and named it Central Park. The park took on its current name in 1890, to honor Charles Loring, first president of the Minneapolis Park Board. The park's 35 acres (designed by Frederick Law

For a quick urban getaway, check out pretty Seven Pools Park, located at Douglas and Bryant Avenues in Minneapolis, just south of the Guthrie Theater and the Walker Art Center. The park is really just a small neighborhood square, named for the seven gurgling pools that cascade across the park and split it in two. A large, romantic arbor covered in wild grapes occupies the park's western edge. The statue of streetcar magnate Thomas Lowry that now rests at 24th Street and Hennepin Avenue once held court in this park. Residents are fighting to return it to its original spot.

The Twin Cities' largest (and cheapest) ice-cream cones are sold in Minneapolis parks, including Lake Calhoun, Lake Harriet, and Minnehaha Park.

Olmstead, the man behind New York City's Central Park) are among the most active in the city. A basketball game is always going on, the ponds teem with ducks, the paths fill with walkers and bikers, and, in winter, the lake is loaded with skaters. On the park's north side, near the Minneapolis Community College buildings, is a statue of Ole Bull, a Norwegian violinist who came to Minneapolis in 1856 and is reputedly the city's first musician. Loring Greenway, a well-traveled pedestrian thoroughfare, connects Nicollet Mall with the park's green acres. The greenway terminates at one of Minneapolis's most amusing curiosities, the Berger Fountain, shaped like a giant dandelion. (Downtown Minneapolis)

MEARS PARK
Bounded by Sibley, Fifth, Wacouta, and Sixth Sts.
St. Paul

Named for philanthropist Norman Mears, this lovely little park is downtown St. Paul's other enormously appealing city square. Originally christened Smith Park when it was platted in 1849, the square was the center of the city's burgeoning commercial district for more than 50 years. By the turn of the century, the area teemed with dry goods wholesalers, shoe manufacturers, and furriers. But when the district seriously declined in the 1960s, the park took a nose-dive, too. An ill-conceived redesign in 1975 did little to enhance its natural beauty, but a 1992 renovation—complete with a stream—restored Mears to its bucolic roots. (Downtown St. Paul)

MINNEAPOLIS CHAIN OF LAKES
612/661-4800

Four large lakes and a series of connected park areas comprise this crown jewel of the Minneapolis park system, located on the southern and western fringes of the city. Each lake has its own distinct personality.

The chain begins at **Cedar Lake**, the cleanest, least urban of the four and the only Minneapolis lake with private homes on its shores. Cedar has two public beaches, to the west and south, as well as a popular (but technically illegal) clothing-optional "Hidden Beach" on its northeastern shore. Cedar is linked by a shallow channel at its southeastern corner to Lake of the Isles, and the overland connection is made by Dean Parkway.

Lake of the Isles is surrounded by some of the city's largest, most well-tended homes, and a walk or bike ride around its shores (2.7 miles) is one of the most pleasant outings in Minneapolis, even during winter. Isles is really a dredged swamp, so swimming is not advised, although the views of downtown and the surrounding neighborhood make the lake a top choice for canoeists.

TRIVIA

Motorized boats are banned on lakes within Minneapolis/St. Paul city limits. However, you can learn how to operate a sailboat on St. Paul's Lake Phalen (651/771-7507), where the city's Parks and Recreation Division offers rentals and lessons.

Lake of the Isles is connected by channel to **Lake Calhoun**, its southern neighbor and the chain's largest, most urban lake. Calhoun's public beaches rest on the north and east shores, and a popular volleyball area sits on the southwest corner.

Calhoun draws a diverse group of walkers, in-line skaters, and bikers to its 3.1-mile perimeter, and the lake itself attracts windsurfers, canoeists, kayakers, and sailors when temperatures permit. Ice-fishing houses dot its frozen waters during the winter. The refectory, located on the northeast corner, offers reasonable refreshments and canoe rentals.

Just south of Lake Calhoun, about a quarter-mile down William Berry Parkway, is **Lake Harriet**. It is named for the wife of Colonel Harry Leavenworth, the first commander of Fort St. Anthony (later renamed Fort Snelling). Lake Harriet hosts a number of attractions, including the Lake Harriet Bandshell and refectory (northwest corner), Como–Harriet Streetcar Line (northwest corner), paddlewheel boat excursions on the Queen of the Lakes (leaving from the refectory, call 612/370-4962), and Beard's Plaisance, a large sheltered picnic area (southwest corner). Some of the city's most palatial homes line the lake's east parkway. Public beaches line the east and south shores.

On Harriet's northeastern corner is **Lyndale Park**, a lovely oasis of rolling hills that features the **Minneapolis Rose Garden**, a meticulously tended and fragrant glen of blooming flowers bordered by two giddy fountains and adjacent to a serene Japanese rock garden.

The five-mile swath of green that is **Minnehaha Parkway** begins on Lake Harriet's southeastern shore, soon connecting with Minnehaha Creek as it winds across south Minneapolis just below 50th Street and heads east to the Mississippi River. The parkway, a meandering roadway with bicycle and walking paths, lush vegetation, and the gurgling creek, is one of the delights of Minneapolis.

At Cedar Avenue, Minnehaha Creek runs into **Lake Nokomis** (to the south) and **Lake Hiawatha** (to the

Walking the Dog

If you're taking your pooch out for a walk, you'll have to put him or her on a leash (up to eight feet in Minneapolis, six feet in St. Paul). Be sure to bring a bag, since you must dispose of all droppings.

north), two popular scenic lakes. Nokomis' northern shore boasts a busy beach plus sailing and canoeing. A stroll around its busy perimeter is 2.7 miles. Hiawatha's beach rests on its eastern shore. (Minneapolis)

MINNEAPOLIS SCULPTURE GARDEN
725 Vineland Pl.
Minneapolis
612/375-7600

This artfully landscaped outdoor extension of the Walker Art Center is the most visited 11 acres in Minneapolis (see Chapter 6, Museums and Art Galleries). 6 a.m.–midnight daily. Free tours (starting in the Walker's lobby) Sat and Sun at 1. Free. (Minneapolis)

MINNEHAHA PARK
Hiawatha Ave. at Minnehaha Pkwy.
Minneapolis

As the Minnehaha Creek makes its way toward the Mississippi River, it culminates in Minnehaha Park, one of the city's most-used stretches of parkland. Currently undergoing an extensive $20 million renovation, the park features several large picnic grounds, formal gardens, playing fields, hiking trails, and pretty Minnehaha Falls.

Minnehaha Parkway turns north at the Mississippi River and becomes West River Road, a scenic drive following the western bluff of the Mississippi to U of M's West Bank campus. The views are spectacular, and the roadway is lined with biking and walking trails. (Minneapolis)

MINNESOTA VALLEY NATIONAL WILDLIFE REFUGE AND RECREATION AREA
3815 E. 80th St.
Bloomington
612/335-2323

This 8,000-acre reserve runs along the banks of the Minnesota River, from its confluence with the Mississippi at Fort Snelling 35 miles upriver to Jordan. The refuge is crisscrossed by hiking and biking trails, birdwatching promontories, and picnic grounds. The visitor's center (a stone's throw from Mall of America) offers unparalleled views of the river valley and a number of interpretive exhibits. (Minneapolis)

MOUNDS PARK
Burns Ave. at Mounds Blvd.
St. Paul
651/226-6400

A 2,000-year-old Indian burial ground is the focus of this 80-acre park, which stretches along the river bluffs and offers superb views of downtown St. Paul and the Mississippi River Valley. (St. Paul)

NORMANDALE JAPANESE GARDEN
9400 France Ave. S.

TRIVIA

Minnehaha Falls, a dramatic 25-foot cataract, inspires contemporary romantics in the same way it led poet William Wadsworth Longfellow to write his epic poem, *The Song of Hiawatha*, even though he never saw the falls himself. A replica of his New England home sits in the park's northwest corner.

Bloomington
612/881-8137
A serene, two-acre getaway on the campus of Normandale Community College, the Normandale Japanese Garden is done up with all the requisite Japanese trappings, including delicate bridges, small ponds, exquisite plantings, and lovely vistas. (Greater Twin Cities)

PEAVEY PLAZA
1111 Nicollet Mall
Minneapolis
The sunken public park outside Orchestra Hall is Peavey Plaza, a remarkable, well-tended inner-city oasis, complete with big shade trees, flowers, a large reflecting pool, splashing water terraces, and quirky tubular stainless-steel fountains. The plaza (designed by M. Paul Friedberg and Associates in 1975) really comes alive during Sommerfest, the orchestra's annual summer music festival, when every square inch of the place is devoted to food vendors, musicians, and outdoor seating. The reflecting pool gives way to an ice rink during winter. (Downtown Minneapolis)

RICE PARK
Bounded by Fourth, Market, Fifth, and Washington Sts.
St. Paul
Any walking tour of downtown St. Paul should begin at Rice Park, undoubtedly one of the prettiest squares in America and the city's oldest public park (1849). Formal but not stuffy, this grassy knoll contains a gurgling fountain graced with Alonzo Hauser's contemplative sculpture *The Source*. The park also contains a bronze statue of author F. Scott Fitzgerald by sculptor Michael Price. During the annual

Greater Minneapolis CVA

Biking by the Lake Harriet Bandshell, p. 128

St. Paul Winter Carnival, the park hosts a popular ice-sculpture contest, and the city festoons the neighborhood in thousands of twinkling lights. (Downtown St. Paul)

THEODORE WIRTH PARK
Theodore Wirth Pkwy. between I-394 and Golden Valley Rd.
Minneapolis
Named for Minneapolis's most influential parks commissioner, the city's largest park is an urban oasis, filled with scenic vistas and recreational opportunities. Located on the western edge of the city, the park includes acres of unspoiled forest and prairie land, an 18-hole golf course, a beach on Wirth Lake, and hiking and biking trails. The fall colors along winding Wirth Parkway can be particularly spectacular. Tucked inside Wirth Park is the Eloise Butler Wildflower Garden and Bird Sanctuary, the nation's oldest wildflower garden. Open April through October, the garden contains dozens of native plants and wildlife in a rolling terrain

Theodore Wirth Park is home to two city-owned golf courses: a challenging 18-hole, par-72 course (612/522-4584) and an easier, 9-hole, par-27 course (612/522-2818). Both begin at the park's chalet, located at the intersection of Theodore Wirth Parkway and Plymouth Road. Reservations are required.

marked by woods, wetlands, and bogs. (Minneapolis)

UNIVERSITY OF MINNESOTA LANDSCAPE ARBORETUM
Hwy. 5
Chanhassen
612/443-2460

This laboratory of 900 carefully tended acres is the state's largest public garden, featuring countless indigenous plants plus a rose garden and Japanese garden. The spectacular scenery is augmented by lectures, classes, demonstrations, and the Snyder Building, a sturdy stone lodge housing a library, gift shop, and one of the loveliest tea rooms you'll ever see. 8–dusk daily. Free seasonal 90-minute walking tours of the gardens surrounding the Snyder Building Tue–Sat at 10; motorized tram tours ($1.50) of the arboretum Tue–Sat at 11:30, 1, and 2:30. Arboretum admission: $4 adults, $1 ages 6 to 16. (Greater Twin Cities)

Greater Minneapolis CVA

9

SHOPPING

The Twin Cities are a shopper's mecca, offering retail thrills to satisfy virtually every taste, whim, and pocketbook. From Mall of America, the nation's largest shopping and entertainment complex, to bustling downtown Minneapolis, to charming neighborhood shopping areas, this area has something for every shopper.

DOWNTOWN MINNEAPOLIS

Most shopping is located on or around Nicollet Mall, downtown's main retail drag and a 12-block pedestrian thoroughfare, open to buses and taxicabs only. Most stores are concentrated between Fifth and Tenth Streets, including three department stores, four enclosed shopping malls, and many fine specialty stores. A number of distinctive shops also exist in the Warehouse District surrounding First and Washington Avenues. Many downtown stores and restaurants participate in the city's "Do the Town" parking validation program. Look for green signs before you park and be sure to ask for a voucher when you make your purchase.

Shopping Malls

CITY CENTER
600 Nicollet Mall
Minneapolis
612/372-1234
This architecturally graceless early 1980s office, hotel, and shopping complex was downtown's first enclosed, suburban-style shopping mall. The sunny shopping atrium houses a large but fairly dull selection of national chain stores and a popular third-floor food court. Sit-down restaurants include TGIFriday's, Ital-

ianni's, Nankin Café (a Minneapolis institution since 1919, complete with campy Cantonese decorations from its original Seventh Street location), and Goodfellow's, one of the city's top white- tablecloth restaurants. The latter is housed in a restored 1929 art deco showplace, meticulously assembled after developers razed its original home to make way for the complex. (Downtown Minneapolis)

GAVIIDAE COMMON
651 Nicollet Mall
Minneapolis
612/372-1222

Neiman Marcus anchors the northern end, and Saks Fifth Avenue has the southern side of Gaviidae (Gah-vid-day, Latin for *loon*, the state bird), an upscale shopping complex straddling two blocks of Nicollet Mall. Gaviidae's northern half includes a number of interesting boutiques, several restaurants—including D'Amico & Sons, a popular cafeteria-style lunch and dinner spot—and a Minnesota State Fair–themed food court (fourth floor). Notable shops include Ann Taylor, Joan Vass, Jessica McClintock, Talbots (women's clothing), and Aveda (Minnesota-made, all-natural beauty products).

Gaviidae Common

Greater Minneapolis CVA

Across Sixth Street is the second—and prettier—half of the mall, distinguished by its thrilling azure and gold barrel-vault skylight, courtesy of architect Cesar Pelli. The upper floors were converted to office space several years ago, but the first two floors still have a number of interesting shops, including Cole-Haan shoes, D. Vincent Jewelers, and the Museum Store. (Downtown Minneapolis)

IDS CRYSTAL COURT
717 Nicollet Mall
Minneapolis
612/376-8000

One of Minnesota's architectural landmarks, the IDS Center is a full-block complex that includes a 57-story office tower (the state's tallest), the Marquette Hotel, and the Crystal Court, home to a Banana Republic, The Gap, Williams-Sonoma, TJ Maxx, and Godiva Chocolatiers, as well as Sola Squeeze, a great little juice bar. The center's underground parking ramp is the most convenient place to park downtown, particularly during winter; enter on Marquette Avenue. (Downtown Minneapolis)

Department Stores

DAYTON'S
700 Nicollet Mall
Minneapolis
612/375-2200

Minnesotans are genuinely devoted to Dayton's. For decades, it was *the* store in the Twin Cities, enjoying a market share that was the envy of department stores everywhere. Although competition and changing shopping habits have loosened

Dayton's grip on the marketplace, the store still has a spot in the hearts of Minnesotans: Residents joke that a Dayton's charge card is the equivalent of a driver's license in terms of identification, and when the company was threatened with a hostile takeover in the late 1980s, the state legislature convened a special session to pass a poison-pill law to thwart the attempt.

The company's flagship store, one of America's last great downtown emporiums, spans the entire block on Nicollet between Seventh and Eighth Streets. The popular Oak Grill and Sky Room restaurants are located on the 12th floor, and the huge eighth-floor auditorium hosts an annual holiday extravaganza that routinely attracts 400,000 visitors between Thanksgiving and New Year's. Every March, the store's annual flower show draws more than 100,000 winter-weary Minnesotans to a blooming feast for the eyes and nose. Dayton's has three don't-miss sales each year: Jubilee in October, Anniversary in March, and Daisy in June. Be sure to visit the Marketplace food and tabletop departments on the store's lower level; third floor's tony Oval Room for de-

The Dayton Empire

When Minnesotans flaunt their much-touted "quality of life," they have Dayton's to thank for at least part of it. In addition to bolstering the local economy as a major employer, the company has long been one of the area's most civic-minded benefactors, contributing 5 percent of its pre-tax profits—more than $350 million—to charity over the past half-century.

One of the country's great retail success stories began in downtown Minneapolis, on Nicollet Avenue at Seventh Street, in 1902, when George Draper Dayton opened the doors of what eventually became Dayton's. George's descendants expanded the company's holdings with a series of suburban and outstate Dayton's outlets. They also created the Target discount chain, the B. Dalton bookstore business, and a number of shopping centers. A 1969 merger with Detroit's J. L. Hudson Company created the Dayton Hudson Corporation. In the mid-1980s, the corporation (now the nation's fourth-largest retailer) spun off B. Dalton, its shopping center holdings, and a number of department-store divisions. In addition to Dayton's, Hudson's, and Target, the company now owns Chicago-based Marshall Field's and Mervyn's, a mid-priced national department store.

TRIVIA

Clothing and groceries carry no sales tax in Minnesota.

signer women's fashions from New York, Paris, Milan, and Tokyo; and the extensive home furnishings and Oriental rug departments on the fifth floor. (Downtown Minneapolis)

NEIMAN MARCUS
505 Nicollet Mall
Minneapolis
612/339-2600
This Texas import hasn't done as well in Minnesota as the company had hoped (the store is consistently outperformed by every other Neiman's location), but its accommodating staff and well-edited stock of furnishings, cosmetics (including the Twin Cities' best perfume selection), jewelry, home accessories, and clothing make it a pleasure to shop. The Last Call clearance outlet occupies the store's fourth floor, and it's full of bargains shipped to Minneapolis from N-M stores across the country. (Downtown Minneapolis)

SAKS FIFTH AVENUE
655 Nicollet Mall
Minneapolis
612/333-7200
Sedate Saks offers a carefully chosen assortment of men's clothing (including a peerless tie department) plus a wide array of women's designer apparel, accessories, cosmetics, and jewelry. As with Neiman Marcus, the store's fourth floor (called Off Fifth) is devoted to marked-down merchandise from Saks stores nationwide, and the prices and selection are often better than N-M's Last Call. Cafe SFA, also on the fourth floor, is one of downtown's best-kept lunch secrets. (Downtown Minneapolis)

Other Notable Stores

AMAZON BOOKSTORE
1617 Harmon Place
Minneapolis
612/338-6560
This 25-year-old store overlooks Loring Park and is the place to head to for new and used books, recordings, and other merchandise of interest to women. (Downtown Minneapolis)

ARCHITECTURAL ANTIQUES
801 Washington Ave. N.
Minneapolis
612/332-8344
The dream store for fans of PBS's *This Old House*, this sprawling place is a treasure trove of old lamps, sconces, ornamental pediments, religious reliquaries, porcelain fixtures, and doorknobs—all salvaged from demolished buildings and waiting for new homes. The sales staff is smart and resourceful. (Downtown Minneapolis)

BILLY GRAHAM EVANGELICAL BOOKSTORE
1201 Hennepin Ave.
Minneapolis
612/338-0500
The world headquarters of the Billy Graham Evangelical Association includes this small bookstore. (Downtown Minneapolis)

CRATE & BARREL
915 Nicollet Mall
Minneapolis
612/338-4000
The national retailer's downtown Minneapolis store, located in the

Young Quinlan building, offers a large and affordable selection of dishes, cookware, and household goods, sold in cheery surroundings. Also at Southdale, 612/920-2300. (Downtown Minneapolis)

HUBERT W. WHITE
611 Marquette Ave.
Minneapolis
612/339-9200
White's is the last of what used to be a thriving downtown haberdasher scene. An institution since 1916, this family-owned operation sells an impressive selection of exclusive men's tailored clothing, sportswear, shoes, and accessories. You'll also find very clubby surroundings, excellent service, and terrific but infrequent sales, including a popular annual trade-in event. (Downtown Minneapolis)

INDIGO
530 N. Third St.
Minneapolis
612/333-2151
This intoxicating, out-of-the-way haunt is curated like a museum. It's devoted to folk arts, textiles, and other exotic must-haves from Africa, Asia, and the Pacific. (Downtown Minneapolis)

INTERNATIONAL DESIGN CENTER
100 Second Ave. N.
Minneapolis
612/341-3441
IDC showcases beautiful furniture, glassware, art, and gifts from Scandinavia on several floors in a sturdy, turn-of-the-century warehouse. (Downtown Minneapolis)

JAMES & MARY LAURIE BOOKS
921 Nicollet Mall

Used Books

Minneapolis's Dinkytown neighborhood is the center of the Twin Cities' used-book trade, with a number of well-stocked stores within a few blocks of one another:

Biermaier's B.H. Books *(809 Fourth St. S.E., Minneapolis; 612/378-0129) stocks nearly 100,000 titles in a well-organized storefront.*

Book House *(429 14th Ave. S.E., Minneapolis; 612/331-1340) is a bit more jumbled but carries 150,000 titles on two packed floors.*

Cummings Books *(318 14th Ave. S.E., Minneapolis; 612/331-1424) maintains a large and varied selection of titles on two spacious floors.*

Dinkytown Antiquarian Books *(1316 Fourth St. S.E., Minneapolis; 612/378-1286) specializes in rare books, carries a stock of 10,000 titles, and is open by appointment only.*

TRIVIA

The Guthrie Theater Costume Rental Shop (718 Washington Ave. N., Minneapolis; 612/341-3683) rents costumes from the famed Guthrie Theater's voluminous storehouse at reasonable rates.

Minneapolis
612/338-1114
This bookstore is stocked floor-to-ceiling with rare, used, and out-of-print books, plus a large selection of prints. (Downtown Minneapolis)

J. B. HUDSON
770 Nicollet Mall
Minneapolis
612/338-5950
This swank, Old World store, tucked just inside Dayton's Eighth Street lobby, sells fine jewelry, expensive china, crystal, and silver, all in ornate surroundings. The shop offers knowledgeable salespeople and the city's best jewelry repair service. (Downtown Minneapolis)

LELAND N. LIEN BOOKSELLER
57 S. Ninth St.
Minneapolis
612/332-7081
This is a first-rate source for rare, out-of-print, and first-edition titles. The store also has a skilled preservation and conservation department. (Downtown Minneapolis)

METRO MATTER
121 N. First St.
Minneapolis
612/376-0239
This charming shop/gallery offers a variety of offbeat arts, crafts, and gifts from a wide range of local and national artists and artisans. (Downtown Minneapolis)

MINNEAPOLIS FARMERS' MARKET
Lyndale Ave. N. between Glenwood Ave. and Hwy. 55
Minneapolis
612/333-1737
Minneapolis's market draws a wider variety of vendors than its St. Paul counterpart (but St. Paul's tidy market has a lot more charm). Here you'll find a wide variety of produce, flowers, meats, baked goods, honey, wild rice, Hmong arts and crafts, cheese, and nursery plants. On Thursday, several dozen vendors set up shop on Nicollet Mall between Fifth and 10th Streets. During the holiday season, Christmas-tree farmers sell their wares. Apr–Nov 6 a.m.–1 p.m. daily. (Downtown Minneapolis)

POLO/RALPH LAUREN
81 S. Ninth St.
Minneapolis
612/338-7700
The vast Polo/Ralph Lauren store occupies the prime first-floor space of the priceless Young Quinlan building. Stop in for men's and women's clothing and the store's large home accessories department, stay for the drop-dead gorgeous ambience and attentive service. (Downtown Minneapolis)

RAGSTOCK
830 N. Seventh St.
Minneapolis
612/333-8520
The warehouse for a large vintage-

clothing store chain has a huge, almost overwhelming selection of used clothing that runs the condition gamut, from ratty to mint. (Downtown Minneapolis)

RAINBOW ROAD
109 W. Grant St.
Minneapolis
612/872-8448
This quirky and entertaining shop is filled with greeting cards, clothing, and gifts geared toward gay men and lesbians. (Downtown Minneapolis)

SHINDER'S
733 Hennepin Ave.
Minneapolis
612/333-3628
This flagship store of the state's largest, most comprehensive newsstand chain is a one-stop source for national and international magazines and newspapers, comic books, trading cards, and paperbacks. The store attracts a fascinating cross section of the city's populace. (Downtown Minneapolis)

SISTER FUN
121 N. Fourth St.
Minneapolis
612/672-0263
Sister Fun is famous for its campy collection of retro toys, wacky collectibles, and kitschy paraphernalia, all at bargain basement prices. (Downtown Minneapolis)

TEENER'S THEATRICAL DEPARTMENT STORE
729 Hennepin Ave.
Minneapolis
612/339-2793
Teener's offers a crazy-quilt jumble of costumes, makeup, fabric, shoes, and other theatrical accoutrements. (Downtown Minneapolis)

Mary Pawlcyn

Indigo, p. 136

DOWNTOWN ST. PAUL

Even with the addition of several large shopping complexes, downtown St. Paul's retail clime is partly cloudy, although some sunny shopping can be had in the capital city.

Shopping Malls

TOWN SQUARE
445 Minnesota St.
St. Paul
651/298-0900
Hailed as the solution to the city's crumbling retail base when it opened in 1980, this dismal, fortress-style complex has proven something of a failure. A recent multimillion-dollar renovation breathed some life into the dreary old place, although most of the storefronts were removed and replaced by offices and a pleasant food court. (Downtown St. Paul)

WORLD TRADE CENTER
Seventh St. and Wabasha Ave.
St. Paul
651/291-1715

This suburban-style shopping mall sits at the base of a dour 1987 skyscraper, offering a paltry selection of local and national chain stores. The best by far is Maud Borup Candies, creators of delicious hometown chocolates since 1907. The mall is slated to undergo a major renovation, which should add some luster—and hopefully a few stores—to the place. (Downtown St. Paul)

Other Notable Stores

CANDYLAND
435 N. Wabasha St.
St. Paul
651/292-1911
Candyland has been making Minnesota's best caramel corn, bar none, since 1932. You'll enjoy other swell sweets, too. (Downtown St. Paul)

DAYTON'S
411 Cedar St.
St. Paul
651/292-5222
Dayton's opened here in 1963 and is now all that remains of a once bustling department store district. This one is a dowdier, downscale version of its downtown Minneapolis counterpart, but it does contain a number of well-stocked departments. Its River Room restaurant is a relaxing place for lunch. (Downtown St. Paul)

NAKASHIAN-O'NEIL
23 W. Sixth St.
St. Paul
651/224-5465
This delightfully musty store has been a St. Paul institution since 1906, specializing in fine antiques and famed for its highly original selection of holiday decorations. (Downtown St. Paul)

ST. PAUL FARMERS' MARKET
290 E. Fifth St.
St. Paul
651/228-8101
Skirting the edge of Lowertown, this charming, manageable market offers competitive prices on farm-fresh produce, plus baked goods, flowers, plants, meats, cheeses, and Hmong arts and crafts. For a java jolt before or after shopping,

St. Paul Farmers' Market

Thomas K. Perry

Textile do-it-yourselfers should thread their way to Linden Hills Yarns (2720 W. 43rd St., Minneapolis; 612/929-1255), the Twin Cities' source for unique knitting materials. If sewing is more your bag, there's no better selection of hard-to-find, high-quality fabrics than Treadle Yard Goods (1338 Grand Ave., St. Paul; 651/698-9690).

stop at the Black Dog Cafe, just down the street (308 Prince St., 651/228-9274). Apr–Nov Sat 6 a.m.–1 p.m., Sun 8–1. (Downtown St. Paul)

MINNEAPOLIS

Uptown

Centered on the corner of Hennepin Avenue and Lake Street, close to both Lake of the Isles and Lake Calhoun, the Uptown neighborhood has shops, restaurants, bookstores, a popular Minneapolis Public Library branch, and cinemas. Uptown is anchored by Calhoun Square (3001 Hennepin Ave. S., 612/824-1240), a two-level enclosed shopping mall with an attached parking ramp. The neighborhood has a healthy mix of national chain stores (The Gap, Urban Outfitters, Pier One Imports) and a fine selection of local merchants.

BAY STREET SHOES
3001 Hennepin Ave. S.
(Calhoun Square)
Minneapolis
612/824-5574

Bay Street is consistently named one of the Twin Cities' top shoe stores by local newspapers and magazines, probably due to its low prices and large selection of men's and women's styles. (Minneapolis)

BORDERS BOOKS
3001 Hennepin Ave. S.
(Calhoun Square)
Minneapolis
612/825-0336

A chain bookstore with an independent atmosphere, Borders is an anchor of the Uptown neighborhood. The store has a knowledgeable sales staff, extensive stock, late-night hours, lots of author readings, and a reputation as a pickup joint. (Minneapolis)

GABRIELLA'S
1404 W. Lake St.
Minneapolis
612/822-1512

Here you'll find beautiful vintage party clothes, jewelry, shoes, and accessories for men and women, as well as the Serious label of naughty vinyl fashions. (Minneapolis)

IN TOTO
3105 Hennepin Ave. S.
Minneapolis
612/822-2414

The store offers fashion-forward men's and women's clothing and accessories by Paul Smith, C. P. Company, Anna Sui, Industria, and Paraboot. (Minneapolis)

ROOM SERVICE
1428 W. 31st St.
Minneapolis
612/823-2640

Room Service hawks objets d'art, including distinctive glassware, pottery, candles, picture frames, and a small line of attractive contemporary furniture. (Minneapolis)

ST. SABRINA'S PARLOR IN PURGATORY
2751 Hennepin Ave. S.
Minneapolis
612/874-7360
The latest in ravewear fills the racks here. The store's Foot Fetish department stocks shoes that are so fashion-forward, they're practically in the next solar system. There's body jewelry, too, and an in-house certified body piercer to make it happen. (Minneapolis)

STICKS AND STONES
2914 Hennepin Ave. S.
Minneapolis
612/827-6121
The store offers two floors of unique designer accessories, lighting, and upholstered furniture, geared toward style-conscious homeowners. (Minneapolis)

South Minneapolis

BROTHERSON'S MEATS
824 W. 36th St.
Minneapolis
612/823-7227
The Twin Cities' best butcher does great things in its smokehouse, providing a large selection of fresh beef, poultry, and seasonal game—even fresh ostrich. (Minneapolis)

A BROTHER'S TOUCH
2327 Hennepin Ave. S.
Minneapolis
612/377-6279
This modest bookstore (with the world's worst name) carries fiction, nonfiction, and magazines for gay and lesbian readers. (Minneapolis)

COASTAL SEAFOODS
2330 Minnehaha Ave.
Minneapolis
612/724-5911
The Twin Cities' most reliable source for fresh fish and seafood offers a large selection, smart staff, and reasonable prices. Also at 74 Snelling Ave., St. Paul; 651/698-4888. (Minneapolis)

DREAMHAVEN BOOKS
912 W. Lake St.
Minneapolis
612/823-6161
Dreamhaven offers the Twin Cities' largest selection of comic books and science fiction. (Minneapolis)

INGEBRETSON'S
1601 E. Lake St.
Minneapolis
612/729-9331
This Minneapolis institution does the Scandinavian import thing better than any other store of its kind in town. It also has an impressive selection of specialty foods and a popular deli. (Minneapolis)

LAVA LOUNGE
3037 Lyndale Ave. S.
Minneapolis
612/824-5631
You'll find inexpensive club clothes for men and women here, aimed at the fake-I.D. crowd. Local designers sell lots of their merchandise here, too. (Minneapolis)

ONCE UPON A CRIME
604 W. 26th St.
Minneapolis
612/870-3785
Mystery and suspense novels line

Upscale Shopping

Across 69th Street from Southdale is the Galleria (3225 W. 69th St., Edina, 612/925-9534), an upscale shopping mall anchored by Gabbert's, a rambling furniture, home accessories, and design studio showplace. This understated mall also includes a number of novel specialty stores, including ***Polly Berg*** *(lingerie and bedding),* ***T.R. Christian*** *(china, crystal, and silver),* ***Cedric's*** *(men's designer clothing and furs),* ***Stroud's*** *(linens), and* ***Oilili*** *(colorful women's and children's clothing from the Netherlands), as well as a huge two-story* ***Barnes & Noble*** *bookstore, large* ***Pottery Barn*** *and* ***Williams-Sonoma*** *stores,* ***Restoration Hardware, Smith & Hawken, Coach****, and a branch of the* ***Walker Art Center****'s gift shop. Its several popular restaurants include* ***Big Bowl, Sidney's Pizza Cafe, Good Earth****, and* ***Ciatti's****.*

the shelves of this friendly shop, which draws a number of authors for readings and book signings. (Minneapolis)

PATINA
1009 Franklin Ave. W.
Minneapolis
612/374-4654
Browse this colorful shop for clever gifts and objects for the home and office, plus toys, books, candles, jewelry, and picture frames. A second store is located at 5001 Bryant Ave. S., Minneapolis; 612/821-9315. (Minneapolis)

ST. MARTIN'S GOURMET IMPORTS
617 W. Lake St.
Minneapolis
612/823-5981
This appealing store sells exotic and hard-to-find foodstuffs from around the world. (Minneapolis)

SCHATZLEIN
413 W. Lake St.
Minneapolis
612/825-2450
Country-western wear begins and ends at Schatzlein, which has been outfitting cowboys and cowgirls since 1907. The store has a huge stock of boots, riding apparel, and hats. (Minneapolis)

SWANK INC.
407 W. Lake St.
Minneapolis
612/822-2242
Here you'll find a carefully selected assortment of vintage 1960s and 1970s fashions and accessories at affordable prices. (Minneapolis)

UNITED NOODLES ORIENTAL FOOD
2015 E. 24th St.
Minneapolis
612/721-6677

A stretch of Nicollet Avenue in South Minneapolis (from 22nd to 29th Streets) is dotted with more than a dozen Asian groceries, but the best bet is a few miles east, at this warehouse-style store that stocks an encyclopedic selection of imported foods and housewares at very low prices. (Minneapolis)

50th and France

This inviting shopping district in suburban Edina, centered around the France Avenue and 50th Street intersection at the southwest Minneapolis border, has a number of shops that bear exploring.

ALOUETTE
5009 France Ave. S.
Minneapolis
612/836-1683
This charming home and garden store is loaded with French-accented merchandise—the kind of baubles you never realized you needed but now suddenly cannot live without. (Minneapolis)

AMPERSAND
5034 France Ave. S.
Edina
612/920-2118
This spacious and expensive store is filled with the latest in dishes, glassware, linens, flatware, stationery, and related geegaws. (Minneapolis)

FASHION AVENUE
4936 France Ave. S.
Edina
612/929-7917
Fashion Avenue is probably the Twin Cities' best consignment store, with a large selection of designer clothing and accessories for men and women. Reasonable prices complement excellent service. (Minneapolis)

ST. PAUL

Grand Avenue

Parts of this busy street, a streetcar commercial district dating from the 1920s, were revived beginning in the mid-1970s. Today the area—especially the stretch from Dale Street to Fairview Avenue—has some of the Twin Cities' most distinctive stores and restaurants.

THE BIBELOT SHOP
1082 Grand Ave.
St. Paul
651/222-0321
This popular women's clothing and home accessories store has a large selection of made-in-Minnesota merchandise. Also at 2276 Como Ave., St. Paul, 651/646-5651; and 4315 Upton Ave. S., Minneapolis, 612/925-3175. (St. Paul)

COOKS OF CROCUS HILL
877 Grand Ave.
St. Paul
651/228-1333
The store offers gourmet foods, kitchenware, cookbooks, dishes, and a popular cooking school, all in a spacious renovated house. (St. Paul)

THE HUNGRY MIND
1648 Grand Ave.
St. Paul
651/699-0587
Many natives consider the Hungry Mind to be the area's best bookstore, probably because of the library-like stock, the bright sales staff, and the store's smart publication, the *Hungry Mind Review*. Its

TIP

Kids can have a ball at the mall, choosing among Amazing Space (612/851-0000), Golf Mountain (612/883-8899), LEGO Imagination Center (612/858-8949), Knott's Camp Snoopy (612/883-8600), and Underwater World (888/DIVETIME). For more information on these attractions, see Chapter 7, Kids' Stuff.

location, next to Macalaster College and the popular Table of Contents restaurant, doesn't hurt, either. (St. Paul)

RESTORATION HARDWARE
791 Grand Ave.
St. Paul
651/228-3033
The national chain's St. Paul store is a mecca for homeowners on the lookout for attractive and affordable fixtures, furniture, floor coverings, and accessories. (St. Paul)

MALL OF AMERICA

This mother of all shopping centers has been a runaway success since its 1992 opening. More than 40 million people visit every year—a steady stream of credit-card-carrying customers from the Twin Cities and all over the world.

MALL OF AMERICA
I-494 at Hwy. 77
Bloomington
612/883-8800
www.mallofamerica.com
Everything about Mall of America ("the Mall") is b-i-g, so big in fact that locals dubbed it the "megamall" long before the first cash register rang up the first sale. The nation's largest shopping and entertainment complex, this $675 million monster is one of the country's top tourist attractions. The mall's 4.2 million square feet—the equivalent of seven Yankee Stadiums—are filled with nearly 450 shops, restaurants, and entertainment venues. There are nearly 13,000 free parking spots within 300 feet of an entrance, located mostly in two huge, seven-story parking ramps.

The building itself, while not exactly an architectural triumph, is something of an engineering marvel, primarily in its ability to comfortably circulate staggering numbers of visitors. Navigating the mall is easy. Picture it as a giant three-story rectangle, with a department store at each corner, all linked by long corridors with distinct (but hardly distinctive) personalities.

East Broadway (Sears to Bloomingdale's) is decked out in high-tech stainless steel with blue accents. South Avenue (Bloomingdale's to Macy's) sports shades of peach faux art deco, while West Market (Macy's to Nordstrom) takes on a town square atmosphere, and North Garden (Nordstrom to Sears) is a tiled garden. The rectangle's center is occupied by Knott's Camp Snoopy, a seven-acre amusement park. A smaller fourth level houses nightclubs, restaurants, and a 14-screen movie theater complex. The basement hosts Underwater World, a 1.2-million-gallon aquarium.

Bloomingdale's (612/883-2500) is the most stylish of the mall's big four, particularly its beautifully merchandised kitchen, tabletop, and bed and bath departments, all on the third floor. Macy's (612/888-3333) is more middle-of-the-road and heavy on its own in-house brands. Nordstrom (612/883-2121), the most successful of the mall's big players, showcases solid clothing and accessories, plus the chain's signature shoe departments. A helpful concierge is stationed on the first floor, near the store's mall entrance. Sears' mall store (612/853-0500) is one of the giant retailer's most up-to-date ventures.

The mall is also packed with the kinds of chains that lease mall space from coast to coast, including oversized branches of the Gap, Banana Republic, Old Navy, The Limited, Structure, Victoria's Secret, Abercrombie & Fitch, Ann Taylor, Sam Goody, Eddie Bauer, and dozens more. Several chain discount stores also call the mall home, include Filene's Basement, Linens 'N' Things and Nordstrom Rack.

The mall does have a number of quirky, interesting shops. Hot Topic pairs CDs with T-shirts of pop music's hottest bands (612/858-9150). Lionel model trains chug overhead at the Great Train Store, which stocks tons of toy train and railroad-related gizmos (612/851-9988). Calido Chile Hot and Spicy Traders is dedicated to the glory of the pepper (612/854-7250). You can shoot hoops in the half-court at Just for Feet, the world's largest athletic shoe store (612/854-5331). Babushka sells imported Russian and Ukranian baubles (612/854-0040). And pick up that hologram you've been searching for at Hologram Land (612/854-9344).

In the West Market area, FAO Schwarz has a large store, including a fabulous Barbie boutique (612/858-9900). Several dozen pushcarts clut-

Where to Eat

The mall boasts more than two dozen sit-down restaurants as well as nearly 50 fast-food outlets, located primarily in two gigantic food courts in North Garden and South Avenue. The most appealing full-service restaurants are ***Twin City Grill****,* ***California Cafe****,* ***Planet Hollywood****,* ***Cafe Odyssey****, and the* ***Rainforest Cafe****. The food courts are full of typical forgettable deep-fried mall fare, but you can get a good meal—at a good price—if you try. Best bets include burgers and fries at lively* ***Johnny Rockets****, inexpensive rice bowls and teriyaki chicken at* ***Hibachi-San****, roast turkey with all the trimmings at the* ***Barn Yard Cafe****, cheese curds and corn dogs at* ***Minnesota Picnic****, and coffee and pastries at* ***Caribou Coffee****.*

ter Market Square's first floor, including Simon Sez (Pez central), the Pin Place (zillions of clever pins), and State Your Name (customized license-plate key chains from every state). Rybicki Cheese Ltd. (612/854-3330) specializes in Wisconsin cheese. You can test athletic equipment before you buy it at cavernous Oshman's Supersports USA (612/854-9444). Air Traffic (612/858-9599) is the one-stop source for kites. And it's strictly tractors and miniature barnyard animals at fun Al's Farm Toys (612/858-9139).

In the North Garden, Brainstorms

Eight Ways to Avoid Getting Malled

1. *If you really want to experience the mall in all its vulgar, excessive glory, wear comfortable shoes (or buy a pair at any of the mall's 25 shoe stores).*
2. *Arrive early, particularly on weekends. During Minnesota's sometimes interminable winter, the mall is a major magnet for snow-crazy natives, and on a hot and humid summer's day, thousands will jam the place to beat the heat.*
3. *Let Bloomie's valet park your car ($5, at the store's east entrance).*
4. *Check your coat and packages ($1) just inside the mall at any of its four first-floor entrances. Lockers (50 cents to $1) go quickly during coat-and-boot season. Nordstrom offers a free coat check during the colder months, too (first floor, mall entrance).*
5. *For event information and money-saving coupons, pick up the* Best of the Mall *newspaper at any entrance.*
6. *Stop by a Guest Service Center, located just inside the mall at its four first-floor entrances. You'll find strollers and wheelchairs for rent, as well as restrooms, directories, a lost and found, telephones, foreign-language guides, cash machines, and shopping bags.*
7. *Rest your weary feet in Bloomie's palatial restrooms (men's on the first floor, women's on the second).*
8. *Get a glimpse of sunlight from the mall's only window to the outside world, at Nordstrom's affordable third-floor cafeteria.*

is dedicated to scientific toys, books, and conversation-starters (612/858-8652). Charlie's Novelties (612/854-8151) sells beer-related collectibles. Trekkies will love Starlog (612/853-9988), a fun sci-fi and comic-book store. Roadside nostalgia from the 1940s, 50s, and 60s is the focus of Runkel Bros. American Garage (612/858-9633). Or put your face on the cover of one of hundreds of magazines at Amazing Pictures (612/858-8680).

Along South Avenue, Brooks Brothers (612/858-8901) brings its preppy look to men and women. And kids will love the hands-on play at the LEGO Imagination Center (612/858-8949), selling a full line of LEGO products.

The mall is designed for one-stop shopping. You can plan a warm-weather getaway at the Florida Vacation Store, then book your ticket next door at Northwest Airlines. Have your teeth cleaned at Health Partners Dental Clinic, then get a physical at the Quello Clinic. You can even tie the knot (at prices ranging from $195 to $745) or renew your vows (from $79 to $295) at the Chapel of Love, which includes a private 75-seat wedding chapel. (The chapel averages three weddings per day.) You can open a savings account at iBank, work toward your high-school or college degree at the Metropolitan Learning Alliance, or cash a check at Daddy's Check Cash. The American Association of Retired Persons even staffs a booth here. The Mall is open Mon–Fr 10–9:30, Sat 9:30–9:30, Sun 11–7. Hours may vary by season, and some attractions have different hours. Children under 16 are not permitted at the mall without a parent or guardian on Fri and Sat evenings. (Greater Twin Cities)

Getting to the Mall

From downtown Minneapolis, drive approximately 15 minutes on I-35W south to Crosstown 62 east and Highway 77 (Cedar Avenue) south. From downtown St. Paul, take Shepard Road west to Highway 5 west to I-494 west, also approximately 15 minutes. From the airport, follow Highway 5 west to I-494 west about five minutes.

Metro Transit bus service makes visiting the mall easy. A shuttle (Routes 4, 7, 43, 54, and 77) runs from the Lindbergh Terminal at Minneapolis/St. Paul International Airport. The Route 80 express shuttle runs from Nicollet Mall in downtown Minneapolis. The Route 54 bus runs from downtown St. Paul via the airport. Fares are $1.50 during peak hours, $1.25 non-peak. Call 612/373-3333 (612/341-0140 TTY/TTD) for schedule information. All buses drop passengers at the mall's transit station, just outside the East Broadway first-floor entrance.

Parking at the Mall

Two seven-story, 6,000-space parking ramps bookend the Mall of America's east and west sides. Negotiating them on a busy day can be a daunting experience, but if you go directly to the mall's top floors, you'll get in and out relatively fast. The large surface lot across 24th Avenue offers a hassle-free alternative to the ramps on especially mobbed days; it's a quick five-minute walk through the ramp to the East Broadway entrance.

OTHER SHOPPING MALLS

If Mall of America is too much mall for you to handle, a number of other shopping centers fill the Twin Cities area. Most contain the predictable mix of department stores and national and local specialty stores, as well as restaurants, movie theaters, and services.

BROOKDALE
Hwy. 100 at Brooklyn Blvd.
Brooklyn Center
612/566-6672
Brookdale is a poor relation to the Twin Cities' other "Dales," with a dreary, run-down environment and low-end retailers. Department stores include Dayton's, JC Penney, Sears, and Mervyn's. (Greater Twin Cities)

BURNSVILLE CENTER
I-35 at County Rd. 42
Burnsville
612/435-8182
This sunny, spacious 1970s mall has a big food court and movie theaters but lots of empty storefronts. Department stores include Dayton's, JC Penney, Sears, and Mervyn's. (Greater Twin Cities)

EDEN PRAIRIE CENTER
I-494 at Prairie Center Dr.
Eden Prairie
612/941-7650
This 1970s disaster has many empty storefronts. Department stores include Sears, Mervyn's, and Target. (Greater Twin Cities)

MAPLEWOOD MALL
I-694 at White Bear Ave.
Maplewood
651/770-5020
Maplewood has been recently remodeled, with a new Dayton's, many new specialty shops, a movie theater, and a booming food court. Other department stores include Sears and Mervyn's. (Greater Twin Cities)

NORTHTOWN
Hwy. 10 at University Ave.
Blaine

Birth of the American Mall

The enclosed shopping mall phenomenon was born in suburban Edina, when Southdale opened it doors on October 8, 1956. Designed by Austrian architect Victor Gruen, Southdale was the nation's first climate-controlled shopping center. More than 40 years later, after several additions and top-to-bottom renovations, Southdale remains, after Mall of America, the area's most successful shopping locale. It even spawned an entire suburban business district that now includes a hospital campus, office buildings, apartments, condominiums, an excellent public library, a few parks, and more than a dozen additional shopping centers.

If shopping's not your bag, come at night and bop 'til you drop at the Upper East Side, the mall's popular nightclub area (fourth floor, East Broadway). The General Cinema multiplex (612/851-0074) is on the same floor. See Chapter 12, Nightlife, for more information.

651/786-9704
At this tired, downscale 1970s center, department stores include Montgomery Ward and Mervyn's. (Greater Twin Cities)

RIDGEDALE
I-394 at Plymouth Rd.
Minnetonka
612/541-8464
This big, popular center has a large variety of specialty stores and restaurants and a big, sunny atrium. Department stores include two Dayton's (one for women's clothing, cosmetics, and accessories, the other for men's clothing and housewares), JC Penney, and Sears. (Greater Twin Cities)

ROSEDALE
Hwy. 36 at Fairview Ave.
Roseville
651/633-0872
This recently remodeled center has lots of shoppers and plenty of national chain stores. Department stores include a big new Dayton's, along with JC Penney and Mervyn's. (Greater Twin Cities)

SOUTHDALE
France Ave. at 66th St.
Edina
612/925-7885
Here you'll find the Twin Cities' best collection of mall chain stores (including J. Crew, Ann Taylor, Crate & Barrel, Disney, and others) and a sunny, appealing food court. Department stores include a particularly large and luxurious new Dayton's, as well as JC Penney and Mervyn's. (Greater Twin Cities)

OTHER NOTABLE STORES

BYERLY'S
3777 Park Center Dr.
St. Louis Park
612/929-2100
Only in the Twin Cities would a grocery store be a tourist attraction. This huge complex houses a popular family restaurant, a cooking school, a branch of US Bank, Wood's Chocolate Shop, Caribou Coffee, and a gift shop (selling everything from greeting cards to $10 baubles to $5,000 statues), along with full-service meat, deli, bakery, and seafood departments, a pharmacy, a photo lab, Chinese and sushi takeout, and a post office. Unlike most supermarkets, this one's decked out with crystal chandeliers, original art, and carpeted isles. This 24-hour store even employs a home economist. The staff is friendly and professional, and the prices match the deluxe decor. (Greater Twin Cities)

KELLEY & KELLEY NURSERY
2325 Watertown Rd.

Zac Mangel

Byerly's—a grocery store attraction, p. 149

Long Lake
612/473-7337
It may not have the vast selection of its chain competitors (including Bachman's, the area's largest-volume nursery), but K&K more than makes up for it in its beguiling setting, the inspiration of countless Twin Cities gardeners. (Greater Twin Cities)

ROOM & BOARD
7010 France Ave. S.
Edina
612/927-8834
The store is a standout resource for casual, contemporary furniture and home accessories. Also at 2480 N. Fairview Ave., Roseville; 651/639-0591. (Greater Twin Cities)

DISCOUNT SHOPPING

BANK'S
615 First Ave. N.E.
Minneapolis
612/379-2803
Bank's is a huge dump, but often full of bargains. The stuff comes from national retailers who have endured some kind of natural or financial disaster, translating into men's clothing by Tommy Hilfiger or Ralph Lauren one week, Schwinn bicycles or Fieldcrest bedding the next. Be sure to check for smoke damage. Call the store's hotline (612/379-4321) for merchandise updates. (Minneapolis)

DAYTON'S OUTLET STORE
701 Industrial Blvd.
Minneapolis
612/623-7111
The department store's giant warehouse has an outlet store that carries a large if somewhat picked- over selection of furniture, rugs, bed and bath items, and more. (Minneapolis)

MEDFORD OUTLET CENTER
1-35 at Exit 48
Medford
507/455-4111
An hour south of the Twin Cities, Medford has 40 factory-direct stores, including G.H. Bass, Liz Claiborne, Jordache, Guess?, Mikasa, Rocky

Fresh Flowers

Minneapolis has a number of exceptionally creative florists who do wonderful things with fresh cut blooms, as well as "smalls," those little bibelots that catch your eye and capture your heart. Each store has its own charms, and all enchant. Here are a few notables:

- ***Larkspur*** *(514 N. Third St., Minneapolis; 612/332-2149)*
- ***Fiori*** *(17 N.E. Fifth St., Minneapolis; 612/623-1153)*
- ***Roger Beck Florist*** *(1904 LaSalle Ave., Minneapolis; 612/871-7080)*
- ***Brown & Greene*** *(4400 Beard Ave. S., Minneapolis; 612/928-3778)*

Mountain Chocolates, Champion, and Geoffrey Beane. (Greater Twin Cities)

OPITZ OUTLET
4320 Excelsior Blvd.
St. Louis Park
612/922-2435
Opitz carries an ever-changing assortment of deeply discounted household goods and clothing for men, women, and children. The store hotline (612/922-9088) provides an updated list of sale merchandise. (Greater Twin Cities)

PRIME OUTLETS AT WOODBURY
I-94 at County Rd. 19 (Exit 251)
Woodbury
651/735-9060
The center contains more than 40 outlet stores, including American Tourister, Book Warehouse, Casual Corner, Eddie Bauer, Fanny Farmer, Fieldcrest, Canon, Hush Puppies, Levi's, Petite Sophisticate, Sara Lee Bakery, Spiegel, Sunglass Hut, and Winona Knits. It's 15 minutes east of downtown St. Paul. (Greater Twin Cities)

ROOM & BOARD OUTLET
4650 Olson Memorial Hwy.
Golden Valley
612/529-6089
The outlet for the contemporary home furnishings store has a great selection of reasonably priced beds, chairs, tables, sofas, and lamps. Open Sat and Sun only. (Greater Twin Cities)

Minnesota Office of Tourism

10

SPORTS AND RECREATION

Twin Citians are a sports-minded people, passionate about their professional teams and dedicated to pursuing a wide variety of indoor and outdoor recreational interests. Blame it on the weather. Rather than fight its extremes, Minnesotans embrace it, hurling themselves into the outdoors with an abandon that few other regions can match.

Precious summertime months find players swarming ballfields, boat enthusiasts skimming across rivers and lakes, and bikers and inline skaters hitting the road. The cool, crisp air of winter puts outdoor sports enthusiasts on ice rinks and cross-country and downhill ski trails. And every season finds Twin Citians turning out in support of the area's many professional sports teams, including the two-time World Series–winning Minnesota Twins. Whatever your recreational passion—spectator or participant, indoor or outdoor—you'll find it in the Twin Cities.

PROFESSIONAL SPORTS

Auto Racing

ELKO SPEEDWAY
26350 France Ave.
Elko
612/461-3395
Bombers, NASCAR late-models, sportsmen, and thunder cars roar around a high-banked asphalt oval. $10 adults, $4 ages 5 to 12; free to children under 5. May–Aug Sat and holidays 7 p.m. (Greater Twin Cities)

RACEWAY PARK
1 Checkered Flag Blvd.
Shakopee
612/445-2257
This modest facility, located two miles east of Valleyfair, has a quarter-mile asphalt track designed for late models, short trackers, hobby stocks, and figure-eight races. $9 adults, $4

TRIVIA

Five Minnesota Twins players have had their numbers retired by the team: Kirby Puckett, Kent Hrbek, Rod Carew, Tony Oliva, and Harmon Killebrew.

ages 5 to 12, under 5 free. June–Aug Sun and Wed 7 p.m. (Greater Twin Cities)

Baseball

MINNESOTA TWINS
Metrodome
Minneapolis
612/375-1366

The two-time World Series champions (1987 and 1991) play in the American League West Division at the cheerless Hubert H. Humphrey Metrodome (Chicago Ave. and Fifth St., Minneapolis), a 1982 multiuse domed stadium that seats 55,000 for baseball and 62,000 for football. The stadium's white Teflon roof is the largest air-supported dome in the world, and has only deflated once, when it was knocked flat during a particularly wicked blizzard in the winter of 1985.

The Twins came to Minnesota in 1961, and the team has had its share of legendary players, including Rod Carew, Harmon Killebrew, Tony Oliva, Kirby Puckett, Frank Viola, and Kent Hrbek.

Team favorites aside, watching baseball here can be a bit of a downer, especially on a sunny summer's day, when many fans long for the old, open-air days of Metropolitan Stadium in Bloomington. In terms of sightlines, the stadium clearly favors football, and unless you can get a seat in the lower decks on the first- and third-base lines, it almost makes more sense to watch the game at home.

Outside the Dome, the city has made an effort at bringing some pre- and postgame life to the area, with the addition of Metrodome Plaza at Chicago Avenue and Fifth Street. While the design is as second-rate as the Dome itself, the pedestrian-friendly space has managed to draw crowds for food, music, and games, making the Metrodome experience a little less sterile. That hasn't kept owner Carl Pohlad from threatening to move the Twins to another city if a new stadium isn't built for the team. Parking is easy to come by around the Dome, though it's just as quick to park downtown and take a shuttle bus down Fourth Street. The team operates a Twins Pro Shop near the Rosedale Shopping Center (2401 Fairview Ave., Roseville; 651/635-0777). (Downtown Minneapolis)

ST. PAUL SAINTS
1771 Energy Park Dr.
St. Paul
651/644-6659

Outdoor baseball returned to the Twin Cities in 1993, and it has been a grand-slam hit from day one. The Saints, part of the Northern League, is minor-league baseball with major-league attitude. Saints tickets are a hot commodity not only among baseball fans who prefer their game under the open sky, but also among folks looking for a fun night out, which the Saints deliver in spades. Fans love the friendly, family-oriented atmosphere, the great food and entertainment (the team mascot is a pig, and lots of zany antics happen on and off the field), and the enthusiastic crowd. One of the team's owners is actor Bill Murray, and he usually appears a few times each season. The team also nabs big-name players (Darryl Strawberry, Jack Morris) every now and then, and St. Paul's comfortable 6,000-seat Midway Stadium brings the action on the field right up to the bleachers. Tickets, unfortunately, are a scarce commodity. (St. Paul)

Basketball

MINNESOTA TIMBERWOLVES
Target Center
600 First Ave. N.
Minneapolis
612/673-1600

Since this NBA expansion team hit the court in 1989, its win-loss record has been a roller coaster. In its first year, the team lost 60 games, a new and rather embarrassing NBA record. But thanks to the leadership of former Celtic, now vice president of basketball operations Kevin McHale and the acquisition of high school superstar Kevin Garnett, the team has lately become a post-season regular with its prospects ever increasing.

Going to a 'Wolves game can be fun, partly because of fans' high energy level and also because of the relative luxury of Target Center, a 16,000-seat arena in the heart of downtown Minneapolis. The arena is connected by skyway to several thousand parking spots in three huge city-owned ramps along Second Avenue North, within walking distance of several dozen bars, restaurants, and clubs for pre- and postgame revelries. (Downtown Minneapolis)

Football

MINNESOTA VIKINGS
Metrodome
Minneapolis
612/333-8828

Under the stewardship of former head coach Bud Grant, the Vikes

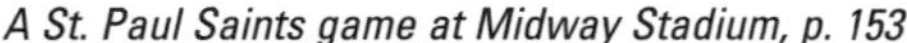

A St. Paul Saints game at Midway Stadium, p. 153

Thomas K. Perry

Golden Gophers

The University of Minnesota's Golden Gophers play a full roster of Big Ten intercollegiate sports, and many attract an extremely loyal following, making tickets hard to get (call 612/624-8080). Men's and women's basketball, both played at the recently renovated Williams Arena (1925 University Ave. S.E.), have fervent followings and are perennial playoff fixtures. Men's hockey also has legions of rabid fans. The team, which plays at sparkling new Mariucci Arena (1901 Fourth St. S.E.), is hardly ever out of the nation's top rankings. Although it's never been a Gopher strong suit (the last time the team made it to the Rose Bowl, John F. Kennedy was in the White House), football is played at the Metrodome, not exactly the best venue for a rousing college game.

traveled to the Super Bowl four times during the team's 1970s heyday; unfortunately, they never took the trophy home, but the fans remain loyal as ever. Now under the watchful eye of coach Dennis Green—as well as new owners—the Vikes still manage to pack the Metrodome, although getting a ticket is easier than it was during the team's glory days at Metropolitan Stadium. The stadium works much better when a football is being thrown across the artificial turf. This 1961 expansion team has had its share of NFL stars, including Fran Tarkenton, Ed Marinaro, Chuck Foreman, Ahmad Rashad, Carl Eller, and Alan Page, who now sits on the Minnesota Supreme Court. The Vikings train at Winter Park, a new facility (9520 Viking Dr., Eden Prairie; 612/828-6500) named for former owner Max Winter. Some events during the team's late-summer training session are open to the public. (Downtown Minneapolis)

Greyhound Racing

ST. CROIX MEADOWS
Hudson, Wisconsin
715/386-6800

This modern facility's best draw is its large, comfortable, air-conditioned clubhouse, which has excellent sightlines. The dogs race May through August, and simulcast racing is also available. 20 minutes from St. Paul in Hudson, Wisconsin, just south of I-94. Adults $1, children under 13 free. Open daily at 11 a.m.; racing begins Wed at 3 p.m., Thu and Fri at 7 p.m., Sat and Sun at 1 p.m. Closed Mon.

Hockey

MINNESOTA WILD
St. Paul RiverCentre
651/333-7825

Hockey was practically born in Minnesota, which makes it hard to believe that this puck-crazy state lacks a National Hockey League franchise.

Disciples of the Pilates Method have a few Twin Cities options, including Ballet Arts Minnesota (528 Hennepin Ave., Minneapolis; 612/340-1071), Lonna Mosow's (6409 Shady Oak Rd., Eden Prairie; 612/942-2900), and the Sweatshop Fitness Training Center (171 Snelling Ave. N., St. Paul; 651/646-8418).

Still, the Twin Cities have been without a pro hockey team since 1993, when the Minnesota North Stars decamped to Dallas. That void will be finally filled with the birth of the Wild in late 2000. The city of St. Paul is currently building the team a handsome new 17,000-seat arena on the site of the old St. Paul Civic Center in downtown St. Paul. (Downtown St. Paul)

Horse Racing

CANTERBURY PARK
1100 Canterbury Rd.
Shakopee
612/445-7223

The excitement of horse racing returns to Minnesota after a half-decade hiatus at this attractive, well-equipped facility, located about 30 minutes southwest of downtown Minneapolis. Horses hit the track late-May to mid-August, and the park's teleracing center is open year-round. Thu–Sat first post at 6:30 p.m., Sun and holidays first post at 2 p.m. $3 adults, under 18 free; seniors free on Sunday. (Greater Twin Cities)

Soccer

MINNESOTA THUNDER
1700 105 Ave. N.E.
Blaine
612/893-1442

This U.S. Interregional Soccer League franchise plays from June to August at the National Sports Center in suburban Blaine. Since it was founded in 1990, the Thunder has had a perfect season (20 wins, 0 losses in 1994) and several near-perfect seasons. (Greater Twin Cities)

RECREATION

Aerobics

THE FIRM
245 Aldrich Ave. N.
Minneapolis
612/377-3003

Nobody serves up a better aerobic workout than the thigh-busting professionals at The Firm, a studio with a wide variety of daily classes—high and low impact, step, kickboxing, and muscle conditioning—for all fitness levels. The Firm also offers Spinning, an intense instructor-led stationary bicycle workout. (Downtown Minneapolis)

JABZ
5812 W. 36 St.
St. Louis Park
612/925-0323

You'll think you've been sent to boot camp when you take a class at this small studio, which specializes in grueling, lung-bursting classes that combine the power and agility of boxing with the stamina of the most challenging aerobics classes. (Greater Twin Cities)

THE SWEATSHOP FITNESS TRAINING CENTER

171 Snelling Ave. N.
St. Paul
651/646-8418
This busy studio offers a huge range of classes for aerobicizers of all abilities and fitness levels, as well as a fully equipped cardio- and weight-training center, Pilates studio, juice bar, and shop. (St. Paul)

Alpine Skiing

Area ski runs don't exactly recall the Rockies, with the steepest drop

Hit the Beaches

In the Land of 10,000 Lakes, finding a public beach is not a problem. Minneapolis's numerous lifeguarded beaches (612/661-4875), open June to August daily from noon to 8 p.m., include: ***Lake Nokomis*** *(4955 and 5001 E. Nokomis Pkwy.),* ***Theodore Wirth Lake*** *(3200 Glenwood Ave. N.),* ***Lake Calhoun*** *(W. Lake St. and W. Lake Calhoun Pkwy., 32nd St. and E. Lake Calhoun Pkwy., and Thomas Ave. and W. Lake Calhoun Pkwy.),* ***Lake Harriet*** *(N. Lake Harriet Pkwy. at Rosewood Rd., and 4740 E. Lake Harriet Pkwy.),* ***Cedar Lake*** *(2100 and 3300 Cedar Lake Pkwy.), and* ***Lake Hiawatha*** *(28 Ave. S. and E. 45 St.). St. Paul operates a guarded public beach at* ***Lake Phalen*** *(just off Wheelock Pkwy., 651/776-9833), open June through August noon to 7 p.m.*

Hennepin County offers seven public beach areas (612/559-9000), with lifeguard service, showers, and changing rooms. All are open June through August 11 a.m. to 8 p.m. daily and charge a $4 daily parking fee. Beaches include ***Baker Park Reserve*** *(2301 County Road 19, Maple Plain),* ***Bryant Lake Regional Park*** *(6400 Rowland Rd., Eden Prairie),* ***Clearly Lake Regional Park*** *(18106 Texas Ave., Prior Lake);* ***Elm Creek Park Reserve*** *(13080 Territorial Rd., Maple Grove), and* ***Lake Rebecca Park Reserve*** *(9831 County Road 50, Rockford).*

Ramsey County (651/777-1707) has 10 lifeguarded beaches, open June through August noon to 6 p.m. daily, including: ***Lake Johanna*** *(3500 Lake Johanna Blvd., Arden Hills),* ***Long Lake*** *(1500 Old Hwy. 8, New Brighton),* ***Lake Owasso*** *(370 N. Owasso Blvd., Shoreview), and* ***White Bear Lake*** *(1300 Lake Ave., White Bear Lake).*

around 350 feet—little more than a molehill for skiers accustomed to mountains. But a number of well-groomed downhill ski areas do exist within an hour's drive of the Twin Cities. Their amenities include snow-making capabilities, nighttime lighting, and chalet facilities. Most are open mid-November through late March. The Minnesota Ski Council (612/673-0828) provides good information about ski schools, race leagues, clinics, equipment swap meets, and more.

AFTON ALPS
County Road 20
Afton
651/436-5245
Located about 15 minutes east of downtown St. Paul, this popular facility has 18 chairlifts, 37 runs, four chalets, a school, and rentals. Open daily 9 a.m. to 10 p.m. (Greater Twin Cities)

BUCK HILL
15400 Buck Hill Rd.
Burnsville
612/435-7174
Just 20 minutes south of downtown Minneapolis, this granddaddy of Twin Cities ski areas has 10 runs and four chairlifts. During the summer, Buck Hill opens the Beaver Mountain Water Slide, an elaborate, six-run water park. (Greater Twin Cities)

HYLAND HILLS
8800 Chalet Rd.
Bloomington
612/835-4604
This 14-run suburban Minneapolis ski area offers day and night skiing about 15 minutes southwest of downtown Minneapolis. (Greater Twin Cities)

Hennepin Parks

One of the 10,000 lakes, p. 157

WELCH VILLAGE
Highway 61 and County Road 7
Welch
612/222-7079
This huge operation, located about an hour southeast of the Twin Cities near the city of Red Wing, maintains 35 runs and a snowboard park. Daily 9 a.m. to 10 p.m.

WILD MOUNTAIN
37350 Wild Mountain Rd.
Taylors Falls
651/257-3550
Located about an hour north of the Twin Cities, Wild Mountain has 23 runs (with great views of the St. Croix Valley), four chairlifts, a ski school, and skiing every Friday until 3 a.m. During warmer weather, Wild Mountain features an elaborate water park, along with a rip-roaring go-cart track.

Bike Racing

NATIONAL SPORTS CENTER VELODROME

1700 105 Ave. N.E.
Blaine
612/785-5600
The nation's only all-weather wood cycling track sits inside this vast suburban recreational sports complex. Its bleachers can accommodate more than two thousand fans. (Greater Twin Cities)

Fishing is a popular pastime in the Land of 10,000 Lakes, but all anglers over the age of 16 must be licensed. Call 651/296-4506 for details.

Bike Rentals

THE ALTERNATIVE BICYCLE SHOP
2408 Hennepin Ave. S.
Minneapolis
612/374-3635
About six blocks east of Lake of the Isles, this popular bike, skateboard, and snowboard store has a top-notch—if arrogant—sales and service staff. It's a great place to rent a wide variety of bicycles, including tandem bikes, for $6/hour or $20/day. (Minneapolis)

CALHOUN CYCLE
1622 W. Lake St.
Minneapolis
612/827-8231
You can rent bikes in all shapes and sizes (tandems run $8 per hour, $32 per day; mountain bikes go for $24 per day) from this shop, conveniently located about two blocks from Lake Calhoun and three blocks from Uptown's shops and cafés. (Minneapolis)

COMO LAKESIDE PAVILION
Como Park
St. Paul
651/488-4297
The city of St. Paul operates a small bike-rental outfit in the park's busy pavilion. Grab a partner, nab a tandem bike for $6/hour, then make your way around the Twin Cities' most popular park. (St. Paul)

Bike Trails

MINNEAPOLIS'S GRAND ROUNDS
For inner-city biking, Minneapolis can't be beat, with more than 40 miles of interconnected dedicated bike trails within its Ground Rounds system of parkways. Bikers can take an off-road tour of Victory Memorial Drive and Theodore Wirth Parkway

Up, Up, and Away

For about $125 per person, ***Apple Express Hot Air Balloon Co.*** *(612/430-2800),* ***Balloon Adventures*** *(612/474-1662),* ***Stillwater Balloons*** *(651/439-1800), and* ***Scenic Adventures Hot Air Balloon Flights*** *(612/432-7009) will send you up, up and away for a hot-air-balloon adventure over the Twin Cities.*

on the city's north side, the Chain of Lakes and Minnehaha Parkway to the south, and the West River Road edging the Mississippi River. The paths are also very popular with in-line skaters (particularly at Lakes Harriet and Calhoun, both recently rebuilt and sporting very smooth surfaces), and all feature adjacent walking paths.

The city's most recent bike-trail addition is an abandoned railroad right-of-way running nearly four miles, from downtown Minneapolis, past Cedar Lake, to suburban St. Louis Park. The city's next project, the Midtown Greenway, is a cross-town trail spanning the length of the city along 29th Street South. Slated for completion in late 1999, the ambitious linear park will extend from France Avenue all the way east to the Mississippi River. During the past five years, Minneapolis has also added more than 25 miles of commuter bike trails along major thoroughfares. For more information, call 612/661-4800. (Minneapolis)

HENNEPIN PARKS

Thanks to a sympathetic board and a well-funded park system, Hennepin County is a very bike-friendly place. While maintaining recreational bike paths in most of its large parks, the county has also created a scenic trail network that follows old streetcar routes. The two most popular, the LRT North and LRT South lines, are both gravel trails starting in downtown Hopkins (free parking available) and extending for about 15 miles.

The north line begins at First Street and Ninth Avenue, winds its way through the woods, darts along the Lake Minnetonka shore, jogs through bustling Excelsior, then moves on to pretty Victoria. From there, it's a pleasant 15-minute ride on country roads to the University of Minnesota Landscape Arboretum.

The south line is the less interesting of the two, starting at Fifth Street and Excelsior Boulevard and rolling its way through a fairly uneventful suburban landscape to Chanhassen. (Greater Twin Cities)

MINNESOTA DEPARTMENT OF NATURAL RESOURCES

Minnesota operates an ever-growing network of bike trails throughout the state (651/296-2216), including several in the Twin Cities area. A popular option is the Luce Line Trail, a scenic 30-mile path that follows an abandoned rail bed from suburban Plymouth to rural Winstead. The trail starts on Plymouth's Vicks-

Lake Minnetonka Boating

Cruise the waters of Lake Minnetonka aboard one of several charter companies. ***Al and Alma's*** *(612/472-3098) will do the driving for you and your party;* ***Rockvam Boat Yards*** *(612/471-9515) rents a wide range of pontoon or fishing boats for your own use, including boats, motors, maps, and even sunblock, lemonade, and ice cream.*

If free-falling out of an airplane is your idea of adventure, you can make it happen about an hour from the Twin Cities, at Freefall Fantasy in Cologne (612/466-5545) and Skydive Hutchinson in Hutchinson (612/433-3633).

burg Lane, between county roads 15 and 6.

The top eastern route is the Gateway Trail, an 18-mile stretch connecting Stillwater with the eastern shore of Lake Phalen in St. Paul. The trail sits on another abandoned railroad bed, offering plenty of shade and very few hills. (Greater Twin Cities)

Billiards

AMERICA'S ORIGINAL SPORTS BAR
Mall of America
Bloomington
612/854-5483
The state's largest sports bar has almost two dozen pool tables, plus a huge video arcade, a half-basketball court, darts, simulated pitching and driving ranges, and a cheap snack bar. (Greater Twin Cities)

CITY BILLIARDS
25 Fourth St. N.
Minneapolis
612/338-2255
This Warehouse District fixture is Minneapolis's largest, most pleasant pool hall, a lively place to knock back a few games of billiards and darts. The airy room boasts nearly two dozen billiards tables, plus several other game tables and a full bar. Offering a large selection of sandwiches, appetizers, pizzas, and desserts, it's one of the few places in downtown Minneapolis (outside Pizza Luce, which is right down Fourth Street) where bar-hoppers can go for something decent to eat after midnight. (Downtown Minneapolis)

Bowling

BRYANT LAKE BOWL
810 W. Lake St.
Minneapolis
612/825-3737
Skirting the edge of Minneapolis's Uptown neighborhood, this small storefront has only eight lanes, but the crowd is young, hip, and friendly, the food far surpasses anything you'd expect at a bowling alley, and the beer and wine selections are tops in their class. $1.50/game; free shoe rental. (Minneapolis)

STARDUST BOWLING LANES
2520 26th Ave. S.
Minneapolis
612/721-6211
The Stardust does bowling big, with 30 lanes, a huge game room, cocktail lounge, and late-night (2 a.m.) hours. $2/game before 5 p.m., $2.50/game after 5 p.m. (Minneapolis)

Golf

EDINBURGH USA
8700 Edinbrook Crossing
Brooklyn Park
612/424-9444

Alice M. Prescott/Unicorn Stock Photos

Canoeing on Lake of the Isles

One of the Twin Cities' newest courses is also one of its most popular. Designed by golf guru Robert Trent Jones, the 18-hole, par-72 course is loaded with water and sand hazards that will vex even the best golfers. Owned by the city of Brooklyn Park, the course also has a large, rather luxurious clubhouse. (Greater Twin Cities)

THEODORE WIRTH GOLF CLUB
1301 Theodore Worth Pkwy.
Minneapolis
612/521-9731

The city of Minneapolis operates this 18-hole, par 72 course, located on the western edge in Theodore Wirth, the city's largest park. The hilly, challenging course has a number of spectacular skyline views. (Minneapolis)

UNIVERSITY OF MINNESOTA GOLF COURSE
2275 W. Larpenteur Ave.
St. Paul
612/627-4000

This notoriously difficult 18-hole, par-71 course is one of the oldest and

Canoeing

Daily canoe rental is available at most Hennepin County park reserves, including Hyland, Lake Rebecca, Clearly Lake, Fish Lake, and French. Call 612/559-9000. Canoes are also available at the Lake Calhoun Refectory (W. Lake St. and E. Lake Calhoun Pkwy., Minneapolis; 612/370-4964), from which you can paddle to both Lake of the Isles and Cedar Lake via channels.

most handsome in the Twin Cities. U of M students, faculty, staff, and alumni association members receive discounted greens fees. (St. Paul)

Health Clubs

BALLY TOTAL FITNESS
3970 Sibley Memorial Dr.
Eagan
651/452-0044

The national Bally's chain has a major presence in the Twin Cities. All eight locations include pools, weight training, aerobics classes, and a wide variety of exercise equipment. Day pass: $12. (Greater Twin Cities)

BODY QUEST INTERNATIONAL
245 Aldrich Ave. N.
Minneapolis
612/377-7222

This gay- and lesbian-friendly gym draws crowds for its excellent personal-training staff, spotless (but cramped) weight- and cardio-workout facilities, peerless juice bar, free parking, convenient edge-of-downtown location, and wonderful skyline views. (Downtown Minneapolis)

LIFETIME FITNESS
3600 Plymouth Blvd.
Plymouth
612/509-0909

The upstart on the Twin Cities fitness scene has grown from one to nine locations in its five short years, and each branch offers a full range of exercise options and free childcare. Lifetime's huge Plymouth facility is a joint effort between the company and the city of Plymouth, featuring extensive gym, weight-training, and swimming facilities, and a popular day-care operation. The company's downtown St. Paul location (340 Cedar St., 651/227-7777) is built inside the luxurious 1920s home of the former St. Paul Athletic Club. As health clubs go, it's rather posh, with six floors of facilities that include a large gymnasium, a beautiful Olympic-size pool, an enormous weight-training room, and a spa. Day pass: $15. Seven other Twin Cities locations.

Warm up your winter—have a hot tub sent to your door. Call In Hot Water (612/938-7913) or Splish Splash (612/427-5241).

LOS CAMPEONES FITNESS & BODY BUILDING
2721 E. Franklin Ave.
Minneapolis
612/333-8181

This small gym isn't much to look at, but it's the place for serious body builders, who come for the extensive, though downscale, weight-training facilities, top-notch personal trainers, and get-down-to-business attitude. Day pass: $6. (Minneapolis)

NORTHWEST ATHLETIC CLUB
600 First Ave. N.
Minneapolis
612/673-1200

This homegrown chain has 11 locations across the Twin Cities. Its flagship is the Arena Club, which is definitely worth a visit. The facilities include an Olympic-size pool, indoor running track, double basketball court, seemingly endless number of machines, in-house café and juice bar, and enormous locker room facilities. Timberwolves members often work out at the club, which is located below the team's Target Center home. Day pass: $10. Nine other Twin Cities locations. (Downtown Minneapolis)

YMCA
30 S. Ninth St.
Minneapolis
612/371-8750

This six-story downtown YMCA branch opened in 1990 to great acclaim, and for good reason. The facility has something for everyone, including an Olympic-size pool, double gymnasium, indoor running track (with swell downtown views), handball and racquetball courts, aerobic exercise rooms, extensive weight-training facilities, a small café, and a convenient skyway location in the LaSalle Plaza complex. Day pass: $16. The Y has 10 other Minneapolis-area locations and 10 St. Paul locations. (Downtown Minneapolis)

YWCA
2808 Hennepin Ave. S.
Minneapolis
612/874-7131

The "Y-Dub" maintains four Minneapolis-area locations and one in St. Paul. This Uptown center includes a well-maintained Olympic-size pool, a holdover from the building's days as the physical fitness center for West High School, (which was demolished in the early 1980s and replaced by the YWCA and an apartment house). The facility also includes a large gym, extensive fitness machinery, and free parking—an Uptown rarity. Day pass: $10. (Minneapolis)

Hockey and Ice Skating

During the cold winter months, neighborhoods across the Twin Cities are dotted with outdoor skating rinks. St. Paul has more than 30 every winter (651/777-1707), and Minneapolis has nearly 50 (612/661-4875). For genuine winter-wonderland recreational skating, check out the rinks near the pavilion at Lake Como in St. Paul and the northernmost finger of Lake of the Isles in Minneapolis (26th Street and East Lake of the Isles Parkway). Both offer beautiful urban scenery, vast expanses of ice, and warming houses. If you prefer skating indoors, the 25-plus ice arenas across the Twin Cities include:

BLOOMINGTON COMMUNITY ICE GARDEN
3600 W. 98 St.
Bloomington
612/948-8842

This sprawling complex in this hockey-crazy suburb has three side-by-side hockey rinks, including one Olympic-size rink. The building also contains extensive food and drink options. (Greater Twin Cities)

Minnesota Office of Tourism

Outdoor skating

Rollin' on the River

Navigate the Mississippi River from both St. Paul (Harriet Island) and Minneapolis (Boom Island) on an old-fashioned steamboat: the Jonathan Padelford, Harriet Bishop Anson Northrup, Betsy Northrup, *or* Josiah Snelling. *The two- and three-hour tours (651/227-1100) can be a relaxing way to enjoy a warm summer's day and see the towns. Memorial Day to Labor Day daily at noon and 2 p.m.*

BRAEMER ARENA
7501 Hwy. 169
Edina
612/484-0268
Edina's recently refurbished ice complex has two rinks. (Greater Twin Cities)

BURNSVILLE ICE CENTER
251 Civic Center Pkwy.
Burnsville
612/895-4650
This 1970s-era facility with arched, wood-framed roofs contains a pair of side-by-side rinks. (Greater Twin Cities)

EDEN PRAIRIE COMMUNITY CENTER
16700 Valley View Rd.
Eden Prairie
612/949-8470
Part of an ambitious community recreation center that includes a huge pool and a number of tennis and racquetball courts, this complex's pair of ice rinks features one Olympic-size rink. (Greater Twin Cities)

MINNETONKA ICE ARENA
3401 Williston Rd.
Minnetonka
612/939-8310
This western suburban complex contains a pair of rinks. (Greater Twin Cities)

ROSEVILLE ICE ARENA AND JOHN ROSE MINNESOTA OVAL
1200 Woodhill Rd.
Roseville
651/484-0268
This new facility has both an indoor and outdoor rink plus one of the state's few regulation outdoor speed-skating ovals, which is used by in-line skaters during the summer months. (Greater Twin Cities)

Nordic Skiing

Cross-country skiers will love the ever-expanding miles of groomed trails that sprout up all over the Twin Cities after the snow flies. Various city, county, and state park boards manage different trails. In Minneapolis, call 612/522-4584; St. Paul, call 651/266-6445; Hennepin County, call 612/559-6778; Ramsey County, call 651/777-1707; state parks, call 651/296-6157. A few standout options include:

CARVER PARK RESERVE
7025 Victoria Dr.
Victoria

TIP

Rent in-line skates for $6 per hour, $12 for an entire day, at Rolling Soles (1700 W. Lake St., Minneapolis; 612/823-5711), about two blocks from the skater-filled paths surrounding Lake Calhoun in Minneapolis's Uptown neighborhood.

612/446-1801
Carver is one of the largest parks in the Hennepin County system. Its cross-country ski loops total more than 14 miles of groomed trails. Located on the western edge of Lake Minnetonka (about 30 minutes west of downtown Minneapolis), the park's scenery is particularly lovely, with paths that wind over gentle hills through woods and prairies and skirt several lakes. (Greater Twin Cities)

CROW-HASSAN PARK RESERVE
11629 Crow-Hassan Park Rd.
Rogers
612/428-2765
This Hennepin County Park, located about 30 minutes northwest of downtown Minneapolis, offers 11 miles of groomed trails on a rolling prairie landscape. (Greater Twin Cities)

Roller Skating

CHEAP SKATE
3075 Coon Rapids Blvd.
Coon Rapids
612/427-8980
Cheap Skate lives up to its name: two- and three-hour sessions, rolled to the tunes of contemporary pop hits and golden oldies, can run as low as $3, with an additional $1 rental fee. Most sessions admit all ages, and a large snack counter caters to skaters who twirl up an appetite. (Greater Twin Cities)

SKATEVILLE FAMILY ROLLER SKATING
201 River Ridge Circle
Burnsville
612/890-0988
A Burnsville landmark for more than 25 years, Skateville offers low rates ($4 per session, plus $1 skate rental) and all-ages fun. Birthday parties can be a hoot here: parties of six or more get skating, hot dogs, ice cream, and a free return pass for $6/person. (Greater Twin Cities)

Soccer

BLAINE SOCCER COMPLEX
1700 105 Ave. N.E.
Blaine
612/785-5600
This well-maintained complex adjacent to the National Sports Center boasts the largest concentration of soccer fields in the state: 55 outdoor fields plus an indoor facility. (Greater Twin Cities)

Tennis

NICOLLET TENNIS CENTER
4005 Nicollet Ave.
Minneapolis
612/825-6844

Hit the Trail

A handful of stables exist in the Twin Cities. They offer saddle rentals, extensive trails, and rates averaging $15/hour. The best include ***Brass Ring Stables*** *(9105 Norris Rd., Elk River; 612/441-7987),* ***Diamond T Ranch*** *(4889 Pilot Knob Rd., Eagan; 651/454-1464),* ***Eagle Creek Stables*** *(7301 Eagle Creek Blvd., Shakopee; 612/445-7222), and* ***Kinni Valley Riding Stables*** *(1181 30 Ave., River Falls, Wisconsin; 715/425-6184).*

The Minneapolis Parks and Recreation Board runs this large new facility, which has 11 indoor courts open to the public. $14/hour. (Minneapolis)

NORTHWEST ATHLETIC CLUB
5525 Cedar Lake Rd.
St. Louis Park
612/546-5474
Northwest Athletic Club maintains the Cities' most extensive indoor and outdoor tennis facilities, with courts at 10 locations. This huge facility is located about five minutes west of downtown Minneapolis. Day passes: $17; free court reservations. (Greater Twin Cities)

REGENCY ATHLETIC CLUB AND SPA
Hyatt Regency Hotel
1300 Nicollet Mall
Minneapolis
612/343-3131
This small, personable health club has four year-round hard courts atop a parking ramp overlooking downtown Minneapolis. Day passes: $11; court reservations: $16/hour. (Downtown Minneapolis)

State Theatre

11
PERFORMING ARTS

Few American cities boast such a wide range of high-quality performing arts as the Twin Cities. Both are blessed with a rich theater scene, and the sophisticated theatergoing audience flocks to major institutions (including the Guthrie Theater and the Children's Theatre Company) and to exciting new local stars like Theatre de la Jeune Lune and the Jungle Theatre.

Minneapolis and St. Paul are also prime destinations for a plethora of touring Broadway shows, nationally renowned music acts, and internationally respected dance companies. This is also the only major metropolitan area in the country that supports two orchestras, in addition to its varied and talented local dance and music scene.

THEATER

CHANHASSEN DINNER THEATRES
501 W. 78th St.
Chanhassen
612/934-1525 or 800/362-3515
www.chanhassentheatres.com
One of the nation's largest theatrical operations, this sprawling complex houses four stages under one roof, including its 600-seat main stage, which produces one lavish musical after another. Other stages include the 231-seat Fireside Theatre, the 120-seat Playhouse, and the 118-seat Club Theatre. (Greater Twin Cities)

CHILDREN'S THEATRE COMPANY
2400 Third Ave. S.
Minneapolis
612/874-0400
www.childrenstheatre.org
A Minnesota institution since 1965, this company is a thrilling way to introduce young imaginations to the theater world. From its beautiful 746-seat facility on the Minneapolis Institute of Arts campus, CTC's hyper-talented company of children and young-at-heart adults produces winning adaptations of classic children's works (including *The Story of Babar, Strega Nona, How the Grinch*

Act One Photography

Chanhassen Dinner Theatres

Stole Christmas, The Hobbit, Linnea in Monet's Garden, A Wrinkle in Time, The 500 Hats of Bartholomew Cubbins, and dozens more), as well as new productions. The handiwork of CTC's amazing technical departments only add to the magic on stage. (Minneapolis)

CHILD'S PLAY THEATRE COMPANY
1111 Mainstreet
Hopkins
612/979-1111

This company is devoted to works geared toward—and performed by—kids. The repertory is heavy on fairy tales and children's classics but includes a smattering of new works, too. The season runs October through June. (Greater Twin Cities)

GREAT AMERICAN HISTORY THEATRE
30 E. 10th St.
St. Paul
651/292-4323

For nearly 20 years this adventurous company has produced new plays (and revived or adapted classics) that explore varied facets of history. Most productions are staged in the Crawford-Livingston Theatre in downtown St. Paul. The cozy, thrust-style stage was originally intended to be the Guthrie Theater's second stage. (Downtown St. Paul)

GUTHRIE THEATER
725 Vineland Pl.
Minneapolis
612/377-2224

One of the nation's leading repertory theaters, the Guthrie started the regional theater explosion when Sir Tyrone Guthrie opened the 1,400-seat house in 1963. Since then, the venue (now under the leadership of artistic director Joe Dowling, formerly of Dublin's Abbey and Gaeity Theaters) has challenged and enriched audiences with a broad repertory of classical and contemporary works. The Guthrie remains one of the most influential cultural institutions in the state. The season runs June through March. (Minneapolis)

HEY CITY STAGE
824 Hennepin Ave.
Minneapolis
612/333-9202

This theater has been home to the long-running hit *Tony 'n' Tina's Wedding* since its doors opened in 1995. (Downtown Minneapolis)

ILLUSION THEATRE
528 Hennepin Ave.
Minneapolis
612/339-4944

For more than 20 years, this company has concentrated on new plays that address contemporary social, political, and personal issues. Illusion's summertime Fresh Ink series showcases a wide and always interesting variety of works in progress. Most performances take place at Illusion's Hawthorne Theater, located on the eighth floor of Hennepin Center for the Arts. (Downtown Minneapolis)

IN THE HEART OF THE BEAST PUPPET AND MASK THEATRE
1500 E. Lake St.
Minneapolis
612/721-2535
At this wild and wonderful puppet theater you may encounter 10-foot puppets, outrageous masks, and everything in between. The theater's highly original and completely enthralling shows take place in a former neighborhood movie house that was rescued from a sad life as a porn theater. (Minneapolis)

JUNGLE THEATRE
709 W. Lake St.
Minneapolis
612/822-7063
Acclaimed productions of American classics, performed in a tiny theater, are the hallmark of this critics' darling. The close confines only add to the intensity of the goings-on. (Minneapolis)

MIXED BLOOD THEATER
1501 S. Fourth St.
Minneapolis
612/338-6131
Here you'll see high-energy, thoughtful Equity productions of new works by American playwrights in an intimate theater housed in an old firehouse. (Minneapolis)

OLD LOG THEATRE
5175 Meadville St.

Buying Tickets

Event USA—800/745-7328*: This ticket broker specializes in sporting events, concerts, and theater. Expect to pay more (prices vary) than the ticket price, plus a handling fee.*

Ticket Exchange—800/800-9811*: This broker offers a wide range of sporting event, concert, and theater tickets. Expect to pay more than the ticket price, plus a handling fee.*

TicketMaster—612/989-5151*: This agent brokers a huge selection of concerts, sporting events, theater, attractions, and special events. Expect to pay a surcharge of $2 to $5 per ticket and a handling fee of $1 to $1.50 per order.*

Ticket Works—612/870-1099*: Ticket Works features a selection of special events, theater, concert, attractions, and sporting events that carry $1- to $2-per-ticket surcharge but no handling fee.*

Greenwood
612/474-5951
The Twin Cities' oldest professional theater produces a steady roster of crowd-pleasing comedies and dramas in its comfortable home near the shores of Lake Minnetonka. (Greater Twin Cities)

OUTWARD SPIRAL THEATER COMPANY
2531 Johnson St. N.E.
Minneapolis
612/789-7622
Outward Spiral is the Twin Cities' only theater company dedicated to producing works for gay, lesbian, bisexual, and transgender audiences. (Minneapolis)

PARK SQUARE THEATRE
408 St. Peter St.
St. Paul
651/291-7005
A typical Park Square season includes a brash mix of Shakespeare, Molière, Tom Stoppard, and Lanford Wilson, all wonderfully produced and marvelously acted in the compact Seventh Place Theatre. Productions run from January through August. (Downtown St. Paul)

PENUMBRA THEATRE
270 Kent St.
St. Paul
651/224-3180
Led by Lou Bellamy, this troupe is Minnesota's only professional company presenting plays by African American playwrights. Penumbra has a rich history with Pulitzer Prize–winning playwright August Wilson. The theater's holiday show, a critically acclaimed musical adaptation of Langston Hughes' *Black Nativity*, is a December tradition. (St. Paul)

RED EYE COLLABORATIVE
15 W. 14th St.
Minneapolis
612/870-0309
The Red Eye is a laboratory for experimental works by new and emerging playwrights. (Minneapolis)

TEATRO LATINO DE MINNESOTA
3501 Chicago Ave. S.

Old Log Theatre

Old Log Theatre

Minneapolis
651/432-2314
The Teatro's original works by Latino playwrights enliven and share the Latino experience. (Minneapolis)

THEATRE DE LA JEUNE LUNE
105 N. First St.
Minneapolis
612/333-6200
This adventurous company with a fanatical following began in Paris in 1978. While the company used to spend half a year in the City of Light and the other half in the City of Lakes, it has now settled here. Its handsome 500-seat theater is a renovated 1889 warehouse. (Downtown Minneapolis)

THEATRE IN THE ROUND PLAYERS
245 Cedar Ave.
Minneapolis
612/333-3010
This dedicated community theater has been producing comedies, dramas, and classics for more than 40 years. Its arena-style stage is an anchor of the Seven Corners area, near the U of M's West Bank campus. (Minneapolis)

CLASSICAL MUSIC AND OPERA

AMERICAN COMPOSERS FORUM
332 Minnesota St.
St. Paul
651/228-1407
www.composersforum.org
This nationwide organization promotes the musical development of composers through commissions, performances, and recordings. (Downtown St. Paul)

DALE WARLAND SINGERS
120 N. Fourth St.
Minneapolis
612/339-9707
This touring choir of superb vocal musicians offers an extensive annual concert series led by conductor Dale Warland. (Downtown Minneapolis)

EX MACHINA
230 Crestway Ln.
West St. Paul
651/455-8086
The Twin Cities' self-described "antique music company" presents vividly produced and beautifully performed operas (most of them slightly

August Wilson

*Playwright August Wilson (*Seven Guitars, Joe Turner's Come and Gone, Ma Rainey's Black Bottom*) lived in St. Paul for a time during the 1980s, in a big house on Holly Avenue in the city's Cathedral Hill neighborhood, not far from the Penumbra Theatre. Wilson was a regular at Sweeney's Saloon (96 N. Dale St., St. Paul; 651/221-9157), where he would sit at the bar, nurse a drink, chain-smoke, and write.*

Greater Minneapolis CVA

Minnesota Orchestra

obscure) from the Baroque period. (Greater Twin Cities)

MINNESOTA CHORALE
528 Hennepin Ave.
Minneapolis
612/333-4866

This 150-voice choir often performs with the Minnesota Orchestra and the St. Paul Chamber Orchestra. (Downtown Minneapolis)

MINNESOTA OPERA COMPANY
620 N. First St.
Minneapolis
612/333-2700

This ambitious company began in the late 1960s as Center Opera, a musical offshoot of the Walker Art Center. In its first 15 years it produced almost entirely new works, premiering—and in most cases, commissioning—works by renowned composers from around the world, including Dominick Argento, Conrad Susa, Yale Marshall, Harrison Birtwistle, Werner Egk, William Mayer, Hiram Titus, and Eric Stokes. The company shifted focus to a more classically oriented repertory when it moved into the Ordway Music Theater in the mid-1980s. Recent seasons have included productions of *Macbeth, Madame Butterfly, Aida*, and *Pelleas et Melisande*. Tickets are hard to come by. (Downtown Minneapolis)

MINNESOTA ORCHESTRA
1111 Nicollet Mall
Minneapolis
612/371-5656
www.mnorch.org

One of the country's finest, the Minnesota Orchestra has been making great music since 1904. Now under the direction of the youthful Eiji Oue, the orchestra has been guided by some of the most influential conductors of the twentieth century, including Edo de Waart, Sir Neville Marriner, Stanislaw Skrowaczewski, Antol Dorati, Dimitri Mitropoulos, and Eugene Ormandy. The regular season runs September through May, with concerts at Orchestra Hall on Wednesday evening, Friday morning, and Friday evening; the Friday concert is broadcast live on Minnesota

Public Radio station KSJN, 99.5 FM. Its vibrant festival of Viennese music, Sommerfest, is the nation's only inner-city summer music festival staged by a major orchestra, luring summertime crowds and stars to Orchestra Hall for more than 20 years. (Downtown Minneapolis)

PLYMOUTH MUSIC SERIES OF MINNESOTA
1900 Nicollet Ave. S.
Minneapolis
612/870-0943
There is never a dull moment with this much-recorded 30-year-old vocal ensemble. PMS focuses on little-known works in the classical choral repertory as well as new works, most specifically commissioned by the series, led by the indefatigable Grammy Award–winning conductor Philip Brunelle. (Minneapolis)

ST. PAUL CHAMBER ORCHESTRA
75 W. Fifth St.
St. Paul
651/292-3248
The nation's only full-time chamber orchestra is also one of the Twin Cities' most cherished cultural institutions. Currently directed by Hugh Wolff, this remarkable 32-member ensemble offers a nine-month concert season in different Twin Cities venues (including its principal home at the Ordway Music Theater), tours constantly, and records often. Wolff follows in the footsteps of Dennis Russell Davies and Pinchas Zucherman. Christopher Hogwood is the SPCO's principal guest conductor, and Bobby McFerrin is the orchestra's musical advisor and a frequent conductor. The SPCO also attracts a heady list of international guest artists and conductors and commissions new works. (Downtown St. Paul)

SCHUBERT CLUB
75 W. Fifth St.
St. Paul
651/292-3267
This producing organization brings internationally renowned musicians to the Ordway Music Theater stage and sponsors an extensive series of recitals and chamber concerts. The club also operates a fascinating (and free) antique musical instruments museum in the basement of Landmark Center. (Downtown St. Paul)

TWIN CITIES GAY MEN'S CHORUS
528 Hennepin Ave.
Minneapolis
612/891-9130
www:minn.net/~lancesch/tcgmc.html

Son of Guthrie

The Guthrie's second theater, the ***Guthrie Lab****, stages its own season of plays, often highlighting new works by leading or emerging contemporary playwrights. The Lab (612/377-2224), which also features works by other area theater and dance companies, is located at 700 North First Street, in Minneapolis's Warehouse District.*

This all-male, 100-voice ensemble produces four major concerts each year for a wide and enthusiastic audience. (Downtown Minneapolis)

DANCE

BALLET OF THE DOLLS
1629 Hennepin Ave. S.
Minneapolis
612/333-2792

For over a dozen years, the Dolls have been presenting outlandish theater-dance works from the bottomless imagination of choreographer/director Myron Johnson. Its season runs October through June. (Downtown Minneapolis)

JAMES SEWELL BALLET
620 N. First St.
Minneapolis
612/672-0480
www.jsballet.org

A gifted chamber-sized ballet troupe showcases the choreography of James Sewell, a former principal dancer with Feld Ballet/NY. The company regularly collaborates with other area performing arts organizations, including the St. Paul Chamber Orchestra and the Plymouth Music Series of Minnesota. (Downtown Minneapolis)

JAZZDANCE BY DANNY BURACZESKI
528 Hennepin Ave.
Minneapolis
612/824-4851

This immensely talented company is inspired by Danny Buraczeski, one of the nation's leading jazz choreographers. (Downtown Minneapolis)

MARGOLIS/BROWN COMPANY
115 Washington Ave. N.
Minneapolis
612/339-4709

This ambitious, imaginative troupe presents theater-dance works with an edge. (Downtown Minneapolis)

MINNESOTA DANCE THEATRE
528 Hennepin Ave.
Minneapolis
612/338-0627

The company of the late Loyce Houlton, MDT was the leading ballet outfit in the Upper Midwest before it fell on hard times in the late 1980s. It is now enjoying a modest comeback under the direction of Houlton's daughter, Lise, a former soloist with American Ballet Theatre. (Downtown Minneapolis)

ZENON DANCE COMPANY
528 Hennepin Ave.
Minneapolis
612/338-1101

Zenon, the Twin Cities' oldest and most successful modern-dance company, boasts skilled dancers and a large repertory of international works. (Downtown Minneapolis)

ZORONGO FLAMENCO DANCE THEATRE
528 Hennepin Ave.
Minneapolis
612/377-0701

This hot-hot-hot dance theater with a definite Latin flavor features flamenco musicians and dancers from all around the world. (Downtown Minneapolis)

CONCERT VENUES

CEDAR CULTURAL CENTER
416 Cedar Ave.
Minneapolis
612/228-2674

Movies and Music in the Park

One of summer's most popular arts events is the Walker Art Center's (612/375-7600) free Monday night film and music series, which pairs vintage films with cutting-edge local bands. An added attraction to the annual Loring Park series, which runs from late June to early August, is superlative people-watching.

A former movie house, the Cedar is a little rough around the edges. It's now used for a wide variety of folk, rock, jazz, and blues concerts. (Minneapolis)

FITZGERALD THEATRE
10 E. Exchange St.
St. Paul
651/290-1221

The beloved home of Garrison Keillor's *A Prairie Home Companion* (heard on 225 public radio stations every Saturday evening) is a prize of a theater. It opened in 1910 as the Shubert Theater, but by the time it received an extensive renovation in 1986, its moniker was the World Theater. It received its current name in 1994, to honor St. Paul author F. Scott Fitzgerald. The small house (with great acoustics) squeezes 900-plus seats on the main level and two balconies, none very far from the stage. (Downtown St. Paul)

LAKE HARRIET BANDSHELL
W. Lake Harriet Pkwy. at William Berry Pkwy.
Minneapolis
612/661-4800

This enchanting, open-air facility on the shores of Lake Harriet is the fourth such bandshell on the site since 1888. An eclectic mix of music (jazz, rock, folk, and classical), free admission, and usually beautiful skies lure crowds from Memorial Day to Labor Day. Many picnic or stroll around the lake (a three-mile walk) before the music starts. Concerts happen Mon–Sat 7:30, Sun 5:30. The Minneapolis Parks Pops Orchestra, a Lake Harriet tradition for more than 60 years, plays light classical, opera, and Broadway favorites every weekend, from late June through late July. (Minneapolis)

McKNIGHT THEATRE
345 Washington St.
St. Paul
651/224-4222

This small theater, located inside the Ordway Music Theatre, seats 300 people and is noteworthy for its fine sightlines, clear acoustics, and comfortable chairs. (Downtown St. Paul)

NORTHROP AUDITORIUM
84 Church St. S.E.
Minneapolis
651/624-2345
www.cee.umn.edu/northrop

Northrup is the state's largest theater, as well as the largest college-campus auditorium in the country. The big old barn dates from 1929 and seats 4,800.

For more than 50 years, Northrop

hosted a two-week spring engagement of the Metropolitan Opera, and the hall housed the Minneapolis Symphony for more four decades, until Orchestra Hall opened in 1974. But Northrop's acoustics are marginal at best. When a reporter once asked Minneapolis Symphony director Eugene Ormandy how he thought the auditorium's acoustics could be improved, he replied, "dynamite."

Since 1977 it has produced a glittering annual dance series featuring internationally renowned companies. Recent guests have included American Ballet Theatre, Mark Morris Dance Troupe, San Francisco Ballet, Frankfurt Ballet, Miami City Ballet, Paul Taylor Dance Company, Urban Bush Women, Mazowsze, Alvin Ailey American Dance Theater, Joffrey Ballet of Chicago, Feld Ballet/NY, Sankai Juku, and Bale Folclorico da Bahia.

The most coveted seats are in the lower balcony and the main floor center after the 15th row. Parking is available in a heated underground ramp (enter on Pleasant Street), and although most patrons use the campus ramps behind University Avenue, a closer and less crowded alternative is the Coffman Union ramp (enter on East River Road). (Minneapolis)

ORCHESTRA HALL
1111 Nicollet Mall
Minneapolis
612/371-5656

This acoustical marvel was built in 1974 to meet the needs of the Minnesota Orchestra. The hall's permanent musical shell is a departure from the traditional proscenium arch, and the design has only enhanced the quality of this superb, 2,400-seat concert hall. The auditorium itself is especially attractive, with its animated ceiling of large plaster cubes and warm rose and periwinkle tones. (Downtown Minneapolis)

ORDWAY MUSIC THEATER
345 Washington St.
St. Paul
651/224-4222
www.ordway.org

The crown jewel of downtown St. Paul is a center of cultural life in the capital city. This elegant horseshoe-shaped opera house is the principal home of the St. Paul Chamber Orchestra, Minnesota Opera, and Schubert Club. It also manages to squeeze in a heady schedule of touring productions as well as its own inter-

On the Radio

Minnesota Public Radio's classical music station, ***KSJN*** *(99.5 FM, 612/290-1212), features regularly scheduled concerts by the St. Paul Chamber Orchestra and the Minnesota Orchestra, plus programs from a variety of other local music-makers, including the Plymouth Music Series of Minnesota, the Dale Warland Singers, the Schubert Club, and the American Composers Forum.*

St. Paul CVB/Tom Steinberg

Ordway Music Theater, p. 177

nationally flavored dance and music series, Planet Ordway. The theater seats 2,000 for classical music and 1,800 for opera. The best seats are in the upper reaches of the orchestra, the center mezzanine, and the center balconies. Steer clear of the boxes; although they afford lots of leg room, the sightlines can be iffy. (Downtown St. Paul)

ORPHEUM THEATRE
910 Hennepin Ave.
Minneapolis
612/339-7007
Once one of the largest stops on the nation's vaudeville circuit, the Orpheum was restored to its glory days in 1994, to the tune of $10.5 million. This 2,700-seat palace now features a constant stream of Broadway musicals (including world premieres of *Victor/Victoria* and *The Lion King*), concerts, and events. (Downtown Minneapolis)

O'SHAUGHNESSY AUDITORIUM
2004 Randolph Ave.
St. Paul
651/690-6700
This intimate, 650-seat theater (with excellent sightlines, due in part to the hall's continental seating arrangement) can be converted to a larger, 1,800-seat hall simply by raising the ceiling and opening the 1,150-seat balcony. Located on the pretty campus of the College of St. Catherine, O'Shaughnessy produces an exciting fall and spring series showcasing the talents of the area's top dance companies. (St. Paul)

SOUTHERN THEATER
1420 Washington Ave. S.
Minneapolis
612/340-1725
A flexible, intimate Seven Corners performance space near the U of M's West Bank campus, the Southern Theater is the favorite venue of a wide variety of theater and dance companies, musicians, and cabaret artists. (Minneapolis)

STATE THEATRE
805 Hennepin Ave.
Minneapolis

612/339-7007

After an $8.8 million renovation in 1991, this restored 1921 vaudeville house of infectious charm and wit is now dressed up for touring Broadway shows, concerts, lectures, and meetings. The theater seats 2,176. (Downtown Minneapolis)

TARGET CENTER
600 First Ave. N.
Minneapolis
612/673-0900
612/673-1688 TDD

Target Center is a major venue for touring rock concerts. For an arena, the acoustics aren't bad, and most of the modern center's 18,200 extra-wide seats provide fairly decent sightlines. Several thousand parking spots (connected by skyway) are within walking distance, and the neighborhood's many restaurants, bars, and clubs offer pre- and post-concert fun. (Downtown Minneapolis)

TED MANN CONCERT HALL
University of Minnesota
2128 S. Fourth St.
Minneapolis
612/626-1892

The concert hall and opera house on the school's West Bank campus opened in 1994 and was named after its primary benefactor, the movie theater mogul. The auditorium, although spartan, has excellent acoustics and wonderful sightlines; it works particularly well for choral concerts. The big lobby offers a panoramic view of the Mississippi River. (Minneapolis)

Fine Line Music Cafe

12
NIGHTLIFE

While it may lack the buzz of Chicago, New York, or Los Angeles, the Twin Cities' nightlife scene isn't without its assets. Jazz and blues are big here, and a number of clubs—particularly First Avenue and the Fine Line Music Café—not only spotlight local artists, but also manage to lure the best talent in the country. The local music scene has also produced a number of nationally prominent acts, including The Replacements, Hüsker Dü, Lipps Inc., and the Artist Formerly Known As Prince.

Much of local nightlife is concentrated in downtown Minneapolis, although clubs, bars, and music venues of note are scattered throughout the metropolitan area. Out-of-state visitors may be surprised to learn that things end early in puritanical Minnesota: Bars must stop serving liquor at 1 a.m., although they can remain open until 3 a.m. A few do. One pleasant surprise is that Twin Citians loathe paying a cover charge, so very few establishments collect dollars at the door. When they do, the fee rarely exceeds $10 and is usually under $5.

DANCE CLUBS

CLUB METRO
733 Pierce Butler Route
St. Paul
651/489-0002
This is one of the Twin Cities' most popular gay and lesbian clubs, with two huge dance floors, a game room, and a number of smaller rooms for conversation, all set in a former indoor-volleyball sports bar. Friday and Saturday evenings draw especially large crowds. (St. Paul)

FIRST AVENUE
701 First Ave. N.
Minneapolis
612/332-1775
The city's biggest nightclub is famous

for its role in *Purple Rain*, the movie that put the Artist Formerly Known As Prince (and the Minneapolis Sound) on the map. Today the Avenue still books the very best on the contemporary music touring circuit, and practically everyone in the business has played here at one point in their careers. Housed in a former Greyhound bus station, the place is big enough to please even the most persnickety of club kids, and on weekend nights the massive crowds can be a little daunting. Inside the Avenue is Seventh Street Entry, a claustrophobic place to hear the cream of the up-and-coming local and national music scene. (Downtown Minneapolis)

GAY 90'S
408 Hennepin Ave.
Minneapolis
612/333-7755
More of a shopping mall than a nightclub, the state's largest gay bar literally offers something for everyone, including heterosexuals, who come for the excellent dance music and the extremely popular (and free) drag show at the La Femme Show Lounge on the second floor. The 90's has nine different bars, including two discos, plus male strippers, a supper club, coffee shop, game room, and leather bar. Friday and Saturday nights are almost obnoxiously packed. (Downtown Minneapolis)

GROUND ZERO
15 N.E. Fourth St.
Minneapolis
612/378-5115
Just across the Mississippi River from downtown Minneapolis, this large club offers a different musical theme every night, including its infamous Bondage A Go-Go, a leather-and-latex evening, every Thursday. (Minneapolis)

O'GARA'S GARAGE
164 N. Snelling Ave.
St. Paul
651/644-3333
Local blues, rock, jazz, and progres-

Luck Be a Lady Tonight

Native American–owned casinos are a booming business in Minnesota, and a number of showy facilities lie within two hours of the Twin Cities. ***Mystic Lake Casino*** *(2400 Mystic Lake Blvd., Prior Lake; 612/445-9000 or 800/262-7700; www.mysticlake.com) is the state's largest and most lavish, conveniently located a half-hour southwest of downtown Minneapolis.*

Other gaming options include ***Grand Casino Hinckley*** *(I-35 at Hwy. 48, Hinckley; 800/472-6321; www.grandcasinos.com/mn) and* ***Treasure Island Casino*** *(5734 Sturgeon Lake Rd., Welch; 800/222-7077; www.treasureislandcasino.com).*

sive music are presented nightly at this venue next door to O'Gara's, a restaurant/bar popular with college students and twentysomethings. (St. Paul)

QUEST
110 N. Fifth St.
Minneapolis
651/338-3383
This high-style club was formerly Glam Slam, a sometimes-hangout for the Artist Formerly Known As Prince. It's still a great place to dance to the latest live and recorded music as well as a prime spot in which to see and be seen. (Downtown Minneapolis)

THE SALOON
830 Hennepin Ave.
Minneapolis
612/332-0835
A younger gay crowd congregates at the Saloon. They come for the good-looking clientele as well as what many consider the best DJs in town. (Downtown Minneapolis)

SOUTH BEACH
325 First Ave. N.
Minneapolis
612/204-0790
A club with a south Florida theme and plenty of attitude (surly bouncers-slash-doormen, a strictly enforced dress code in the land of 10,000 Dockers). Several bars, a dance floor, and a restaurant share a single roof. The motif, including everything from salsa to disco, changes nightly. (Downtown Minneapolis)

TROPIX BEACH CLUB
400 Third Ave. N.
Minneapolis
612/333-1006
If you're young, uninhibited, and looking for a no-holds-barred night on the town, consider Tropix, which packs in a rowdy, post-college crowd for heavy drinking, dancing, and pickups. Cover varies. (Downtown Minneapolis)

Jeff Johnson—The Dakota

The Dakota

MUSIC CLUBS

Jazz

CAFE LUXX
1101 LaSalle Ave.
Minneapolis
612/332-6800
Enjoy great live jazz in a charming café setting just inside the lobby of the Doubletree Hotel, a half-block from Orchestra Hall. (Downtown Minneapolis)

THE DAKOTA
1021 E. Bandana Blvd.
St. Paul
651/642-1442
The Twin Cities' premier jazz club, staging a heady combination of local and national acts, is set in a renovated railroad switching house. You'll

enjoy excellent food and a wonderful summertime patio. (St. Paul)

THE TIMES BAR AND CAFE
1036 Nicollet Mall
Minneapolis
612/333-2762
Dark, clubby, and grown up, this Nicollet Mall fixture (kitty-corner from Orchestra Hall) features live music every night, interesting food, and welcoming surroundings. (Downtown Minneapolis)

Blues

BLUES SALOON
601 Western Ave.
St. Paul
651/228-9959
You'll hear local and national blues acts in a crowded, snug setting every Thursday through Monday night. The Blues Saloon Maniacs' Open Jam takes the stage every Monday night. (St. Paul)

BUNKER'S MUSIC BAR & GRILL
761 Washington Ave. N.
Minneapolis
612/338-8188
Live blues, R&B, and funk are the hallmarks of this cramped and always-crowded hangout, located off the Warehouse District beaten path about seven blocks north of Hennepin Avenue. (Downtown Minneapolis)

FAMOUS DAVE'S BLUES & BBQ
3001 Hennepin Ave. S.
Minneapolis
612/822-9900
The Famous Dave's franchise blew into Uptown's Calhoun Square a few years ago, with crowd-pleasing results. The barbecue is the same as Dave's other outlets (so-so), but this huge operation, designed to resemble a 1930s-era El station in downtown Chicago, also offers a full bar and the Blues All-Stars, a kicking 11-player house band. Lots of fun and no cover. (Minneapolis)

Other Clubs

THE CABOOZE
917 Cedar Ave.
Minneapolis
612/338-6425
This is one of the Twin Cities' top live music venues, with a nightly double bill of rock, blues, progressive, or reggae. A devoted crowd enjoys the big dance floor. (Minneapolis)

FINE LINE MUSIC CAFE
318 First Ave. N.
Minneapolis
612/338-8100
An engaging blend of local and national folk, rock, blues, jazz, and gospel acts play this concert hall/restaurant/bar. The Fine Line's sightlines and acoustics are excellent, and while the food's nothing special, it's not bad, either. The Sunday gospel brunch is a blast. (Downtown Minneapolis)

RIVERVIEW SUPPER CLUB
2319 N. West River Rd.
Minneapolis
612/521-7676
National and local jazz, blues, and funk artists bring this spendy and predominantly African American club alive seven nights a week. (Minneapolis)

Country and Western

MEDINA ENTERTAINMENT CENTER
500 Hwy. 55

The Cabooze, p. 183

Medina
612/478-6661
Located about 30 minutes west of downtown Minneapolis, this enormous facility (which started life as a ballroom) books a surprisingly large number of national country acts. Its second stage hosts big band, swing, rock, and oldies. The center also features a bowling alley and restaurant. (Greater Twin Cities)

PUBS AND BARS

AMERICA'S ORIGINAL SPORTS BAR

Fourth Floor, East Broadway
Mall of America
Bloomington
612/854-5483
What better location for probably the country's largest sports bar than the nation's largest shopping mall? This gargantuan good time has something for everyone, including billiards, video games, a basketball half-court, live music and dancing, countless video monitors, and more bars than you thought possible. Huge crowds. (Greater Twin Cities)

BRYANT LAKE BOWL

810 W. Lake St.
Minneapolis
612/825-3737
An unlikely South Minneapolis hot spot, this neighborhood bowling alley was reinvented in the early 1990s as a hip hangout for young and old alike. You'll find great people-watching, excellent beer and wine selections, good cheap food, and bowling. The adjacent cabaret offers a steady and eclectic diet of reasonably priced comedy, music, performance, and movies. (Minneapolis)

CHAMPP'S

100 N. Sixth St.
Minneapolis
612/335-5050
This huge Butler Square sports bar features a big bar fronting First Avenue, as well as the celebrated summertime bar, wedged into an adjacent alley, which packs in revelers by the

hundreds. Champ's offers a standard sports-bar menu here and at its other locations, in St. Paul, Richfield, Minne-tonka, Burnsville, New Brighton, and Maplewood. (Downtown Minneapolis)

CHANG O'HARA'S BISTRO
498 Selby Ave.
St. Paul
651/290-2338
Jazz, blues, and Latin are the musical draws in this renovated fire station, which boasts a snug bar, a spacious dining room, and a charming and secluded garden. (St. Paul)

CITY BILLIARDS
25 N. Fourth St.
Minneapolis
612/338-2255
Eight Ball never looked so good as in this upscale billiards hall, which also serves a light lunch, dinner, and late-night menu, as well as a full bar. (Downtown Minneapolis)

ELI'S BAR & GRILL
1225 Hennepin Ave.
Minneapolis
612/332-9997
Downtown's best kept culinary secret, this long and narrow boîte—housed on the first floor of a nineteenth-century apartment house—provides surprisingly inventive lunch and dinner fare. The atmosphere is genuinely friendly, and the bar is great. (Downtown Minneapolis)

FREIGHT HOUSE
305 S. Water St.
Stillwater
651/439-5718
Of all the bars and clubs in pretty Stillwater, this one draws the largest crowds. Inside you'll find a restaurant, several bars, a huge outdoor deck, and a large nightclub with a sizeable dance floor. (Greater Twin Cities)

GLUEK'S RESTAURANT
16 N. Sixth St.
Minneapolis
612/338-6621
The only place in town to get a tall, cold mug of Gluek's beer on tap, this quasi-German beer hall also serves a vaguely Teutonic menu. The crowd is young, loud, and fun-loving. (Downtown Minneapolis)

IVORIES
605 N. Hwy. 169
Plymouth
612/591-6188
The piano bar to end all piano bars, Ivories also serves lunch, dinner, and a champagne Sunday brunch. (Greater Twin Cities)

JOHNNY'S BAR
2251 W. University Ave.
St. Paul
612/645-4116
Don't let the dreary exterior fool you. A center for this emerging area of artists and artisans, Johnny's offers up a huge selection of beers and a friendly, congenial atmosphere. (St. Paul)

LINGUINE & BOB
100 N. Sixth St.
Minneapolis
612/332-1600
The handsome bar of this D'Amico brothers' Butler Square restaurant screams Pottery Barn, but it's a comfortable place to enjoy a glass of wine or a drink before setting out for the Warehouse District's more animated watering holes. The bar in D'Amico Cucina (L&B's expensive downstairs sibling, 612/338-2401) can

Wine Bars

A number of wine bars have sprouted up across the Twin Cities in the past few years. The most pleasant options include:
Bobino *(222 E. Hennepin Ave., Minneapolis; 612/623-3301)*
Bev's Wine Bar *(250 N. Third St., Minneapolis; 612/337-0102)*
Giorgio's Wine Bar *(1601 W. Lake St., Minneapolis; 612/822-7071)*
Jitters Café *(1026 Nicollet Mall, Minneapolis; 612/338-8511)*
Lucia's Wine Bar *(1432 W. 32nd St., Minneapolis; 612/823-7125)*
New French Bar *(128 N. Fourth St., Minneapolis; 612/338-3790)*
The Vintage *(579 Selby Ave., St. Paul; 651/222-7000)*

be a quieter alternative to the Warehouse District/Target Center hubbub. (Downtown Minneapolis)

LOON CAFE
500 First Ave. N.
Minneapolis
612/332-8342
The city's first downtown sports bar still packs 'em in before, during, and after Metrodome and Target Center games. The throngs come for the clubby atmosphere and stay for the three-alarm chili, burgers, and other delights. Get a seat in one of the tables near the big picture windows and watch the world go by on First Avenue and Fifth Street. (Downtown Minneapolis)

LORD FLETCHER'S ON THE LAKE
3746 Sunset Dr.
Spring Park
612/471-8513
Fletcher's is the center of action on Lake Minnetonka during warm weather. Its labyrinthian dock leads up to an even larger deck, which is mobbed on lazy summer afternoons. Divided into three separate sections, the restaurant is considerably more formal than its outdoor counterparts. (Greater Twin Cities)

THE LORING BAR
1624 Harmon Place
Minneapolis
612/332-1617
The Loring is one of the most interesting places in town for a glass of wine or beer, nibbly things, conversation, and people-watching. The giant windows offer priceless views of Loring Park, the furniture recalls an upscale garage sale, the lighting is romantically dim, and the service can be politely described as haughty. Live music nightly. (Downtown Minneapolis)

THE LOUNGE
411 Second Ave. N.
Minneapolis
612/333-8800
Another quiet respite from the loud downtown bar scene, this collection of small rooms is furnished with plush, comfy sofas and chairs de-

signed to encourage conversation and mingling over food and drink. The mid-30s crowd is up, prosperous, heterosexual, and on-the-make. (Downtown Minneapolis)

LYLE'S BAR & RESTAURANT
2021 Hennepin Ave.
Minneapolis
612/870-8183

A South Minneapolis landmark for decades, this dark and smoky neighborhood hangout draws a diverse crowd for drinks, chatter, games, and terrific burgers. (Minneapolis)

MANCINI'S CHAR HOUSE
531 W. Seventh St.
St. Paul
651/224-7345

This see-it-to-believe-it blend of Las Vegas show lounge and Minn-ee-soh-tah supper club has a large bar that draws one of the Twin Cities' most unlikely cross sections of people. Live music includes an inevitable polka band or two. (St. Paul)

NIKKI'S BAR AND CAFE
107 Third Ave. N.
Minneapolis
612/340-9098

Here you'll enjoy piano and vocals in a cluttered setting. The kitchen does nice pastas and pizzas, and the large outdoor garden is a frequent summertime destination. (Downtown Minneapolis)

NYE'S PIANO BAR
112 Hennepin Ave. E.
Minneapolis
612/379-2021

Lovely Lou Snider holds court at her organ six nights a week—as she has for more than a quarter-century—at this singalong bar, drawing one of the most varied clienteles in the Twin Cities. (Minneapolis)

OLD CHICAGO
508 First Ave. N.
Minneapolis
612/338-8686

Another entry in the sports bar wars, this chain draws the crowds for its burger/pasta/pizza routine, zillions of beer varieties, and large span of billiard tables. Other locations include Uptown Minneapolis and Eagan. (Downtown Minneapolis)

ROCK BOTTOM BREWERY
825 Hennepin Ave.
Minneapolis
612/332-2739

A branch of a Colorado-based chain, this is the city's most ambitious brewpub, and the suds aren't bad. The atmosphere is rather cookie-cutterish and the food won't win any awards, but that doesn't keep a good-looking yuppie crowd from mobbing the place. (Downtown Minneapolis)

ROSEN'S BAR & GRILL
430 First Ave. N.
Minneapolis
612/338-1926

A popular sports bar owned by Mark Rosen, sports anchor for the local CBS affiliate, this place is known for its big friendly crowds, decent food, and proximity (two blocks) to Target Center. (Downtown Minneapolis)

RUNYON'S
107 Washington Ave. N.
Minneapolis
612/332-7158

Still a draw for the post-college, first-job crowd after more than a decade, Runyon's makes a wicked buffalo chicken wing, and the long, narrow bar and attractive surroundings are

Kevin Laukkonen

William's Uptown Pub & Peanut Bar

designed to make meeting strangers easy. (Downtown Minneapolis)

SHERLOCK'S HOME
11000 Red Circle Dr.
Minnetonka
612/931-0203
The Twin Cities' first brewpub cranks out a number of excellent beers—just don't order any food. The atmosphere is that of an English pub, which should come as no mystery, given its name. (Greater Twin Cities)

URBAN WILDLIFE BAR & GRILL
331 Second Ave. N.
Minneapolis
612/339-4665
By day, this corner bar serves up a mean burger and fries to local office workers. By night, the Lowlife is often packed cheek-to-cheek with good-looking, predominantly single twentysomethings. (Downtown Minneapolis)

WILLIAM'S UPTOWN PUB & PEANUT BAR
2911 Hennepin Ave.
Minneapolis
612/823-6271
William's ground-floor restaurant has been an Uptown fixture for years. The downstairs peanut bar and its countless beers by the bottle draw a fairly young crowd. (Downtown Minneapolis)

COMEDY CLUBS

ACME COMEDY COMPANY
708 N. First St.
Minneapolis
612/338-6393
In the 1980s, when stand-up comedy was king, it seemed like clubs popped up on every available corner. Acme is one of the few remaining comedy rooms in the Twin Cities from that era, and with good reason: It books an entertaining mix of local and national acts and offers a series of dinner packages with Sticks, the restaurant next door. (Downtown Minneapolis)

KNUCKLEHEADS
Fourth Floor, East Broadway

Mall of America
Bloomington
612/854-5233
The premier Twin Cities comedy club draws from a national roster of comedians. Its spacious surroundings and animated crowds make for a fun night out. (Greater Twin Cities)

MOVIE HOUSES OF NOTE

More than 350 screens in 64 theaters fill the seven-county metropolitan area, but unfortunately, few of the screens are exceptionally large, and the majority are located in characterless suburban shoebox multiplexes. However, a number of distinctive and comfortable places to enjoy a good movie or two still exist.

ASIAN MEDIA ACCESS
3028 Oregon Ave. S.
Minneapolis
612/349-2549
This nonprofit group imports a heady roster of the latest in Asian cinema, as well as little-known films and classics. Most screenings take place at the delightful Riverview Theater. (Minneapolis)

THE CINEMA CAFE
1925 Burnsville Pkwy.
Burnsville
612/894-8810
This suburban operation combines dining with moviegoing. All seats are $2.50, most movies are rated G, beer and wine are served, and while the food isn't exactly haute cuisine, it's not bad. Other locations at 2749 Winnetka Ave. N., New Hope; 612/546-2336, and at Valley Creek Mall, Woodbury; 651/714-5500. (Greater Twin Cities)

GENERAL CINEMA
MALL OF AMERICA 14
Mall of America
Bloomington
612/546-5700
Among multiplexes, the biggest screens, cleanest facilities, and best film picks belong to this huge

Movie Stadiums

The latest craze in movie theaters—steep, stadium-style seating—has hit the Twin Cities. A number of newer suburban cineplexes offer the sightline-friendly feature, including ***Chanhassen Cinema*** *(570 Pauly Dr., Chanhassen; 612/974-1000),* ***Hastings Theatre*** *(1325 S. Hwy. 55, Hastings; 651/438-9700), Lakeville Theatre (County Road 70 and I-35, 612/777-3456, ext. 539),* ***Plymouth Cinema 12*** *(3400 Vicksburg Ln., Plymouth; 612/551-0000),* ***Coon Rapids Showplace 16*** *(Hwy. 10 at Foley Blvd., Coon Rapids; 651/757-6608), and* ***Inver Grove Showplace 16*** *(Hwy. 52 at Upper 55 St., Inver Grove Heights; 651/453-1016).*

For movie information, call 777-FILM. For mini–film reviews, call The Line (612/222-1000 ext. 4800), the audio service of the *St. Paul Pioneer Press.*

complex. The runner-up is Centennial Lakes Cinema 8 (7311 France Ave. S., Edina; 612/546-5700), just a few blocks south of Southdale. (Greater Twin Cities)

LAGOON CINEMA
1320 Lagoon Ave.
Minneapolis
612/825-6006
After a week's run on the big screen at the Uptown, most flicks move down the street to the popular Lagoon Cinema, a comfortable five-screen multiplex devoted to small art-house movies. Both theaters offer a money-saving discount card, with five admissions for $25. (Minneapolis)

OAK STREET CINEMA
309 Oak St. S.E.
Minneapolis
612/331-3134
Oak Street is the Twin Cities' sole revival house. Located near the U of M, this enterprising operation screens an astonishing range of films, and the marquee often changes daily. (Minneapolis)

PARKWAY THEATRE
4814 Chicago Ave. S.
Minneapolis
612/822-3030
A bit of a dump, this low-key neighborhood theater features a quirky selection of titles, cheap popcorn, and low-low admission prices. (Minneapolis)

RIVERVIEW THEATER
3800 42nd Ave. S.
Minneapolis
612/729-7369
The Riv hasn't changed one iota since it opened in 1948. The space-age lobby predates the Jetsons (be sure to check out the bathrooms), and the vast auditorium and its wide screen remain intact. Movies are generally a few months old, and all seats are $1.75. The bargains continue at the refreshment counter. (Minneapolis)

ROSEVILLE 4 THEATRES
1211 Larpenteur Ave. W.
Roseville
651/488-4242
If a comfortable seat is all that matters, then park it at this small multiplex. The plush seats cost merely $2 per ticket. (Greater Twin Cities)

SKYWAY 6 THEATRES
711 Hennepin Ave.
Minneapolis
612/333-6100
The main auditorium here shows Hollywood's biggest blockbusters on the Twin Cities' largest movie screen. Unfortunately, this tired 1970s multiplex cries out for a renovation or, at the very least, a good hosing down. (Downtown Minneapolis)

SUBURBAN WORLD THEATRE
3022 Hennepin Ave. S.

Bargain and Drive-In Theaters

*At the bargain theaters, seats cost a buck or two, and the films aren't new but haven't yet jumped to video. The pick of the litter includes the six-screen **Apple Valley Theatres** (7200 W. 147th St., Apple Valley; 612/432-1199), **Hopkins Cinema 6** (1118 Main St., Hopkins; 612/931-7992), **Plaza Maplewood** (1847 Larpenteur Ave., Maplewood; 651/770-7969), and the **Excelsior Dock 1, 2 and 3** (26 Water St., Excelsior; 612/474-6275).*

*Although they are definitely a dying breed, a few drive-ins remain on the outskirts of the Twin Cities. They include the **65-Hi** (10100 Central Ave. N.E., Blaine; 612/780-3063), about 25 minutes north of downtown Minneapolis; the **Cottage View** (9338 S.E. East Point Douglas Rd., Cottage Grove; 651/458-5965), about 20 minutes southeast of downtown St. Paul; and the **Vali-Hi** (11260 Hudson Blvd., Lake Elmo; 651/436-7464), about 20 minutes east of downtown St. Paul.*

Minneapolis
612/825-6688
If you like a little atmosphere with your popcorn, catch a show at the Sub World. The ceiling twinkles with stars, and the interior is done up like a Moorish palace. It has good sightlines, too, particularly from the loges. (Minneapolis)

U FILM SOCIETY
10 Church St. S.E.
Minneapolis
612/627-4430
The fiefdom of director Al Milgrom for more than a quarter-century, U Film shows every kind of foreign, little-known, and fascinating film and hosts both the annual Rivertown Film Festival and the Twin Cities Gay, Lesbian, Bisexual and Transgender Film Festival. Screenings take place in a somewhat uncomfortable lecture hall in Nicholson Hall (10 Pleasant St. S.E.) and at U Film's main venue in the roomy, recently renovated Museum of Natural History auditorium. (Minneapolis)

UPTOWN THEATER
2906 Hennepin Ave. S.
Minneapolis
612/825-6006
The Twin Cities' best single-screen theater and an Uptown anchor, this 1930s treasure has a large auditorium complete with a cozy balcony—the only one left in the Twin Cities—perfect for necking. It serves up a steady diet of indie films. (Minneapolis)

Minnesota Office of Tourism

13

DAY TRIPS FROM THE TWIN CITIES

DAY TRIP: Duluth

Distance from the Twin Cities: 150 miles

The city on the lake is also Minnesota's window to the world. When the St. Lawrence Seaway opened in the late 1950s, Duluth's harbor (the world's largest freshwater port) became a destination for ocean vessels. Large boats still crowd the city's docks from April until October.

Nearly 100,000 people call this rugged and very hilly city home, and a visit here can be a pleasant diversion in any season. One of the best views of Duluth is from I-35, at the spot where it begins its downhill journey into the city. All of the harbor, the St. Louis River, and the city lie below. Look for the wayside rest operated by the state highway department; it offers a great vantage point for some of the state's most thrilling scenery. For a self-guided orientation of the vertiginous city, take a spin on **Skyline Parkway**, a winding hilltop drive providing breathtaking views of the lake, harbor, and surrounding areas.

The city's **Spirit Mountain** recreational area (218/628-2891) offers great alpine and Nordic skiing in winter and camping and hiking in summer—just 10 minutes from downtown Duluth. When the weather's warm, everyone heads down to the lakefront, much of which has been handsomely redesigned for recreational uses.

You can learn about the history of Lake Superior shipping at the fascinating **Canal Park Marine Museum** (Canal Park, Duluth; 218/727-2497). To find out when to expect a big ship, call the **Boatwatcher's Hotline**, 218/722-6489. No visit to Duluth is complete without a pilgrimage to the

TWIN CITIES REGION

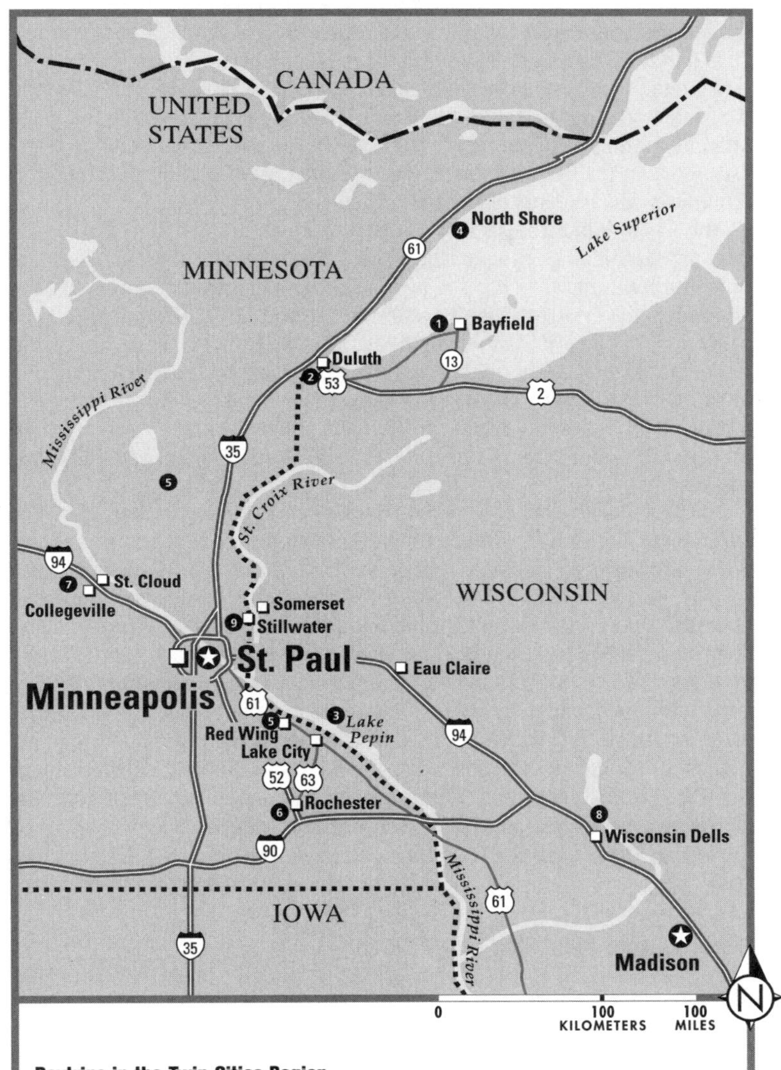

Daytrips in the Twin Cities Region

1 Bayfield, Wisconsin
2 Duluth
3 Lake Pepin Area
4 The North Shore
5 River Tubing Areas
6 Rochester
7 St. John's Abbey and University
8 Seth Petersen Cottage
9 Stillwater

Aerial Bridge, which spans the canal connecting harbor to lake. The 1905 landmark is one of only two of its kind in the world, and it's a treat to watch the 300-foot roadway fly up the bridge's towers, making the 50-foot journey in less than 15 seconds.

Another highlight is the ***William A. Irvin*** (218/722-6218). This 600-foot U.S. Steel ore carrier sailed the Great Lakes from 1938 to 1978. It's now open for 60-minute guided tours from May through October at its mooring just opposite the Duluth Entertainment Center near Canal Park ($6 adults, $5 seniors and students, $3.50 ages 3–12).

The Canal Park area, where Minnesota Point juts out from the shoreline, offers stunning views of the harbor, the lake, and the city itself. Its renovated warehouses are full of shops and restaurants. The neighborhood's big player is **Grandma's Saloon and Grill** (522 S. Lake Ave., 218/727-4192), a sprawling, constantly mobbed joint. Grandma's hosts the state's largest marathon every June. From Canal Park, take a quick stroll up the **Lake Walk** to **Fitger's Brewery** (600 E. Superior St.), which was transformed in the 1980s into a festival shopping center with interesting stores, a brewpub bearing the Fitger's name (218/726-1392), and the very fine Fitger's Inn.

Another Duluth attraction is the **Depot** (506 W. Michigan Ave., 218/727-8025), a restored 1892 railroad station that now houses arts organizations and a popular train museum. And be sure to visit stately **Glensheen** (3300 London Rd., Duluth; 218/724-8864), a 39-room mansion of lush Jacobean splendor. Built on the shores of Lake Superior in 1908 for the Congdon family, this opulent home owned by the University of Minnesota is open for public tours. If you're staying overnight, book a room at **Fitger's Inn** (218/722-8826) and ask for a lake view; **The Mansion** (3600 London Rd., 218/724-0739), a bed-and-breakfast housed in another Congdon-built mansion next door to Glensheen; or the city's largest hotel, the **Radisson Duluth** (505 W. Superior St., 218/727-8971), a round 1970s curiosity just down the street from the city's fine Beaux Arts enclave of government buildings.

Getting There from the Twin Cities: *Take I-35 north.*

DAY TRIP: The North Shore

Distance from the Twin Cities: 150 to 300 miles

The Lake Superior coastline stretches for 150 exceedingly scenic miles to the U.S.-Canadian border, and its sightseeing and recreational opportunities are boundless. The vistas are unlike anything else in Minnesota: craggy cliffs, deep forests, low-lying mountain ranges, and pounding waves. Highway 61 journeys all the way north from Duluth to Grand Portage, the North Shore's final Minnesota town.

The best scenery begins 12 miles north of Two Harbors, a small town about 45 minutes north of Duluth. That's where you'll find **Gooseberry Falls State Park** (218/834-3855), one of Minnesota's most visited state parks. It offers breathtaking scenery, hiking, picnicking, and camping (call 800/246-CAMP to reserve one of the park's 70 sites).

Eight miles to the north, the Minnesota Historical Society operates **Split Rock Lighthouse** (218/226-6372), a turn-of-the-century landmark perched atop a sheer 100-foot cliff with awesome lake views. May–Oct daily 9–5. $4 adults, $3 seniors, $2 ages 6–16.

Lutsen (about 25 minutes north of Two Harbors, 218/663-7212), attracts hordes of wintertime weekenders to its challenging lake-view ski slopes and gorgeous wood-timbered lodge and cabins. Although Lutsen's condos are comfortable, they're charmless; request a room in the lodge, which was built in the late 1940s. If you can't snare a room at Lutsen, try **Bluefin Bay** in nearby Tofte (218/663-7296), about 10 minutes south. The facilities are modern, and many of the condos open directly onto the lake.

Continue north on Highway 61 to pretty Grand Marais, one of the oldest fur trading settlements on the lake. Fifteen miles past the city on the shores of Lake Superior is **Naniboujou Lodge** (218/387-2688 or ourworld.compuserve.com/homepages/naniboujou), a splendiferous 1929 hunting club that has to be seen to be believed. The main dining hall is a whirlwind of color, the handiwork of Canadian artist Antoine Goufee. Shaped like an upside-down canoe, every surface of the room is awash in stylized abstractions of Cree characters. The lodge is open May through October and some weekends in winter. Some rooms have fireplaces, all have private baths ($65 to $75 per night).

Thirty-five miles north of Grand Marais is Grand Portage, site of the **Grand Portage National Monument** (218/387-2788), a late-seventeenth-century fort and fur trading post that's definitely worth a visit.

Split Rock Lighthouse

Phyllis Kedl/Unicorn Stock Photos

Northeastern Minnesota is also home to several major recreational areas, including the pristine **Boundary Waters Canoe Area**, **Voyageurs National Park**, and **Superior National Forest**, all of which contain hundreds of thousands of acres of virgin forest, several thousand (yes, thousand) crystal-clear lakes, and wilderness lands of unspoiled beauty. The town of **Ely** is a major stopping point for all three. From Duluth, take Highway 61 northeast just past Silver Bay, then continue northwest, away from the lake, on Highway 1.

Getting There from the Twin Cities: *Take I-35 north to Duluth, then take Highway 61.*

Minnesota Office of Tourism

Lake Superior

DAY TRIP: Bayfield, Wisconsin

Distance from the Twin Cities: 250 miles

The southern coast of Lake Superior is nothing like its rocky, wave-pounded counterpart to the north. From the bustling ports of Duluth and its sister city of Superior, Wisconsin, the southern shore's long stretches of calm, sandy beaches eventually lead to the **Apostle Islands** (a 22-island chain, preserved as a National Lakeshore and run by the National Park Service, 715/779-3397) and the hill-hugging town of Bayfield, about 90 minutes east of Duluth-Superior.

Bayfield was founded in 1856 and thrived until the turn of the century as a fishing, lumber, and mining center. Most of the brownstone used in New York City, Cleveland, and Chicago was mined nearby, and the town boomed until the material went out of fashion.

Bayfield's shops and galleries are quaint without veering too far into cloying, and a few restaurants are worth checking out. Grab a tasty lunch—and save room for the peanut butter–chocolate pie—at **Maggie's** (257 Mannypenny Ave., 715/779-5641). Step back in to the 1940s for genuine roadhouse fare at **Gruenke's** (17 N. First St., 715/779-5480). Ask for the stool where John Kennedy Jr. sat. Or, if you really feel like putting on the dog, have supper or book a room at the **Old Rittenhouse Inn** (301 Rittenhouse Ave., 715/779-5111), a massive, overdecorated Victorian mansion with magical views of the Apostles. Each room has a private bath and a fireplace, and rates run $100 to $200, including breakfast.

During the warm months, rent sailboats and kayaks from Bayfield's Marina, or catch the auto ferry (715/747-2051) for the 20-minute journey to picturesque **Madeline Island**, the largest of the Apostles and home to **La Pointe**. Founded in 1667, it's one of oldest European settlements west of the Hudson River. The island provides a relaxing getaway with a number of lodging possibilities. Pamper yourself at lovely **Woods Manor** (715/779-3102 or 800/822-6315), a seven-room B&B with fabulous views of the lake and Bayfield. Rates run $110 to $190 per night, including breakfast. The **Inn on Madeline Island** (715/747-6315) offers lakeside condos just off the La Pointe marina, an 18-hole golf course, and a fine restaurant. If tenting is more your speed, try the well-maintained campground at scenic **Big Bay State Park** (715/779-3346), about six miles outside of La Pointe. If you prefer a little privacy, more than a dozen cottages and homes scattered across the island are available for rent through the Inn on Madeline Island; call 715/747-6315.

Getting There from the Twin Cities: *Take I-35 north to Duluth, Highway 2 south to Superior, Highway 13 east to Bayfield.*

DAY TRIP: Seth Petersen Cottage

Distance from the Twin Cities: 250 miles

Frank Lloyd Wright aficionados—or those with a romantic streak a mile long—should consider an overnight stay in one of the master architect's little-known treasures: the Seth Peterson Cottage. About the only negative thing that can be said about this late-1950s Wright prize is that it is dangerously close to one of the tackiest tourist traps in the United States, the Wisconsin Dells.

Happily, the nightmare that is the Dells will fly out of your head the minute you lay eyes upon this amazing house, available for overnight stays since a nonprofit group purchased it in 1992 and invested more than $300,000 into a much-needed restoration. Laid out to take advantage of its superb site, high above the woods of Mirror Lake State Park on a secluded ridge overlooking pristine Mirror Lake, the 900-square-foot cottage is designed within an inch of its life, so much so that Wright's son-in-law described it as having "more architecture per square inch than any other Taliesin-designed structure."

Built as a summer retreat for Petersen, the house is packed with details that exemplify a late-career Wright at the peak of his form: a beautifully detailed sandstone and wood exterior that's sheltered by deep overhangs and punctuated by panoramic picture windows, soaring ceilings, smooth flagstone floors, a huge stone fireplace, and cozy rooms flooded with natural light. Both the kitchen and bath have been discreetly modernized, and the coffee table is stocked with plenty of Wright-related reading material.

Although the cottage technically sleeps four, thanks to a queen-size hide-a-bed in the living room, it's a good idea to rent a deux—not only because the cottage is very romantic, but also because access to the sole bathroom is through the bedroom, placing privacy at a premium.

Nabbing a reservation can be exasperating, since weekends are often booked a year in advance and even a plain old Tuesday can be reserved three or four months ahead of time. Rents run $225 per night or $995 per week. Call the Sand County Service Company at 608/254-6551, or write P.O. Box 409, Lake Delton, WI 53940. If you can't stay overnight, the cottage is open for public tours ($2) on the second Sunday of every month from 2 to 5.

The area in and around Madison (about 45 minutes southeast of the cottage) is a treasure trove of Wright architecture. **Taliesen**, Wright's home, school, and farm complex, is in nearby Spring Green, and the bucolic site has a number of extraordinary Wright structures, as well as an excellent bookstore. Guided tours are available from May through October; call 608/588-7900.

For brand-new Wright, check out **Monona Terrace** (608/261-4000), Madison's new $68-million convention center. The beautiful, 80,000-square-foot facility, built on the shores of Lake Monona, is based on a 1938 Wright design. To learn more about Wright sites in and around Madison—or arrange for a self-guided Wrightian tour—contact the Frank Lloyd Wright Heritage Tourism Program at 608/221-4111.

If you get a little peckish during the drive, stop for a slice of pie at the famous **Norske Nook** in Osseo, Wisconsin (about two hours east of St. Paul on I-94). The Nook (207 W. Seventh St., 715/597-3069) bakes at least two dozen varieties daily, and pie this good rarely comes out of a commercial kitchen.

Getting There from the Twin Cities: *Take I-94 south and east to the Wisconsin Dells, then follow the signs to Mirror Lake State Park.*

DAY TRIP: St. John's Abbey and University

Distance from the Twin Cities: 80 miles

The small town of Collegeville is home to the world's largest Benedictine monastery, as well as some eye-popping midcentury architecture. Architect Marcel Brueur crafted an amazing assemblage of buildings at this men's college and preparatory school during the late 1950s and early 1960s. A visit to the 2,500-acre campus should be on the itinerary of any Brueur fan—or anyone searching for a contemplative retreat.

Brueur devised a 100-year plan for the school (the original handsome brick buildings were centered around a European quadrangle) and designed its remarkable science hall and library, plus four dormitories. The campus's biggest jaw-dropper is Brueur's monumental, 2,000-seat **Abbey Church**. Probably the most dramatic building in Minnesota, this 1954 poured-concrete masterpiece is simplicity itself, starting with a sanctuary of sloping walls and cleverly placed windows that give the appearance of supporting the massive concrete ceiling. The thrills continue in the bapistry—flooded with light from an immense stained-glass window—and the adjacent bell tower, an overpowering sculptural slab looming over the church and dominating the entire campus. Mass in this otherworldly place is a transcendent experience.

The **Hill Monastic Manuscript Library** (320/363-3514) is a world-famous scholarly center with an unparalleled collection of early Christian manuscripts, as well as 85,000 volumes of priceless European archival manuscripts on microfilm. On a lighter note, the monks bake a famous loaf of cracked-wheat bread, and you shouldn't leave campus without stocking up or buying a prepackaged kit for your bread machine. Pottery is also big at St. John's, with a very active studio open weekdays; call 320/363-2930.

Guests can take advantage of a number of opportunities to share the quiet life of the Benedictine community, including staying overnight at the monastery. Weekends are often booked months in advance; for reservations, call 320/363-2011.

Getting There from the Twin Cities: *Take I-94 west to Collegeville, about 10 miles past St. Cloud.*

DAY TRIP: Rochester

Distance from the Twin Cities: 90 miles

Life in this company town revolves around the world-famous **Mayo Clinic**. Dr. William Mayo and his sons Will and Charlie helped start St. Mary's Hospital in 1889, and their revolutionary surgical techniques drew patients and other physicians from around the country. In 1914 they founded the Mayo Clinic. Unlike other practitioners of the time, the Mayos offered a wide variety of specialists for promoting total patient care, a widely copied model that the clinic has retained to this day.

Today the clinic is one of the world's most respected health care institutions, as well as home to a prestigious medical school and a giant research unit. More than 700 physicians and 7,000 other medical personnel are on staff. Free tours are available Monday through Friday at 10 a.m. in the Judd Auditorium (200 First St. SW, 507/284-9258).

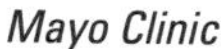

Mayo Clinic

By permission of the Mayo Foundation

Glimpse how the Mayos lived at **Mayowood** (3720 Mayowood Rd. SW, 507/287-8691), their palatial and rather ungainly 1891 mansion. The 57-room house, located on 3,000 acres with commanding views of the Zumbro River Valley, is now owned by the Olmstead County Historical Society. It's open to the public for an interesting one-hour tour. $8 adults, $5 under age 16. Hours vary.

Another magnificent doctor's residence is **Plummer House** (1091

Plummer Ln., 507/281-6160), a 1924 Tudor now owned by the Rochester Parks and Recreation Department. Dr. Henry Plummer joined the Mayo Clinic in 1901 and played a significant role in its development. His house is most noteworthy for its carefully manicured 11-acre gardens, open to the public daily from sunrise to sunset.

The Plummer name is also attached to the clinic's most beloved building, located at Second Street S.W. and Second Avenue S.W. Built in 1928, the **Plummer** is a wedding cake of a tower. Its open belfry houses the **Rochester Carillon**, a 56-bell, 4-octave collection—the largest of its kind in North America. Recitals are regularly scheduled; call 507/284-2511 for details. Look for an image of Dr. Plummer clutching a handful of drawings, carved into the corner of this richly detailed tower.

Pedestrian-friendly downtown Rochester has had quite a renaissance over the past five years, including construction of a fine new public library and a handsome civic center. A pleasant park lies along the Zumbro River. The lodging of choice is the mighty **Kahler Hotel** (20 Second Ave. SW, 507/282-2581), a 1920s grand dame of more than 700 rooms and suites across the street from the Mayo Clinic.

Getting There from the Twin Cities: *Take Highway 52 southeast 90 miles to Rochester.*

DAY TRIP: Lake Pepin Area

Distance from the Twin Cities: 50 miles

One of the Mississippi River's most beguiling charms is Lake Pepin, where the landscape changes from rolling hills to dramatic cliffs, and the Father of Waters widens—at some points up to a mile—for some of the state's most beautiful scenery. This region boasts plenty to see and explore.

Start upriver from the lake, at **Red Wing**, one of the state's great river towns. The city has a charming collection of nineteenth-century commercial buildings, churches, a fine courthouse, and several public squares. Its levee attracts major boating traffic, including periodic visits from the *Delta Queen* (800/543-1949), a luxury paddlewheel passenger boat that plies the Mississippi and Ohio Rivers. The **Sheldon Theatre** (443 W. Third St., 612/385-3667), a 1904 beauty and the nation's first municipal theater, was fully restored in the late 1980s and now lures an impressive roster of musical and theatrical talent.

Lots of antiques stores here accompany a number of pottery outlets, including the famous **Red Wing Pottery Company** (1995 Old W. Main St., 612/388-3562). The city's top hotel is the **St. James** (406 Main St., 612/388-2846); ask for a room in the old section. The best bet for breakfast and lunch is the **Blue Plate Cafe** (416 1/2 W. Third St., 612/388-7573).

You can follow the scenic Cannon River from Red Wing to Cannon Falls via the **Cannon Valley Trail**, (612/388-5984), a 19-mile paved hiking and biking trail. Rent a bike at Ripley's Rental (612/388-5984) in Red Wing or at the

Welch General Store (612/388-7494) in tiny Welch, about midway on the trail. Learn more about Red Wing by contacting the city's Visitor's and Convention Bureau (800/498-3444 or www.redwing.org).

Cross the Mississippi at Red Wing and proceed south on the Wisconsin side (the Minnesota side, Highway 61, is a plain four-lane highway, while the Wisconsin alternative, Highway 35, winds and curves its way over hills on the top of the bluffs). Drive south to Stockholm, home of several antique stores, art galleries, and a good restaurant, the **Star Cafe** (715/442-2023), open April through October.

For another memorable meal, consider lunch or dinner at the **Harbor View Cafe** on the riverbank in nearby **Pepin** (715/442-3893), open May through October. The ambitious and inviting restaurant draws a devoted clientele that endures the no-reservations, no-credit-cards policy. Tiny Pepin (known by *Little House on the Prairie* fans as the home of Laura Ingalls Wilder) also has a number of antiques stores, art galleries, a professional summer theater company (the Pepin Players, 715/442-3109), and a handful of bed-and-breakfasts.

Continue south to Nelson and cross the river to Wabasha, where you'll encounter more small-town delights, including antiques, a bustling marina, and several B&Bs. If it's a hot day, have an ice-cream cone at **The Cooler** (612/565-2585), in the old city hall.

Head back upriver to **Lake City**, which is crawling with boating, swimming, and other lake-related activities. Grab a burger (and a root beer) at the **Root Beer Stand** (805 N. Lake Shore, 612/345-2124). The town is just downriver from **Frontenac State Park** (612/345-3401), a pretty park with panoramic river views, camping, hiking, picnicking, and fishing.

Getting There from the Twin Cities: *Take Highway 61 south to Red Wing, cross the river to Wisconsin Highway 35, and head south to Nelson; cross the river again and head north on Minnesota Highway 61.*

DAY TRIP: Stillwater

Distance from the Twin Cities: 20 miles

Minnesota's oldest city is also one of its most charming. Picturesque Stillwater has been hugging this stretch of the St. Croix River for more than 150 years. Its well-preserved nineteenth-century downtown is a magnet for locals and out-of-towners, who come for the shopping, restaurants, and the state's largest concentration of bed-and-breakfasts (see Chapter 3, Where to Stay). Stillwater can be mobbed on warm weekends (traffic can be a nightmare), so weekdays are the best times to enjoy its quiet pleasures.

Antiques are big business in Stillwater. **The Mill Antiques** (410 N. Main St., 651/430-1818) has 200 dealers on three levels. Ditto the **Isaac Staples Sawmill Complex** (410 N. Main St., 651/430-1816). Others worth a peek include **American Gothic Antiques** (236 S. Main St., 651/439-7709), **Main Street Antiques** (118 N. Main St., 651/430-3110), **Midtown Antique Mall**

(214 S. Main St., 651/430-0808), and **More Antiques** (312 N. Main St., 651/439-1110).

Stillwater is also a town for book lovers. **St. Croix Antiquarian Booksellers** (232 S. Main St., 651/430-0732) has 25 vendors under one roof. Philosophy and theology are the specialties of **Loome Theological Booksellers** (320 N. Fourth St., Stillwater; 651/430-1092).

Downtown Stillwater is crawling with interesting restaurants, including **La Belle Vie** (312 S. Main St., 651/430-3545), **Savories** (108 N. Main St., 651/430-0702), **Harvest Inn and Restaurant** (114 E. Chestnut St., 651/430-8111), and **Orleans** (342 S. Main St., 651/430-9790).

The town is also the gateway to the recreational possibilities of the St. Croix River, and its docks are packed during summer with an amazing array of pleasure craft. The river itself is a federally protected waterway, and much of its sylvan beauty remains intact.

Getting There from the Twin Cities: *Take Highway 36 east from St. Paul. Exit at Highway 95.*

DAY TRIP: River Tubing Areas

Distance from the Twin Cities: Welch, 50 miles; Somerset, 50 miles.
There's no better way to cool off and relax on a humid summer's day than to float down a river on an inner tube. Two places, both about an hour's drive from the Twin Cities, are especially designed for such sun-soaked folly. At **Welch Mill Canoeing and Tubing** (14818 264th St. Path, Welch; 800/657-6760, $5 gets you a large tube, a 15-minute shuttle ride, and a quiet, exceedingly scenic three-hour sojourn down the Cannon River. The river runs through a

Kayaking at Welch Mill

Welch Mill

county park. The surroundings are wooded and unspoiled, and the rolling topography and clean, waist-deep river (complete with gentle rapids) are a treat from the vantage point of a big ol' inner tube. Pack a picnic lunch (rent an additional tube for your cooler) and a ton of sunscreen, and make a day of it for the whole family. The mill also rents canoes at very reasonable rates. Weekends and holidays are naturally the most popular days, but on most weekdays it can feel as if you have the entire valley to yourself. Welch is approximately one hour southeast of the Twin Cities, about 10 minutes west of historic Red Wing. Mon–Fri 10 a.m.–dusk, Sat–Sun 8 a.m.–dusk.

Tubing connoisseurs prefer the Cannon to the shenanigans at the much more established **Float-Rite Park** in Somerset, Wisconsin (715/247-3453 or 800/826-7096). A lot happens here, including camping, miniature golfing, volleyball playing, video arcading, and more. These activities translate into more crowds, more noise, more litter, and less relaxation. What's worse, the decidedly unspectacular **Apple River** lacks the natural beauty of the Cannon. It's also much shallower, meaning that unwanted scrapes are a lot more common. Tube rates are higher, too: $8 on weekends and holidays, $7 during the week.

Getting There from the Twin Cities: *Welch: Take Highway 52 south 25 miles to Highway 50, head east for 15 miles to County Road 7, then 2 miles south to Welch. Somerset: Take Highway 36 east, cross the St. Croix River at Stillwater, then take Highway 64 northeast 25 miles to Somerset, Wisconsin.*

EMERGENCY PHONE NUMBERS

POLICE/FIRE/AMBULANCE
911

ALCOHOL AND DRUG INTERVENTION AND REFERRAL
612/879-3501

CRISIS INTERVENTION CENTER
612/347-3161
612/347-5711 (TTY)

FIRST CALL FOR HELP (UNITED WAY)
612/335-5000

GAY AND LESBIAN HELPLINE
612/822-8661

POISON CENTER
612/347-3141
612/337-7474 (TTY)

SUICIDE PREVENTION
612/347-2222

HOSPITALS

CHILDREN'S HEALTH CARE MINNEAPOLIS
612/813-6100

CHILDREN'S HEALTH CARE ST. PAUL
651/220-6000

FAIRVIEW SOUTHDALE HOSPITAL
612/924-5000

FAIRVIEW-UNIVERSITY MEDICAL CENTER RIVERSIDE CAMPUS
612/672-6000

FAIRVIEW UNIVERSITY MEDICAL CENTER UNIVERSITY CAMPUS
612/626-3000

HENNEPIN COUNTY MEDICAL CENTER
612/347-2121

NORTH MEMORIAL MEDICAL CENTER
612/520-5100

REGIONS MEDICAL CENTER
651/221-3456

UNITED HOSPITAL
651/220-8000

RECORDED INFORMATION

MINNESOTA HIGHWAY CONDITIONS
651/296-3076

ROUND-THE-CLOCK WEATHER UPDATES
612/512-1111

VISITOR INFORMATION

MINNEAPOLIS CONVENTION AND VISITORS ASSOCIATION
612/661-4700
www.minneapolis.org

ST. PAUL CONVENTION AND VISITORS BUREAU
651/297-6985
www.stpaul.gov

BLOOMINGTON CONVENTION AND VISITORS BUREAU
612/858-8500
www.bloomington.org/visit.html

MINNESOTA OFFICE OF TOURISM
800/657-3700
www.explore.state.mn.us

CITY TOURS
Capital City Trolleys
651/223-5600

MEDICINE LAKE/GREY LINES
612/469-5020

METRO CONNECTIONS
612/333-8687

RIVER CITY TROLLEYS
612/673-5123

CAR RENTAL

AVIS
800/831-2847

BUDGET
612/727-2600

ENTERPRISE RENT-A-CAR
800/325-8007

HERTZ
800/654-3131

NATIONAL CAR RENTAL
800/227-7368

RENT-A-WRECK
612/474-6554

THRIFTY CAR RENTAL
800/367-2277

DISABLED ACCESS INFORMATION

ACCESS PROJECT
651/405-2482

COURAGE CENTER
612/520-0520

MULTICULTURAL RESOURCES

CENTRO CULTURAL CHICANO
612/874-1412

GERMANIC AMERICAN INSTITUTE
651/222-7027

MINNEAPOLIS AMERICAN INDIAN CENTER
612/871-4555

SONS OF NORWAY INTERNATIONAL
612/827-3611

VIETNAMESE CULTURAL ASSOCIATION OF MINNESOTA
651/297-5451

BABYSITTING AND CHILD CARE

CLUB KID
612/831-1055

KID'S PLAY
612/566-2114

KID'S QUEST
612/941-1007

SICK CHILD CARE
612/780-6600

NEWSPAPERS

ST. PAUL PIONEER PRESS
651/222-5011
www.pioneerplanet.com

STAR TRIBUNE
612/673-4000
www.startribune.com

CITY PAGES
612/375-1015
www.citypages.com

FAMILY TIMES
612/922-6186

LAVENDER MAGAZINE
612/871-2237
www.lavendermagazine.com

MINNEAPOLIS ST. PAUL CITYBUSINESS
612/288-2100
www.amcity.com/twincities/

MINNESOTA LAW AND POLITICS
612/335-8808
www.lawandpolitics.com

MINNESOTA WOMEN'S PRESS
651/646-6938

SKYWAY NEWS
612/375-9222

TWIN CITIES REVIEW
612/375-9222

MAGAZINES

ARCHITECTURE MINNESOTA
612/338-6763]

CORPORATE REPORT MINNESOTA
651/338-4288

MINNESOTA HISTORY
612/296-6126

MINNESOTA MONTHLY
612/371-5800

MPLS/ST. PAUL
612/339-7571

TWIN CITIES BUSINESS MONTHLY
612/339-7571

RADIO STATIONS

KBEM 88.5 FM, jazz
KMOJ 89.9 FM, soul, jazz, reggae, blues
KFAI 90.3 FM, community-based alternative
KNOW 91.1 FM, Minnesota Public Radio news/talk
KQRS 92.5 FM, rock
KEGE 93.7 FM, modern rock
KSTP 94.5 FM, contemporary pop
KNOF 95.3 FM, religious
KTCZ 97.1 FM, progressive rock
KSJN 99.5 FM, Minnesota Public Radio/classical music
KDWB 101.3 FM, contemporary rock
KEEY 102.1 FM, rock
KCFE 105.7 FM, contemporary
KQQL 107.9 FM, oldies
KTCJ 690 AM, progressive rock
KUOM 770 AM, University of Minnesota alternative
KMZZ 980 AM, hard rock
KTIS 900 AM, religious
KMJZ 950 AM, 104.1 FM, jazz

KFAN 1130 AM, sports, talk
KLBB 1400 AM, '40s, '50s, '60s
KDWA 1460 AM, '50s and '60s country
KBCW 1470 AM, country
KSTP 1500 AM, news, talk
KKCM 1530 AM, Christian music
KYCR 1570 AM, religious
WCAL 89.3 FM, public classical
WLKX 95.9 FM, country
WBOB 100.3 FM, country
WLTE 102.9 FM, contemporary pop
WCCO 830 AM, news, general interest
WMIN 740 AM, '40s, '50s, '60s
WCTS 1030 AM, religious news and music
WIMN 1220 AM, nostalgia
WWTC 1280 AM, children's, radio AAHS
WMNN 1330 AM, news and information
WIXK 1590 AM, 107.1 FM, country

TV STATIONS

KTCA Channel 2, PBS
KSTP Channel 5, ABC
WCCO Channel 4, CBS
KMSP Channel 9, WBN
KARE Channel 11, NBC
KTCI Channel 17, PBS
KLGT Channel 23, independent
WFTC Channel 29, Fox
KXLI Channel 41, independent

BOOKSTORES

AMAZON BOOKSTORE
1612 Harmon Place
Minneapolis
612/338-6560

B. DALTON BOOKSELLERS
Miracle Mile, 5001 Excelsior Blvd.
Minneapolis
612/920-8140

City Center, 40 S. Seventh St.
Minneapolis
612/332-8363

5001 France Ave.
Minneapolis
612/922-1252

Southdale Center,
66th St. and France Ave.
Minneapolis
612/920-2677

183 Northtown Dr.
Blaine
612/786-9110

Highland Village Shopping Center
2024 Ford Pkwy.
St. Paul
651/699-1350

48 Signal Hills
West St. Paul
651/457-4378

Mall of America
Bloomington
612/851-9476

Southport Center, 15050 Cedar Ave.
Apple Valley
651/891-4654

BARNES & NOBLE BOOKSELLERS
3216 W. Lake St.
Minneapolis
612/922-3238

2080 Ford Pkwy.
St. Paul
651/690-9443

710 N. Hwy. 10 N.E.
Blaine
612/786-0686

8049 Wedgewood Ln.
Maple Grove
612/420-4517

BORDERS BOOKS & MUSIC
3001 Hennepin Ave. S.
Minneapolis
612/825-0336

800 W. 78th St.
Richfield
612/869-6245

1501 S. Plymouth Rd.
Minnetonka
612/595-0977

BOOKS FOR TRAVEL
Victoria Crossing, 857 Grand Ave.
Minneapolis
612/341-3333

A BROTHER'S TOUCH
2327 Hennepin Ave. S.
Minneapolis
612/377-6279

DREAMHAVEN BOOKS
912 W. Lake St.
Minneapolis
612/823-6161

HUNGRY MIND BOOKSTORE
1648 Grand Ave.
St. Paul
651/699-0587

JUST THINKING BOOKSTORE
12085 Vermillion
Hastings
651/438-3696

MICAWBER'S BOOKSTORE
2238 Carter Ave.
St. Paul
651/646-5506

NATURE OF THINGS
4306 Upton Ave.
Minneapolis
612/920-6670

ONCE UPON A CRIME
604 W. 26th St.
Minneapolis
612/870-3785

ORR BOOKS
3043 Hennepin Ave. S.
Minneapolis
612/823-2408

SAINT MARTIN'S TABLE
2001 Riverside Dr.
Minneapolis
612/339-3920

SHINDER'S READMORE BOOKSTORE
733 Hennepin Ave.
Minneapolis
612/333-3628

WALDENBOOKS
505 Rosedale Circle
St. Paul
651/636-8332

Northtown Mall
575 Northtown Dr.
Blaine
612/780-1264

INDEX

ABOUT THE AUTHOR

Rick Nelson was born and raised in suburban Minneapolis and now lives in the city's Uptown neighborhood. He writes about restaurants for the Minneapolis *Star Tribune*. He is a former staff writer at the *St. Paul Pioneer Press,* former restaurant critic for *Twin Cities Reader*, and the cofounder and former editor of *Q Monthly*.

You'll Feel like a Local When You Travel with Guides from John Muir Publications

CiTY-SMaRT™ GUIDEBOOKS

Pick one for your favorite city: *Albuquerque, Anchorage, Austin, Calgary, Charlotte, Chicago, Cincinnati, Cleveland, Denver, Indianapolis, Kansas City, Memphis, Milwaukee, Minneapolis/St. Paul, Nashville, Pittsburgh, Portland, Richmond, Salt Lake City, San Antonio, St. Louis, Tampa/St. Petersburg, Tucson*

Guides for kids 6 to 10 years old about what to do, where to go, and how to have fun in: *Atlanta, Austin, Boston, Chicago, Cleveland, Denver, Indianapolis, Kansas City, Miami, Milwaukee, Minneapolis/St. Paul, Nashville, Portland, San Francisco, Seattle, Washington D.C.*

TRAVEL✦SMART®

Trip planners with select recommendations to: *Alaska, American Southwest, Carolinas, Colorado, Deep South, Eastern Canada, Florida Gulf Coast, Hawaii, Illinois/Indiana, Kentucky/Tennessee, Maryland/Delaware, Michigan, Minnesota/Wisconsin, Montana/Wyoming/Idaho, New England, New Mexico, New York State, Northern California, Ohio, Pacific Northwest, Pennsylvania/New Jersey, South Florida and the Keys, Southern California, Texas, Utah, Virginias, Western Canada*

Rick Steves' GUIDES

See *Europe Through the Back Door* and take along guides to: *France, Belgium & the Netherlands; Germany, Austria & Switzerland; Great Britain & Ireland; Italy; Russia & the Baltics; Scandinavia; Spain & Portugal; London; Paris; or the Best of Europe*

ADVENTURES IN NATURE

Plan your next adventure in: *Alaska, Belize, Caribbean, Costa Rica, Guatemala, Honduras, Mexico*

JMP travel guides are available at your favorite bookstores. For a FREE catalog or to place a mail order, call: 800-888-7504.

John Muir Publications • P.O. Box 613 • Santa Fe, NM 87504

JOHN MUIR PUBLICATIONS and its CitySmart Guidebook authors are dedicated to building community awareness within CitySmart cities. We are proud to work with the Minnesota Literacy Council as we publish this guide to the Twin Cities.

The Minnesota Literacy Council, founded in 1972, is a nonprofit volunteer organization dedicated to providing a variety of cost-effective literacy services to Minnesotans. MLC provides training for volunteer tutors and trainers, a referral service for learners and volunteers, and support to a network of almost 130 associate community- and school-based literacy programs. Last year, through this network, 13,343 students were tutored by approximately 3,500 volunteers.

For more information, please contact:
Minnesota Literacy Council
756 Transfer Road
St. Paul, MN 55114-1404
651/645-2277 or 800/225-READ (7323)
fax: 651/645-2272
e-mail: KKOSHIOL@theMLC.org